Baggage
Check

Curtis Bunn

UpStream
Publication

UpStream Publication is am imprint of
A&B PUBLISHERS GROUP
1000 Atlantic Ave.
Brooklyn, NY 11238
(718) 783-7808

COVER DESIGN: *A & B Publishers Group*
TYPESETTING: HART2HART GRAPHIX

Library of Congress Cataloging-in-Publication Data

Bunn, Curtis
  Baggage check / Curtis Bunn
          p.   cm.
   ISBN 1-886433-47-X cloth   ISBN 1-886433-X paper

   1. Single men—Fiction. 2. Afro-American men—Fiction. 3. Male friendship—Fiction.
   I. Title

813'.6--dc21   00-048715

00 01 02 03 04   7 6 5 4 3 2 1

Manufactured and Printed in Canada

Dedication

This book is dedicated to my role models:

My late father, *Edward Earl Bunn*

My mother, *Julia Bunn*

My grandmother, *Nettie Royster*

My cousin, *Warren (Button) Eggleston*

*A portion of the proceeds will go to the
Tom Joyner Foundation that aides Historically Black Colleges.*

Acknowledgement

There were many who aided me with their support and were gracious enough to take the time to read *Baggage Check* when it was just a vision. You encouraged me to push this novel to fruition. And so, I say a heartfelt thanks to:

Deborah Anderson, Patricia Baines, Yvonne S. Benton, Marilyn Bibby, Monya Bunch, Vera Burns, Jeri Byrom, Giselle Chalmers-Turner, Regina Collins, Verla Cook, Kellie Crawford, Tisha Dease, Michelle Easley-James, Wayne Ferguson, Keith Gibson, Shelia Harrison, John Hatfield, Attorney Sharon Adams, Sidney "Elder Sid" Williams, Kyle Greene, Ed DeJesus, Lisa Benton, Humberto Roberts, Carlton Barnes, Renwick Edwards, Felicia McDade, Francine McCarley, Delia McIntyre, Arlene McPhee, Joan Napoleon, Ndidi Opia, Panesa (Penny) Payne, Gloria Shepherd, Kimberly Shotwell, Sandra Smith, Sophia Stewart, April Tarver, Gloria (D.D.) Turner, Tracy Van and Sylvia Wilkins, Michael Easter, Darryl Williams Jr., Deidre Goldbeck, Romi, A.P. Ri'chard, Jose Vasquez, Ronnie Akers, Cecile Mitchell, George Hughes, Bill Rhoden, Brian Yeldell, Stephanie Brown and Rita Owens, Blakphut, Robert 'Bo' Little, Peter Aviler, Crooze.

Much thanks also to David Black, Paul Chung, Anita Diggs, Scott Moyer and Tamaira Thompson. Also thanks to David Drummond for the cover design.

Special thanks to Deirdre Barrett-England, whose support, love, wisdom, encouragement and effort are so meaningful, unforgettable and appreciated. And special thanks to Trevor Nigel Lawrence, who, from the outset, offered great support in sharing in the vision of "Baggage Check."

Very special thanks—and kudos—to Clifford Benton of

AUDACITY *The Literary Consortium* and his team. It would be too simplistic and too weak to call you "my agent." You're family. And your expertise, effort, enthusiasm, insight and encouragement were significant . . . and lasting. The publishing world is yours!

Very, very special thanks to A&B Books—Eric, Wendy and Maxwell. Fortunately, you guys acted when others would not, and the rewards will be yours. I'm eternally grateful.

The utmost thanks to my family, which is very special to me and a source of strength and ambition: my mom, Julia Bunn and grandmother, Nettie Royster; my kids, Curtis Jr., and Gwendolyn (Bunny) and my nephews Gordon and Eddie Jr.; my niece Maya (Bink Bink); my brothers Billy and Eddie and sister, Tammy, and brother-in-law Derek and Derek Jr.; uncle Al and aunt Thelma, my grandfather, Williams Irons, and aunt Barbara and family; my cousin Warren (Button) and his family; my cousin Greg Agnew and his mom, Rosa Bogar; and the Braswell family.

I'd be remiss if I did not acknowledge and thank so many people who have been generous with their time and friendship: my Alpha Phi Alpha brothers, especially those from the notorious Epsilon Pi chapter at Norfolk State University, Michael Brown of BlackSingles.com, Len Burnett of Vangarde, Terry Carmon, Darryl (D.J.) Johnson, Larry Lundy, Terrie Williams of the Terrie Williams Agency, Dwayne Gray, Denene Milner, D.L. Cummings, Paul Spencer, Lyle Harris, Ralph Howard, Derek Dingle, Crystal Bobb-Semple, Jai Wilson, Anita Muhammad, Roland Louis, Tara Ford, Hadley Evans, Linda Vestal, Sam Myers, Olivia Alston, Cliff Brown, Kimberly Fogg, Val Guilford, Randy Brown, Angela Tuck, Roger B. Brown, Michael Holley, Andre Aldridge, Brad Turner, Natanyi Carter, Linda Gadsby, Darryl Caine, Bruce Lee, Skip Grimes, E. Franklin Dudley, Danny Anderson, Clarence Roberts, Clarence Roberts, Andre Johnson, Claire Batiste, George Willis, Kerry Muldrow, Anthony Hall, Sherri Kelly, Garry Howard, Glen and Deirdre Robinson, Derek (Nick) Lambert, Tony Starks, Debra Ray, Jeff Stevenson, Donna Scott, D. Orlando Ledbetter, Ron Simms, Rob Parker, Dexter Santos, Carmen Carter, Tyrone Wyche, Ed (Batman) Lewis, Pam Rachel, John Hughes, Cynthia Gray, Garry Raines, Dennis (Slick) Wade, Julian Jackson, Shelanda Anderson, Alisa Wrenn, Alicia, Miller, Tonja Lee, Theresa, Broomfield, Kimberly Yeager, Gwen Bell, Mark Webb, Jacques Walden, Mark

definition

¹**Baggage check** \ba-gij chek *n* (2000) **1:** an examination of thoughts, feeling and behaviors that may be injurious to a relationship {if I had done a baggage check on him, I wouldn't be going through all of this drama} **2:** the prevention of negative psychological and emotional residual effects stemming from a previous relationship(s) that may adversely affect a new relationship(s) {You better do a baggage check on yo' self before you wreck yo'self}

²**Baggage check** *vb* **baggage check·ing**; *vt* **1:** to investigate for potentially detrimental ideas, beliefs, and practices about relationships {Oh, you know I *baggage checked* him first before going out with him, Girrrlfriend} **2:** to discard possibly harmful ideas, beliefs and practices about relationships {I want to come correct so next time I will *baggage check* myself before trying to get with someone}

(B.J) Bartlett, Marvin Burch, Leslie Hanesworth, Linda Jord\
Marty McNeal, Clarence Hill, Travis Stanley, Stephen A. Smit\
Michelle Lemon, Pam Sims, Alvin Whitney, Denise Taylor, Gre\
Willis, Sonya Perry, Kimberly Royster, Patricia Hale, Zack Withers\
Ballou Senior High (especially the Class of '79), Norfolk State\
University (especially the Class of '83) and Kwame (The King)\
Ofori-Atta.

I owe thanks to my journalism guiding lights: Leon Carter, sports
editor of the New York Daily News and David Squires, metro editor
of the Detroit Free Press. And much thanks to the Atlanta Journal-
Constitution, particularly my editors in the sports department.

And certainly and resoundingly, above all, I thank God. I know
where my blessings come from, and nothing can be accomplished
unless it is His will.

ONE:

Sister Girl

Julian

Her legs were on my shoulders, which was not a bad thing, except I didn't know whose legs they were. The room was dark, faintly lit by two candles on a windowsill, and I could not see her face. She was screaming my name—"Oh, Julian. Oh, Julian"—but I did not recognize her voice. Neither of these facts, however, were reasons enough for me to stop stroking her.

Such was the dangerous combination of five shots of straightup Hennessey, a Long Island Iced Tea, and a horny brother. I could feel the sweat rolling down my back, an indication that we had been at it for a while.

It was amazing how difficult it was to walk or drive straight after so much alcohol, but in the bed I was perfectly coordinated. So I dug into this mystery woman from many angles and positions, pleasing her with a ferocity and passion as if she was the love of my life. And when I was done, I rolled over and passed out.

I awoke about the time the sun did, wearing a dried up condom—and a headache that seemingly pulsated each time I exhaled. She rested peacefully next to me, in the fetal position, with her back turned. Who was she? I almost didn't want to know. I contemplated sliding out of the bed, into my clothes, and out the door. But curiosity is a mother.

I surveyed the surroundings. The room was not that large, but it was tastefully decorated. Whoever this woman was had order in her life. She liked Black art, candles, and cherrywood. She was in a sorority—apparent by the paraphernalia all over the room.

From the high-post bed, I could see a colorful dress that looked familiar in her open closet. Maybe I knew her after all.

As it turned out, I wished I didn't know her at all. Before I could

9

awake her, she rose from her fetal position, stretched, and turned toward me. I was startled by what I saw. Not the healthy, round breasts she exposed, but her face. Oh, I knew her, all right. The only mystery to this woman was why she would sleep with me when for the last nine months I'd been dating her sister.

"Donna," I managed to get out. "How did this happen?"

She didn't speak. Then my memory began to click in. I ran into her at the Ritz during happy hour. I remembered thinking that her being there was slowing my roll; I couldn't very well try to meet any other honies when my girl's sister was there.

And it also came to me that we ended up dancing and that she threw her big, juicy ass on me as we did, despite my weak attempts to back up. The Long Island I had was courtesy of one Donna Copeland, a chocolate, 5-foot-6, 130-pound package of beauty. She had thick lips adorned with an orangish gloss. She had cut her long hair and dyed it auburn, but it went wonderfully with her round, smooth face.

I remembered her telling me that she needed a ride home because she caught the subway to work, and she walked to the club from the job.

I volunteered to take her home, but I didn't have getting with her in mind. However, I was not blind. I had noticed her stunning body during gatherings with her family. And my ego even told me she was attracted to me. But having her in bed was more of a fantasy that I never expected to be a reality.

"Did I make this happen?" I asked her as I slipped into my wrinkled shirt, which looked to be hastily thrown aside. "I remember dancing with you and giving you a ride home and walking you to your door and even coming in. But how did we end up here? Please tell me I didn't push up on you."

"You don't remember?" she said. "Now, I could be insulted by that. But, no, you didn't come on to me. I asked you to come into my room and I, well—I just kissed you. It was on after that."

I shook my head.

"Now, if you tell me that you don't remember what we did," she said, "I really would be insulted."

I couldn't lie. Although hung over, I remembered how good she felt, how many positions we tried, how in sync we were.

"I remember," I said, almost embarrassed. "Now what?"

"Joanne is my big sister. I love her. But this kind of just happened. I'm going to be honest with you. I'm not trying to hurt

Joanne. I didn't plan this—until I saw you at the club. I just thought: 'If she really wanted this man, she'd be here.' She's so into her job and other stuff that, to me, she ignores you. I know she cares about you, really cares about you. But I also know from being around you that I do, too. This might sound cold to you. But I'm not a cold person. I know what I want."

"And you want your sister's man?"

She stepped off the bed and onto the floor. Wearing nothing but a seductive smile, she sashayed around the bed and flopped down on it, next to me. I noticed her titties bounced as if they were dribbled.

"I think you want me, too. I believe you do. It seemed that way last night," she said. "I'm not going to say anything to Joanne. And I'm not going to sweat you about this. But I'm not going to let you just walk away, either."

That sounded kind of scary to me. I had dealt with women who seemed fine and then eventually went psycho. One had keys made to my apartment and went in when I wasn't there, going through my belongings and taking shit she had no business when she found a letter from another woman. Another tried to run me off the road in a car when she saw me driving with someone else. That kind of foolishness.

And it was not that I was so special that rejection from me triggered this irrational behavior. At least I didn't think so. I was confident enough in myself to believe I was a good catch. I had an advanced degree, a good job. I kept myself in shape. I was tall, dark, and handsome if you looked at me from just the right angle. But at times, women just jumped in so deep, so quickly, with visions of love and shit that they messed up their own minds. Next thing you knew, they're talking about, "I'm not going to let you walk away."

Immediately, I pondered if Donna—my girlfriend's sister—was a Glen Close-in-Fatal Attraction-type. Maybe that was paranoia or an overreaction, but that was how I felt at that moment.

"What do you mean, you're not going to let me walk away?" I said as I searched for my underwear.

"Looking for these?" she said, holding my drawers and ignoring my question. "You don't need these just yet."

With that, she tossed them across the room and began rubbing my leg and kissing my neck. Suffice it to say that I did not leave for another forty-five minutes or so.

TWO:

Say What?

Julian

The overwhelmingly popular "thinking" of women was that men wanted what they could not have and did not want what they had. Or they simply wanted it all. With me, I wasn't so conventional, not like I had been. I was content with Joanne because we had grown close over nine, mostly blissful, months. She was strong, independent, smart, charming, and elegant. And, oh yeah. She was strikingly beautiful with a body to match. Sexy and sensual. Her and her younger sister Donna favored in most every physical way: height, complexion, weight. Only Joanne's eyes were bigger, brighter, more captivating. More alive.

I didn't get smitten about women very often. Mostly I enjoyed them for the sex, a handful of good times and then I'd be bored and on to something—or someone—else. I could detach myself with virtually little emotional maintenance or regret. That was a flaw of mine. Or a virtue.

But Joanne gave me hope that I could be rid of that passionless state. She did not have children, which was a requirement for me. The "instant family" thing was something I could not get with. Without exception, when I learned a honey had a kid, I was outta there.

And the fact that Joanne turned down a job offer in Charlotte meant something to me, too. I refused to get down with a long distance relationship. No one I'd met made me want to deal with her when she lived hours away.

With Joanne, I actually wanted to spend time with her. I felt that way with other women to some degree, but I did not feel as close to others as I did with Joanne.

And then I go and fuck her sister. Twice. What could have been more messed up than that? I had been faithful to her for our nine

12

months together, which was a feat in itself. And I knew I was really into Joanne when it ate me up inside every time I thought about doing her sister. It was an accident, sort of, but, if I wanted to, I could have stopped it, I guess.

I saw Donna three days after our, uh, encounter, at, of all places, Joanne's house. Talk about awkward. Well, at least it was for me. Donna seemed to bask in the secret we shared. When Joanne had to take a call in her bedroom, Donna immediately switched from the single chair to the sofa cushion next to me.

"Don't you want to do it right here, right now?" she said with a look in her eyes I never before had seen.

I knew she was crazy then. "Listen, I don't want to tell Joanne what happened the other night," I said. "She'd be mad at me and hurt. But she'd be more mad and hurt with you, and I don't know if she'd ever forgive you. You're her sister. But if you force me to tell her, I will. I'd rather we make like it never happened, because it won't happen again."

My sternness shook Donna. She was twenty-nine and had a lot going for her, but she didn't want me. Once I put aside my considerable ego, I realized that there was much competition between the sisters. Mostly, Donna was jealous of Joanne. Only one year separated them in age, but there was a wide gap in maturity.

Joanne had been a woman for a long time. She was poised and assured. She attracted guys pretty much all her life. Donna did not bloom physically until late. It wasn't until a few years before that men paid her much attention, her sister said. Before then, the men she was attracted to were attracted to Joanne. Hence, the one-sided rivalry.

"If you want it to be over, it's over," Donna said. "I'm not going to press you."

I didn't believe she meant it, mostly because she placed her hand on my thigh as she spoke. I quickly got up. "Don't do that," I said with a hint of anger. "Is this a game to you?"

"OK, OK," she said. "Fine. It's over. But don't come back to me later talking about you changed your mind."

Just then, Joanne returned from her room. She looked concerned about something, but what? I hoped she did not hear me and Donna.

Donna didn't seem to notice. She stayed a few minutes—never making eye contact with me again—and made up an excuse to leave, without saying goodbye to me. Joanne said nothing was wrong with her, but then began a surprising line of questioning.

"Do you love me, Julian?"

"Of course I do."

"Then say it. Say, 'I, Julian Morgan love you, Joanne Copeland.'"

"What's wrong? What's this all about?"

"That was my doctor on the phone," she said in a voice so low I had to strain to hear her.

"I'm pregnant."

I had no problem hearing that. Sounded, in fact, like she yelled it.

"What?" My heart literally stopped beating for a few seconds. I thought: Nah, no way. I wasn't ready to be a father. And I wondered if I'd ever be. But I did not fully convey that to Joanne. She knew I was surprised—shocked even—but somehow, amid the shock, I thought about her and how she must have felt. Having a child then was not something she anticipated or wanted either, from what she had told me. And the burden of carrying the child would be hers. So I thought composure was in order right about then, but I wasn't sure how much I had.

"Are you sure? How could this be, Joanne?" I tried really hard to not appear rattled. "We always used a condom."

"I don't know," she said, tears in her eyes. "It happens. But I did a home pregnancy test on Friday that was positive. That's why I did-n't see you or call you this weekend. I was too upset. Then I went to my doctor this morning to be doubly certain. That was him on the phone with the news."

I ran my fingers through my hair, wiped my face, and checked my watch. Nervous energy had taken over. But I regrouped quickly. I held her hand. "Baby, I don't know what to say. Yes, I do love you. But you know I was not planning on a child before getting married."

I paused and chose my words carefully. She was on the verge of breaking down and needed some comforting words. So I delivered.

"I never told you this, but I did not meet my natural father until I was twenty-three years old. At that point, I didn't want to; he aban-doned me and I didn't see any need to meet him then. But my mom really wanted me to, so I did. But there was no connection there, none at all. He was a stranger, and I never saw him again. I thank God that the man I've always known as my father came along and raised me as if I were his own. I said that to say this: If it turns out that we have a baby, I'll never let my child have the feeling I had about that man I met at twenty-three. I'll always be there, in every way."

Joanne began to cry as she lay in my arms. But they were more like relief tears—if there was such a thing—than tears of distress.

"It's going to be all right," I whispered to her. "It's going to be all right." And I meant it.

THREE:

Ooooh La La

Julian

The five-hour flight to Los Angeles was only interesting when there was an attractive black female flight attendant working it or an eye-catching passenger. Not necessarily to flirt with, but to admire. There was nothing—I mean NOTHING—more beautiful than the grace, elegance, and strength of a black woman. Why a so-called brother would even consider dating a white woman, I simply could not fathom.

And that really was not a racial thing as much as it was holding a firm, committed allegiance to sisters. That's where my heart was and would always remain.

This flight west was completely boring: an all-white crew and no attention-grabbing sister on board, which meant reading the newspaper and Walter Mosley's novel, *Always Outnumbered, Always Outgunned,* until I fell asleep. And I would need the rest because waiting for me at the airport would be my boys, Larry Thompson and Greg Gibson. And we were sure to keep each other busy. They were the ultimate friends.

"Friends" was a word loosely thrown around. I came to learn the hard way that I had far more acquaintances or associates or just people I knew than friends. Larry and Greg were truly friends.

Larry lived in L.A., an aspiring actor, like half the population there. Only he had talent. Until he made it big, "L" worked as an assistant manager at Pacific Bank, performing a job I was not exactly certain of. As for Greg, he lived in Chicago, making it very nicely as the owner of a black bookstore and card shop.

We grew up together in southeast Washington, D.C., becoming friends as seventh-graders on the basketball court. We were strangers on the same team during a pickup game, and, when a fight broke out,

15

we defended each other with a fervor. Back then a fight ended without bloodshed as a result of gunfire. Eventually the fistfight was broken up, and you either continued playing ball or moved on to something else.

Larry, Greg, and I walked to the corner candy store that day and put our money together to buy some Now & Laters, sodas, and potato chips. We hung out virtually every day since then.

We remained tight as we got older, despite my going to college in Virginia, Greg doing eight years in the Army all over the world, and Larry up and bolting one day to Cali, presumably to avoid the law. Greg and I were more conservative in our lifestyles, while Larry always had an angle, a "hookup," legal or otherwise. It was not until he moved 3,000 miles away that he abandoned the flimflams.

This visit to Los Angeles was all about fun. We all needed a break from the monotony of home and the rigors of work. But I had the extra burden of Joanne's news. For a day or so after she told me, I was somewhat in a trance and did not tell anyone. Now, I was OK with it, had accepted it to a degree, and I would tell Larry and Greg about it on this trip. At some point.

But that would wait. I did realize, however, that the fact that I did not tell them—or my family—about it immediately meant I wasn't so OK with it as I was trying to convince myself. I didn't know how my boys would take it, and I didn't want to dampen the vacation for any of us.

This was a time for partying foremost and whatever else next. We had no regard for time—except knowing when the party started. We picked L.A. for the obvious reasons: the gorgeous weather and even more gorgeous women.

In Los Angeles, a brother from the East Coast in a lot of instances was like a prize to West Coast women. After you sorted through the self-centered, materialistic airheads, you found in L.A. beautiful women who wanted gentlemen who reveled in treating women with chivalry and respect and not the glitter-pants-wearing, pop-dancing, curly-kit-hair-sporting weirdoes out there. In other words, it was a haven if you knew how to treat a women, as we did.

I was mindful that I had Joanne back in D.C., more so than ever. I really liked her—shoot, even said I loved her—and was committed to her. But I really did not limit myself to what I'd do while on vacation. I did not plan on doing anything. But the truth was, I was incredibly weak to a woman that attracted me, meaning I was prone to being unfaithful. It was part of my *baggage*—my weakness for women that is. In that way, unfortunately, I was a typical man.

As for Larry, he was the consummate playa. He kept a handful of women content enough to feel good about their connection to him but not happy enough to think they had a real relationship. That was an art, and he was definitely an artist.

Greg was in his second year of a serious relationship with Brianna. He did not want to admit it, but it was clear one day they'd get married—if he stayed the course. She was strong-willed, outspoken, and independent. Greg was a man of conviction, and he spoke of Brianna in a way that said she was right for him. That was more than enough for me.

But hanging with me and Larry would not make it easy for him to be faithful to her. We adored the beauty and mystique of women and being around them. We needed to make acquaintances. And it wasn't for the sexual conquest, not all the time, anyway. It was the challenge.

Larry summed it up best when he said, "I like it when a woman resists. That makes me more determined to break her, to make her succumb to my will. Next thing you know, she's asking me over at midnight—a booty call. But at that point, it's not about sex. I've already made love to her mind."

Larry thought philosophically like that about most everything. Usually I agreed with his assessments. We thought alike on the matter of women, that was for sure. And in the '90s, Larry and I were the chosen ones: tall and dark. That was a reversal from the previous decade, when women treated dark-skinned brothers with disdain and light-skinned brothers like jewels.

But in that wave of Afrocentric consciousness, blacker was better. Wesley Snipes and Michael Jordan seemed to carry the torch in that enlightenment. In any case, neither Larry nor I complained. Greg was not as dark or as tall, but he was distinguished, funny, and a gentleman like us, which were key elements in attracting women. Plenty of them. And he sported a bald head, which became en vogue, too.

Even though we had it going on, it was hard to hook-up with a quality woman. They all had hang-ups, or as we would say, "baggage." Maybe not all but far too many did. You were judged by their past experiences which generally weren't pleasant. Not only were you judged by their past experiences with men, but you were dealing with the experiences of their sisters, aunts, cousins, grandmothers, girlfriends, and co-workers, all of whom had strong opinions—all of whom had negative opinions, all of whom would pass on their experiences like it was a contagious disease. They wanted their hang-ups to be everybody else's. They couldn't check their *baggage*, and they would make it impossible for another woman to check hers. It's like they took an oath. "You must bring your *baggage* into the relationship."

Greg's flight arrived an hour earlier than mine, and the notoriously late Larry remarkably was on time to pick him up. So there they were outside the United baggage claim at LAX waiting for me, the rear door of Larry's black Pathfinder open so I could toss in my bags, and we could get on with the business of funning.

I greeted Larry with a big smile and a hug. "What's up, L?"

"Everything is everything," he said.

"Yo, G, it's on!" I said, greeting Greg.

"Let's do this," he said loudly.

At that moment, a sense of contentment and utter joy went over me. We talked on the phone via conference calls regularly, but we did not get together that often, maybe three times a year. I loved those guys, and each gathering was a special occasion.

And, of course, a special occasion called for drinks. Lots of them. We knew better than to drink while in the truck, but hey, we were on vacation. It was all good. And so, I pulled up the top to the cooler that rested in the back seat with me, reached in, and passed out Heinekens all around.

As Larry pumped the latest Ronnie Jordan CD, we toasted to the weather, to the beaches, to the women, and to a wonderful five days we were certain to have.

FOUR:

What Ya Got Cookin'?

Larry

I lived in West Hollywood, off Ventura Blvd., in a nice li'l one bedroom spot in one of those large complexes with a clubhouse and
pool. It was not much, but I was proud of it because I had come a long
way since my days back home in D.C., when I was a pseudo-hustler. I
slung a little weed every now and then, and robbed a couple of people
at gunpoint.

I don't know why I did it really, because I was brought up to abide
by the law. My family originated in Trinidad, and my parents were
adamant about being a proud, hard worker. It built character, my
father told me, virtually every time I started whining about something. I got to D.C. and caught up with some wild dudes. All of a sudden, I'm all wrapped up in making some dough—and the warped
thrill of doing something I knew I shouldn't have been doing.

It wasn't until I had a close call that I stopped trippin'. I had
arranged to purchase some marijuana from a dealer at his apartment
one night. I'd then break it down and sell it in nickel bags and make
a nice little profit.

On the way, I noticed I needed some gas and decided to fill up
first and then make the deal. Turned out that those five minutes
saved me from certain jail time. After filling up, I drove to the dealer's place. As I got out of the car in front of his building, I was almost
knocked over by DEA agents who rushed his crib, confiscated all the
drugs, and arrested everyone in sight.

I would have been in handcuffs too if I hadn't stopped for gas. If
that was not a sign to kick the bad boy habit, I didn't know what else
could be. So, I did. But since I owed a couple dudes some money, I
couldn't clean up my life looking over my shoulder in D.C. So, I
picked L.A. as a new locale. It was far away, had a reputation for

beautiful women, and had year-round sunshine. That was six years ago, and I've never looked back.

When I first moved to California, I didn't know a soul, had no money to speak of, and lived for a short time in a YMCA. I worked for a short time as a waiter, security guard, and telemarketer for one of those long distance carriers. There were many nights when I rested in bed at the Y and wondered if I'd ever get my life together.

But I did—slowly. I got a room in a house in Inglewood and later an apartment in Gardena. The Valley was my latest and best stop. I was handling my business. Legitimate business as a bank assistant manager.

And I was excited about showing my boys how far I'd come. As the host of the getaway, it was my responsibility to set a loose agenda, which was easy, really. All I had to do was have some honies on call and know where the parties were. I was straight on both counts.

"I'm loving it out here," I said to Greg and Julian. "But it would be better if I had you two to flow with. I've met some brothers who have been cool. But that D.C. flavor is missing. It's just not the same. You know how we roll into a spot and our aura just consumes the place. Here, I have to roll solo, create the atmosphere by myself."

Julian and Greg frowned. They knew that I'd approach a women with the ease of a vagrant confronting strangers for change. Rolling solo was hardly a problem for me. And those two, of all people, knew just that.

"Who do you think we are?" Greg said to me. "Man, your monkey ass don't need a soul to roll with. Shit, anytime we've ever rolled, we barely saw you anyway. You were always doing your thing. We just gave you a ride to the party."

We all laughed. Part of being so tight was to regularly talk about each other or, as we called it in D.C., "jone." This was a constant thing with us, which required a thick skin and a broad imagination. If people were around us who did not know we were so tight, they'd think we despised each other. The attacks were that personal at times.

And if we felt like it, we'd "jone" on people we just met, too. It wasn't about being mean. Really, it was about being friendly, keeping the mood light.

Laughing uplifted the soul, made the blood flow more freely, Julian used to say. And we all agreed that if you could make a woman laugh, it would relax her and make her feel good about you.

That was a critical element in our approach to women. Not

jokes, but conversing with them and making them laugh naturally through wit. Julian was the smoothest at making a tense woman more at ease, to make her feel like he was not coming on to her, but just talking to her.

Brothers who use those so-called lines— "Haven't we met before?" "You look so good I'd sop you up with a biscuit," and on and on—were so tired they almost offended me. I loved words, creative analogies, metaphors, especially when dealing with women.

What was even more to me was that some women accepted those guys' weak lines as compliments. A lot of things about women puzzled me, and, during the L.A. trip, Julian, Greg, and I would discuss them quite a bit, as we always did.

Since neither of us lived near the other, we'd run up crazy phone bills each month. We'd do three-way calls at least once a week, with them lasting as long as an hour each. It was an expensive way to keep in touch, but we absorbed the cost because talking to each other was that important.

As much fun as we liked to have, we always had very serious conversations too. The subjects would range from women and relationships, to race relations, to work, to sports. And it was always thought provoking. And many times it would lead right back to women. They were sort of an obsession for us.

Knowing that, I gave Greg and Julian the rundown when we got to my apartment: "Put your baggage down and let's roll," I said. "Here's the deal: We're going to Marina Del Ray to have lunch at Aunt Kizzie's. We can get a good meal and see some honies too. From there, we're going to stop by this little honey's office I know downtown, on Wilshire. She's bringing two of her partners over tonight to cook dinner for us. I haven't met her friends before, but I gave her the run-down. I told her just like this: 'Listen, my boys are high caliber. Don't bring any poo-butt women into my domain to meet my people. My boys are kings like me. Bring queens.' "

Julian and Greg knew I told her just like that. I could be arrogant at times, lots of times. I couldn't help it. Other times I could be insensitive, or viewed as insensitive because I was very carefree, almost aloof. Definitely I was direct. And when it came to my boys, I made my points clear.

"What did she say?" Greg asked.

"She said, 'Don't worry. They are good women,' " I said. "And I told her, 'Naw, I mean queens. Good is not good enough. They've got to be on point.' She finally just promised that you guys would be satisfied."

And it turns out, they were—at least from their physical appearance. After lunch, some girl-watching, and some down-time at my place, the trio of women came over with groceries in hand. To the eye, the three were off the hook.

My girl was Simone, a statuesque sister with long, smooth legs and a tight, firm build. She was light-skinned, which was not my flavor, but she was cool. She had long, flowing brown hair. But she had an irritating, high-pitched voice. It probably bothered me more than it would others because I was particular like that.

The two for Greg and Julian were tight. Simone had come through in a big way: big breasts, big legs, and big butts. Tara, who was for Julian, and Greg's Angie had the goods, and they wore deep-cut blouses and short skirts to accentuate them. When they came through the door, I could tell by their expressions that they liked what they saw.

Before they headed for the kitchen, we insisted they take a few moments to chat with us. I was anxious to start the feeling-out process. And I took the initiative.

"Thanks, Simone, for bringing two queens with you for two kings—at least that's the look of things," I said.

The girls smiled and thanked me. Tara let it be known from the start that she was for Julian by the way she looked at him during the introductions. And Julian being Julian, he let her know he felt the same way by not letting her hand go after shaking it.

"We appreciate you guys spending some time with us," Julian said, "welcoming us to Los Angeles. Cooking is a bonus. And Greg and Larry will be glad to do the dishes while Tara and I sample the CD collection."

Tara smiled. Greg, who stood beside Julian, gave him a playful forearm to the shoulder. "Anyway," Greg said, "since this is Larry's home and we're all guests, he and Simone should tackle that while I get to know Angie and Julian bores Tara to death."

Everyone laughed. The mood was set for a nice evening. Simone, who was sitting on the arm of a black leather recliner with me, got up after laughing. "OK," she said, "we're going to get started. You guys look hungry."

"Yeah, hungry in more ways than one," Greg said under his breath.

FIVE:

Chit-Chatting

Greg

The meal was slammin': salmon, dirty rice, spinach. The search for the total woman often started with her ability to cook. Not that we were exactly searching. After all, I had Brianna, a potential wife, and Julian had Joanne, a good woman, and Larry had, well, he had a number of women, no one who really meant anything to him. But Simone's crew impressed for sure with their ability in the kitchen. They threw down. It was a trip because they did not exactly look like chefs.

"If it's true that the quickest way to a man's heart is through his stomach," I said, "then you guys just took the express train."

The food devoured, we got into some conversation while listening to music and sipping champagne. It was a Wednesday night, and I assumed the women had to work in the morning, but they did not seem to be concerned about time—and we certainly were not going to make it an issue.

As the champagne flowed, the conversation among the six of us got more personal, more free. I knew of the dangers of too many drinks, having listened to Julian's mistake of a lifetime just last week and recalling my own mistakes on the impact of alcohol. I reminded myself of that, but still downed the Moet like it was apple juice.

Before long, the subject of debate was relationships. No surprise there. As curious as women were about what made men react or not react to women, what made us lie and cheat, and not reach our full potential as mates, men were just as interested in learning why women were so seemingly hell-bent on luring a man into a relationship and why their insecurities ruled once they were in one.

"You guys seem intelligent, so maybe you can give us an answer to a question all women want to know," Tara said. "Why is it that men are so reluctant to commit?"

I wanted to answer truthfully. I wanted to say that men often avoid committing because they know they CAN'T commit. Or will not do it. I didn't know if it was something innate or some chemical imbalance or just plain weakness, but the lure of other women was so strong that even having a woman that is good, and real, and inspiring many times just was not enough.

Larry, Julian, and I talked about this pretty regularly. We did consider ourselves intelligent, but we were stumped on this one. Just last week, I told them on a conference call: "I can't explain it at all. I know I have a good woman. But it's almost like I can't help myself. It's like I have this strong love for women that, no matter what, I just can't fight it. It's like a sickness. I'm cursed."

A talk came to mind that I had with an elderly black man as he shined my shoes one night in Las Vegas. As beautiful young women with half their asses hanging out passed, the man shared his experiences. And when older people talked, I listened closely.

"I tell you, it's hard on a man out here," the shoeshine man said. "I just divorced my third wife last year. Now I ain't got n'ar one. But I ain't mad. I just got it bad. I love women. Black women. The temptation is hard on any man. You might be in love with a woman, but you've got eyes. You can see. So it's hard. I married the prettiest woman in Louisiana. She was sweet, too. But, man, I would tell her, 'I'm going out tonight and I won't be back until tomorrow.' I did. For real. I couldn't help myself."

All those thoughts rushed to my head when Tara asked her inevitable question. But there was no way I could come with that. And I didn't feel right saying simply, "I don't know." Instead, I gave her a measure of reason and a dose of bullshit.

"You know," I began, "women are quick to think that. But the reality is that if the woman is right for the man, he will be the kind of man she expects and deserves. Now, there are cases where men just have no regard for this person they supposedly care about, and they do whatever. I know women are not calling men dogs for no reason; men have done some wild stuff. I KNOW men who have done stuff that blows me away. But the real problem is that he's not with a woman he respects enough to be faithful. Either that, or men don't want to commit because they know that eventually they won't act as committed men should act—because the women they have are not the ultimate. That's no excuse, but that's my thinking."

And it really was. I actually believed what came into my head a moment earlier. It made sense. Sort of. Right on cue, Julian chimed in as if we had rehearsed it as a skit. "That's true," he said. "Plus, the thing that really gets me when women bring up this subject is that they always portray themselves as the victims. There are cases where men just have no control over their hormones or whatever. But I'm willing to bet that these men who don't commit or aren't faithful with their mates are driven to do some of these so-called bad things. They don't commit because the woman who wants the commitment is short of what he needs to be monogamist. I love women, but let's keep it real here: women nag you and pressure you sometimes to the point where it's overbearing. And women do their dirt, too. They sneak around with other men, lie, whatever. Women are just better at hiding their dirt. They'll sleep with their friend's man or have a one-night stand and not tell anyone, not even their tightest girl because they are afraid their friend will think of them as a slut. With men, they can't hold in their escapades. They'll actually brag about it.

"Ultimately," Julian went on. "I believe if a good man finds a good woman, it is not automatic that he'll be afraid to commit or that he'll be unfaithful. Why bother if you've got what you need right there in that person?"

Our positions were so well argued that Larry did not even contribute. He just kind of sat back with an expression that said, "Yeah, those are my boys. They were lying like shit, but they did it well."

The women seemed satisfied enough with our responses to not pursue it any further, probably because Julian put them on the defense by talking about women's misdeeds. Whatever the case, there was not much debate about that anymore. It was about 11 o'clock, and the conversation switched to sex. No surprise there, either.

Angie wanted to know what we thought about the importance of sex in a relationship. Who were better experts on that subject than us? After all, sex was a big part of our lives. It kind of drove us. We even bragged about the type of women we slept with, the circumstances, everything. Once, Larry listed some of his sex partners by jobs. I bragged about having women in their office, in the car, in the elevator, in a parking lot, wherever.

Together, we pulled off many sexual twists, getting women to sleep with us after just meeting at, say, a club or a party. Wherever. And once or twice, we ALL ended up in the bed together.

Yet that hardly made us experts on the importance of sex in relationships. But we DID understand the importance of sex if there was to BE a relationship.

So to Angie's question, Larry jumped right on it. "We're all adults here, so let's be candid," he said. "I understand the importance of communication in a relationship and love and honesty and trust. You must have those elements for it to succeed. But if the sex is not good and you have all those other elements, it's not going to work. Period. It seems people, especially women, try to trivialize sex as just part of a relationship that doesn't matter much. It is a part, all right—a BIG part."

There was no need for neither Julian nor I to interject. Larry had it covered, to the point where even the women agreed. "That's true," Simone said, "and not just for men. In reality, a woman might stay with a man because he's a good man who is honest and can provide for her. But if he's not doing it for her in bed, eventually the woman is going to get completely bored with it. She's going to think about straying. She's going to fantasize about it. Then she's going to DO it." Her partners nodded in agreement.

SIX

2 On Two

Julian

Time was lost amid the conversation. If something was going to happen on that night with those women, the move had to be made. It was nearly 1 a.m.

With Simone in pocket, Larry was straight. The three women rode together to dinner, but Simone clearly had staying the night on her mind, based on the way her hands consistently found Larry's chest and back, despite our presence.

So, what were Greg and I going to do with Tara and Angie? Larry and Simone disappeared without a word into Larry's bedroom. Greg quickly but smoothly moved closer to Angie. I heard him softly say something about admiring her smile all night. And she flashed all thirty-two then.

I knew Greg extremely well, and I could tell he genuinely liked Angie. Or at least he had serious lust. We developed a chemistry over the years, frequenting the D.C. club scene like nighthawks: The Chapter III, RSVP, the Black Crystal, the Black Tahiti, Triples, Seasons, the Racquetball Club, the Ibex, Hogates, the Classics, L'Enfant Plaza, the Paragon Too, The Buck Stops Here. We hit them all over the years, always together.

Greg was a man of discipline—especially when it came to money. He worked at a pizza parlor in high school and later at a government office, all the while saving his money as if his intent were to rival Donald Trump before he was twenty.

He guarded and cherished the money he earned. If he were going to part with it, it would not be hastily. Basically, Greg was a tightwad. He did not deny himself quality clothes or the essentials and occasionally he sprang. Greg was nothing like another friend of mine, Vernon Keith, who once refused to take his girlfriend to a movie because it cost more than matinee price. Vernon also would ask a woman to walk out of a restaurant without paying; he was so stingy. And we're talking Pizza Hut, not Morton's.

Greg was hardly that ridiculous. But while stationed in D.C., he could afford an apartment and craved the independence that came with having his own place. Instead, he stayed at home with his mom for two years to save money. That was discipline.

And I was very grateful for Greg's conservative nature. Along with my parents, he was very much responsible for me attending college. As the date for enrollment neared, my mom's and stepdad's finances dwindled. They hardly could afford to send me to college out of their pockets, yet we were denied financial aid. It was two weeks before I was to head south on Interstate 95 for school, and their scraping left them still $500 short with no apparent source of money available.

I told Greg of the situation only because I told Greg everything. Without hesitation, he lent the money I did not even know he had. I went on to college, got academic scholarships for the three remaining years and earned a degree in education. Then, I attended Temple University and got my graduate and doctoral degrees in African American History. So, I was grateful to him, as his love for me at eighteen years old ultimately was responsible for my job as a professor of African-American studies at Bowie State College in Maryland.

That he had enough money to open a bookstore after eight years in the Army spoke for his discipline, his love for books, and his love for money. It was of no surprise to anyone who knew him. He knew how to make money and save it. With women, he knew how to get them and get rid of them. Women easily impressed him physically, but not mentally. He would probe their minds, and not always in a subtle fashion. He'd provoke heated debates, put them on the defensive, and then make an assessment about their mental strength. If they did not stand up to his grilling, he got to steppin'.

Yet he was much gentler with Angie. Noting her smile was not his usual style. As a compliment, he'd usually point out a woman's position on an issue that he agreed with. But not with Angie.

"I think a smile tells a lot about a woman," he said to her.

"What does mine say about me?" Angie said.

"That you're kind," Greg answered quickly, looking directly into her eyes. "That you're genuine. That you're soft. Not to the touch—although I'm sure you are—but soft and gentle in how you deal with people. I'm sure you have a side to you that's not so soft and pleasant. We all do. But you have to be pushed to that unpleasant side."

"Men have a way of doing that," she said.

"The right man will make you smile far more than not," Greg retorted.

"And you're the right man?" Angie said.

"You're smiling, aren't you?" Greg said.

Angie's smile grew—and so did her attraction of Greg. It was evident. "I'm sort of reluctant to ask this," he said, "because it might seem like I'm trying to end this night when I'm really trying to extend it, but do you have to work in the morning?"

"Why?" she said.

"Because if you do," he said, "I'd understand it if you were ready to go, but I'd like to have lunch with you tomorrow. If you don't, I'd like to have breakfast AND lunch with you."

Angie smiled some more. "Actually, I'm off," she said. "I work at Pacific Bell. We're going through some things in the office right now, some layoffs and reorganizing, so my days off fluctuate every two weeks. I don't go back to work until Saturday, of all days."

"So . . . " Greg said.

"So I don't have a curfew," Angie said. Five minutes later, Angie asked Tara for a moment in the kitchen. I was not sure what was said, but clearly the plan was for Angie to take the car— and Greg—while I took care of Tara. It was the identical plan Greg and I quietly planned in the living room.

Greg played it off by saying they were going out for a ride and late dessert, with dessert having a double meaning. I knew I would not see him again until the next day.

So it was just me and Tara. I asked her if she liked movies. She labeled herself an avid theatergoer, with dramas and science fiction her favorites. I told her I loved dramas, too, but liked only a few sci-fi flicks because realism mattered to me.

I asked her what interest she had, if any, in politics. She said she voted for the presidency and local officials, but that was the extent of her interest. I told her I voted, too, and was mildly interested in politics, but I had two people in that political arena that I admired.

I knew the first would throw her, but at least I could be honest about something. "Marion Barry, former mayor of D.C., is a guy I supported. I know he was seen on TV smoking crack. It was an awful thing, and I almost cried when I saw it. There is no excuse, no defense for that. But this man did not fold under at a time when he could have. White folks—the government—spent several millions and many years trying to entrap Barry. I'm not big on conspiracy theories, but there was a big one working here to get that man. Still, he cleaned up his life. He looks better than ever because, hopefully, he's living right. And then he came back and won reelection, which means I'm not alone in this thinking. We're always talking about role models, well, he's shown that you can rise from the depths of hell and still reign over the Nation's Capital. If nothing else, Marion Barry has shown that drugs can be beaten, which in this day and age, needs to be reinforced. He fought his way back, and as terrible as his crack behavior was, his comeback was as strong a testament to recovery and perseverance."

I sounded like I had rehearsed my position, but I had not.

"Well, I see your point, but I just can't get pass that video tape," Tara said. "Who else do you admire in politics, Nixon?"

I laughed. "Nah. I liked Bill Clinton. I don't know how you felt about the him, but he was cool with me. I know he got a little shaky on the scandals that flew out of the White House and later admitted to them. But I think that was a product of just trying to be perfect. I was down with him because he was a real person. He talked to people, not down at them. Any man who ruled over the free world and went on "Arsenio" with sunglasses on, playing a saxophone, you had to love. He did things that real people do, something we haven't seen in a president. Ever.

"As for the state of the country in the '90s, it wouldn't have been better off with a Republican in there. It would have been worst. The economy was good under Clinton, unemployment was down, relatively speaking. And let's not forget that he hired more African-Americans to his cabinet than Reagan, who had two terms, and Bush combined."

"And don't forget the reason he was so cool," Tara chimed in. "He had a brilliant wife. Hillary was BAD. She was so bad, MEN were intimidated by her. Together, they were tough. I respect her for throwing her hat into the political arena."

Tara's stock rose at that moment. I agreed totally with her assessment on the former First Lady. And if we agreed on something that I was so adamant about, well, that meant something to me.

So I upgraded the conversation. "What's the deal with you?" I said. "Why aren't you home in bed? What's keeping you here?"

This was a spur-of-the-moment tactic. Normally, I'd take the subtle approach, work out a way for the woman to say what I wanted to hear without asking it. I was very good at that, but it was nearly two in the morning, and I was getting tired.

"You're keeping me here," she said. "I mean, I've enjoyed the conversation. I'm surprised how easy you are to talk to. Men usually make me feel like I have to guard myself all the time. But I haven't been that way with you. You've been very easy to talk to. You have a way about you. You're very mellow."

SEVEN:

Truth Be Told

Julian

Sometimes you can sense when a woman wants you, when she's eschewed her instinct to be tight with the booty and says to herself, "Fuck it. I want to do this now. Why wait?" Then she does it.

I contemplated this as Tara worked her tongue inside my mouth. Without warning or trepidation, she slowly placed her wet, soft lips on mine. Last I remembered, we sat directly in front of each other, talking, smiling, feeling good. Next thing I knew her tongue was like a loose water hose in my unsuspecting mouth.

"I'm sorry," Tara said after the sustained kiss.

"Don't be," I said, pulling her back to me.

We exchanged kisses for several more minutes. I didn't realize I could hold my breath that long. I was not in the habit or comfortable deeply kissing someone I'd just met. But at that point, I was like Michael Jordan on a fastbreak: unstoppable.

In the process of kissing, my hands did the natural thing, which was to explore that luscious body. I caressed her arms from her wrists up to her shoulders. Delicately, I slid both hands over her tender mounds of breasts, an act that caused her to moan with pleasure. My hands stuck there for a few moments.

She responded by fondling me, her target was bulging steadily between my legs. With a gentleness that matched her persona, Tara rubbed and caressed my groin area. It got more and more hot the longer we played touch with each other's bodies.

Finally, Tara pulled back. Greg had flicked out the lights on his way out, leaving only the single bulb over the stove in the kitchen to barely illuminate the living room. Tara was more of a silhouette now, but I could still identify her beauty. She was breathing heavily, panting. She slowly licked her lips and then rubbed her own breasts. Her

32

look and actions said, "Come and get me . . . now."

And I wanted to so badly. Any other time I would have brandished my dick as if it were a weapon, without hesitation and with serious intentions. But before I dozed off to sleep on the flight to L.A., I thought about the impending responsibility of being a father. I thought about Joanne, whom I truly adored and respected. She deserved better than someone like me—a man who succumbed to his wildness.

This was the ultimate test of willpower, especially for someone who had never really exerted much willpower when it came to women. Here was a lady I was attracted to throwing herself on me while I was on vacation. I could do what I had to do, enjoy it, and Joanne would never know. I had done it before with impunity.

But not then. I just wouldn't. However, I needed to graciously refute her advance without offending her, or worst, leaving her to think I was gay. A woman that fine could easily believe something was wrong with me before thinking I was trying to do the right thing.

After a moment, I resorted to something I had seldom done when dealing with a woman in this type of situation. I told her the truth.

"Tara," I said, wiping my face, "you know I'm very attracted to you. No doubt, I want you. But it would not be the right thing for me to do. I have a girlfriend back in D.C. I told her when we got serious that I'd be faithful to her. And that's what I want to do now. If you really knew me, you'd know that this is a difficult thing for me to do. Something I've never done. You've felt how much I want you. But I really can't."

She looked at me as if I were crazy. I'm sure it was seldom—more likely never—that she had been rejected sexually. Clearly, an attractive woman understood that she controlled the situations with men. If she did not want to have sex, there was no sex. If she wanted just kissing and touching, that's what it was. And if she decided, "Fuck it," and wanted sex, then it was hot sex on a platter.

I needed her to say something, although I knew my mind would not change. It felt GREAT to be honest, to do the right thing. Tara shook her head. No words came out. Finally, I said, "You know it's not you. It's not about rejecting you. It's about respecting a relationship I already have."

"But why all this kissing and stuff?" she said.

I could see that Tara was more confused than hurt. "Weakness, my weakness for a beautiful woman," I said. "You're beautiful. I got lost in that, as I've done before. But I'm respecting you now by being honest. I . . ."

She interrupted. "OK," she said. "I'm just surprised. This has never, well, it's not something I've done a lot, but . . . you know men. I liked you before, and I like you even more now. I respect that."

Tara pulled down her tight little skirt that had slipped up so high I could see her satin white panties. "So, tell me about your girl-friend," she said.

"Well, I'm not sure what to tell. She's a good woman, smart, pretty." I felt very awkward, talking about one woman to another woman, especially one I was trying to get with. "She's a quality person."

"What does she do?"

"She's an accountant for a firm in Maryland. Sort of like me as a professor, it's the only job she ever wanted. You can tell she loves her job by the way she lights up when she talks about it. Dealing with numbers all day is boring to me, but it's a joy for her."

"Are you in love with her?"

"Yeah, I love her, I guess. And what's interesting is that I've told her that before, and I believed it. But I don't think I ever really felt like I did until right now, this moment. For me to resist you and then sit here and actually talk about her to you, well, it must be love. It may not be significant to you, but this is a very big moment for me."

Then I couldn't stop. "And you know what?" I said. "She's pregnant." This was a rather strange admission from me. I wanted to take the words back as soon as they left my mouth.

"What?"

"Yeah, I learned about it a few days ago."

"Are you excited?"

"At first I wasn't, but I've gotten a chance to get used to the idea and now I've accepted it. I think I'm ready to handle the responsibility. I have to be because the baby is coming."

"You want a boy or girl?"

"A girl. They are so sweet, so beautiful. And they usually love their dads. But a boy would be great too because he's your little man. You can be rough with him, play sports with him, toughen him up. So, I guess that means either one would be great."

We talked for a few more moments before I borrowed Larry's Pathfinder and took Tara home. At her door, I hugged her good night. "I'm glad we met," she said. "Good luck with everything."

"I'm glad I met you too, Tara. You're good people," I said.

The ride back to the Valley was great. I was on a high. I had DONE THE RIGHT THING and it felt GREAT. I found Patti La-Belle's "Right Kind of Lover" on the radio and blasted it.

When I got back to Larry's, I tossed the keys on the coffee table and changed into shorts and tee shirt. It was about 6:30 a.m. in D.C., but I called Joanne anyway. I missed her.

Her answering machine came on, so I left her a message: "Hey, J, I hope you're good. The fellas are fine out here in Cali. I just wanted you to know that you're missed and that I love you. It'll be a great trip, but I'm already looking forward to getting back to see you. Eat healthy. Bye."

I hung up the phone and in no time went to sleep on the couch. I was happy to be sleeping alone.

EIGHT:

Thanks But No Thanks

Larry

Greg and Julian slept so hard that they did not hear when Simone left at about 11:30 the next morning. Greg was knocked out on the loveseat, mouth open and snoring. He did not look as if he got much rest at Angie's. And Julian was wrapped up in covers on the couch.

I decided I'd awake them by blasting an old cassette of Rare Essence, a go-go band from southeast D.C. Most of the band members—Foots, L'il Benny, Funk, D.C., White Boy, Jungle Boogie, David—went to high school with us at Ballou. Go-go music was hard to explain, except to say it was dominated by the sounds like an African drumbeat complemented by a horn section and congas. Some people said it sounded like guys banging on trashcans, which was not far from the truth. But if you were from the District, you bobbed your head when go-go was played.

So Julian and Greg vibed to Essence as they struggled to adjust to Pacific time. I pulled up a chair. Greg and Julian were awake but remained stretched on the loveseat and couch. It was confession time, and I was the priest.

"Talk to me," I said, meaning I wanted all the juicy details of the previous night.

Greg was eager to interject, which I took to mean that he hit with Angie.

"Yo, I don't believe what happened last night," he said, the excitement detectable in his voice. "She took me to her house, over in Inglewood. I tried to play the gentleman role. I didn't touch her. I let her make the moves, and she did. She said it was too late to sit up in the living room and talk, and she told me to come into her bedroom.

"She had this big platform bed with mirrors on the headboard.

She asked me what did I usually sleep in, and you know I told her, 'I usually sleep naked.' "

We all laughed.

"So she said, 'Fine,' and grabbed a black teddy or something out of a drawer and went to the bathroom to change. She sat on the bed beside me and told me the usual.

Greg started talking in a high-pitched, squeaky voice just like Angie, for effect: "I've never done anything like this before. I don't want you to think I'm a tramp or something. I just like you. I'm very comfortable with you. So I'm thinking, why wait? But there's just one thing: Do you have a condom?"

Greg laughed at the thought and said, "Shit, I had two of them. But I didn't want to sound too eager, and I didn't want to act like I walked around with them in my pocket or like I knew I was going to hit it. I didn't know how to sugarcoat it, so I just nodded my head.

"It was on then. She turned on some music; I think it was Sade. She went into the bathroom to change. I could hear the water running and her slipping out of her clothes."

We knew what was next. Greg was going to give us his version of power sex. He was a trip in talking about that. He came up with wild sayings like he "jet-rocked" a woman or "power drove" or "ram-rod-ded" or his favorite—"performed reconstructive surgery." Since he paused before reaching the crescendo, I knew he had come up with a new one.

"And . . ." I said to Greg.

"And I . . . fell asleep."

"What?" I said, standing up. "I give you an assist like that and all you have to do is make a lay-up and you dribble the ball out of bounds? You went to sleep? What's wrong with you? Julian, you believe this?"

"G, what happened?" Julian said.

"Man, I was tired. It was about five in the morning, Chicago time. I worked Tuesday and got up at 5:30 to fly yesterday. I was tired. More tired than I thought, plus, we had been drinking since we got here."

"Well, you still had time when you woke up. What happened in the morning?" Julian said.

"By the time I got up, she was fully dressed and cooking break-fast," he said. "I couldn't believe I had missed out like that. My dick was harder than a frozen Cornish hen too. But all I could do at that point was get dressed. It was a trip. But, you know, it's no biggie."

"How did she act?" I said. "You know you're messing with my reputation when you don't follow through like you should."

"Angie was cool. She was pleasant," Greg answered. "I told her I was sorry that I went to sleep like that. Guess what she said. She said she tried to wake me up, pushed me, shook me, even kissed me. She said I didn't budge."

We shook our heads.

"Yo, I was exhausted," Greg said.

I sat back down. "Hey, it happens," I said. "I've gone to girls' houses at all hours of the night, got there, got undressed, in the bed, she's butt-ball naked, and the next thing I know it's the next day. But you got off good since she was cool. The girls I fell out on gave me the blues."

Julian got up and went to the bathroom. He said he never felt truly awake in the morning until he brushed his teeth. "I could take a shower and get dressed, but I would not really feel like I was up until I brushed my teeth," he said. "It's my version of a Bloody Mary."

When Julian returned, it was his turn in the confession booth, and there were now two presiding priests. Since Greg had told of his night, he switched roles. Our eyes were on Julian as he flopped back down on the couch. He peeped how we looked at him and knew we were ready to hear the deal. And it wasn't about being nosy. If you could not share your supposed private affairs with your boys, what was the use of even having them?

"So, Ju, what's up with Tara?" Greg said. "When I left here, it seemed like she was on your jock."

"She was," Julian said. "She basically threw the booty right here, in my lap."

"Yeah, but did you catch it?" I said.

"Nope."

"What do you mean, 'nope?' " Greg said with a quizzical look.

"I was going to crush it," Julian answered. "When she slammed her tongue down my throat, I just knew she was going to ride me like a mechanical bull."

"Wait a minute," I said. "You're telling us that she kissed you like that and you didn't . . ."

"No," Julian interrupted. "I had it right there, but I, I couldn't."

"You mean you couldn't get hard?" I said, mouth open. That wasn't so far-fetched. There had been times when a honey set it out for me, but I couldn't get it up. It was embarrassing, for sure. And I didn't know why it happened. But I always made her pay for it when whatever came over me went away.

Julian said that was not his problem. "Hell, no, fool," he said. "I mean I couldn't do it because it wasn't the right thing to do. Look, I've been kind of waiting for the right time to tell you some important shit."

Our eyes were really transfixed on Julian then. Usually, when any of us had news, we just told it. There was no setup, no hesitation. Waiting for the right time? With us, anytime was the right time. That was the kind of time we were on. So, his delay was alarming to us. Why would he wait with good news?

"What's up, Ju?" Greg said.

"Joanne is pregnant."

"Get the *fuck* outta here!" Greg yelled.

"Julian, you sure?" I said.

"She told me about a week ago. At first, I didn't know how to react. I was totally caught off guard. But, yep, she's pregnant. I've accepted it. And if I'm not ready at this moment, I will be by the time it comes. I have to be."

"Damn, Ju, that's deep," Greg said. "And you refused Tara? Good. That's a big step for you."

Then he rose from the love seat and approached Julian, arms extended. He stood up and Greg hugged him. "Congratulations," he said. "You can handle it. I don't know anything about being a father, but I've got a nephew and a niece so I know how to be an uncle."

Greg looked at me and continued. "We'll be good uncles to Little Julian or if it's a girl, Julia or whatever. You'll probably name her Nakeesha Aretha Monika, or some wild shit like that. But you know we'll be there for you and Joanne and the baby. I've got just one question: When's the wedding?"

"You better stop tripping," Julian said. "No shotgun wedding here. Joanne is good people, but marriage is another story. I'm not ready to give up my whole life."

In probably too many instances, that was exactly how men felt about marriage—like life as they knew it was over. I'd never felt even close to considering marriage. The things I did for my peace of mind—shooting ball as much as possible, hanging with the fellas for drinks at happy hour, partying when I felt like, and really just being irresponsible—would be unacceptable to most wives. But those things were still very important to me. I didn't want to give that up, and I wasn't sure when I'd be ready. Or if I'd ever be ready.

And I knew I wasn't the only man who felt that way. If men felt women were possessive and clingy as girlfriends, forget about it when they were wives. They believed they had legal grounds to turn your leisure time into shopping trips and never-ending conversation— anything other than what you wanted it to be. I was not ready for such a dramatic lifestyle change. Really, I wasn't sure if I'd ever be.

"If I know women at all, and I do," I said, "you'd better believe that marriage is on Joanne's mind. That's just how women think. You might as well prepare for that subject to come up."

"I don't give a damn if she does bring it up," Julian said. "I'm not going to be forced into anything. You think people get married when they don't want to?"

"Happens all the time," I said. "Right, Greg?"

NINE:

Blah, Blah, Blah

Greg

Julian and Larry thought that if anyone was going to be married anytime soon, it would be me. Brianna was my ace. We met at a library. I talked too loudly and Brianna, outspoken woman that she is, asked me to be quiet. I later learned that she would assert herself to most anyone at any time.

Once, she was at the post office and this teenager had his rap music just blasting in his car. Kids were out there and the lyrics were filled with profanity. Brianna coolly walked over and told the guy to turn down his music. Now, he could have gotten funky about it and told her where she could go—or worse—but she didn't think about that. She just stepped to him.

That's how she did me. "Excuse me," is what she said to me that day we met, "but this IS a library. You can't talk so loudly here, if you don't mind."

I apologized and told her I'd hold it down—with one condition: That she help me locate some books on tax preparation. I had an accountant, but I wanted to know more about it. She agreed, and I took that time with her to make inroads. Before long, we were dating.

Brianna had a house on the south side of Chicago, on Justine. I had a really good feeling for her the first time I visited her place, for a house warming. She was a person you just felt comfortable around. She was funny and graceful and poised.

My older brother, Ricky, told me that the way a woman handled duress told a lot about her ability to handle a man. If her first reaction was to snap or fall apart, you could bet she'd be confrontational and overly emotional with her man when composure would serve better. Brianna was not fazed by the inevitable snafus of hosting. And she had me under control because she seldom bit the bait I'd throw her to incite an argument. A clearer indication was that I did a lot of talking and flirting with women, but I did not cheat on her. Not once.

"Hold up," Julian said. "Let's be serious for a minute here. Greg, what's the deal with you and Brianna?"

"It's not what you think," I said.

I knew that was definitely alarming to them. I couldn't hide the concern on my face. Plus I knew they'd realized that I had not once mentioned Brianna since we'd been in L.A., which was highly unusual. Usually, whether in-person or during one of our weekly conference calls, I'd have something to say about her—good, bad, or indifferent.

"We used to talk about marriage," I added. "But not anymore. She used to always bring it up. But she's changed. Believe it or not, we haven't even slept together in the last two weeks. And, trust me, that's not like us at all."

Larry said, "I know you, Greg. You have this pride that a lot of times is stubbornness. Talk to your woman and clean it up. I mean, what happened before she cut you off?"

"I just told her until I get her a ring, all this talk about getting married is premature," I said. "I just got tired of her talking about it, as if it were a foregone conclusion. To me, it's a process: I get a ring and then propose. She accepts and then we go on from there. I don't want to hear all this planning stuff now. It's premature."

Larry turned to me. "I think you're tripping," he said. "Women live for that stuff. You tell a woman you want to marry her, and no way she's not going to be excited about it. It's her dream."

I was so defensive that I jumped right on Larry's shit. "When did you become an expert on women and relationships?" I said. "When was the last time you had a relationship that really meant something to you? Oh, you might have been upset about losing a honey you liked in bed. Or one who was a good cook or gave you money. But what about one that meant something to you? Hasn't happened."

I said that in a joking manner, but I was serious, too. And he knew it, so he addressed it.

"I love women in general, but individually, I've never been in love with one," Larry said. "And I know that my aunt got engaged BEFORE she got a ring and she still went on and made wedding plans. That's just how women are. As for me, I don't know if I'm capable of being in love. If there is a woman out there who can change that, I haven't met her. And I've met enough with all kinds of backgrounds to believe she doesn't exist.

"You remember when I used to live with Emma? I really cared about her. We got along great for a while. She wanted marriage, I didn't. Because I didn't, she thought that must have meant that I was messing with someone else. When I was with her was one of the few times that I actually gave it a real chance by not stepping out.

"How could I see someone else when she made sure she knew where I was every moment that I wasn't with her? She bought me a pager to keep up with me. But, still, that did not stop her from going through my briefcase, through my pants pockets, my wallet, my suit jackets, my desk. Then she had the balls to tell me about it by questioning me about what she found, which, through all that searching, was a business card of a woman who handled casting calls."

There was hardly a man who had not experienced, at least once, a woman violating him by going through his stuff. Women always talked about their "instincts" told them to do it. Yeah, right. I didn't care what they found or thought they found through the search. And I didn't care what drove them to do it. There was NO excuse that justified being so underhanded, sneaky, and disrespectful. It was a violation. And it was an express ticket out of my life.

I remember when Larry went through that with Emma. I kind of liked her, but she showed herself to be a typical, paranoid woman with that move. I lost total respect for her. Larry gave Emma the boot, and good.

"You know what was really wild about Emma?" Larry said. "She never would apologize for going through my shit. She didn't see anything wrong with it. It was crazy. Since her, I just don't think I can be overwhelmed by a woman. I know who I am in this world. I've accepted who I am."

We had gotten a little off the path of vacation and into one of our countless debates about women. We could not get away from them.

"All right, all right," I said. "Get off your soapbox, and let's just get on with the day. What's on the agenda—besides depressing talk about how hopeless we are?"

"I don't think we're hopeless," Julian said. "I got a baby coming. You have a woman who loves you and wants to marry you. Larry knows who he is in this world—whatever that is. What's hopeless about that?"

"Well, I'm saying let's do some vacation stuff," I said. "We can talk about this stuff in the car. But let's get out of here. Let's go to Venice Beach, shoot some ball. It's about time to get out of this apartment."

And so we did. We piled into the Pathfinder, but the conversation switched from women in our lives to the prospect of meeting new women. It was such a contradiction to one moment talk proudly about having a good woman and, the next, talk about meeting other women. But we just could not help it. We loved women.

As we rolled along the 101 Freeway toward Interstate 10, Larry pointed this out to us. "Let me get this straight: you turned down a woman last night because you're going to be a father. And you're glad you fell asleep on another woman because you have a good woman in Chicago. Now, twenty minutes later, it's 'Where are the honies?' You guys are a trip. And to keep it real: you're just like me. It's about lust."

"That's what you want it to be about because you don't want to be left out there alone," Julian said. "I'm still holding out hope that there's somebody out there who can change my emotions from lust to love. But I won't hold my breath that it'll happen."

TEN:

Act Like Ya Know

Greg

Venice Beach was, well, Venice Beach. Even on a Thursday afternoon, it was vibrant. Smog took a break on this day, and the reflection of the brilliant sun shimmied off the Pacific Ocean in a way that drew postcard images. You could stand on the beach, sink your feet into the sand, and get lost in your thoughts staring out at the water.

The boardwalk had the usual horde of roller-bladers, bikini-clad women, hustlers, tourists, and vendors. The group of weight lifters was smaller than on Saturdays and Sundays, but the buffed-up crew was represented.

Against this backdrop, we played basketball, having made our way up the boardwalk, across the playground, and to the courts. A steady breeze was a respite for the board walkers, but it was a hazard for a jump shooter like me on the court. The wind affected my shot, so I focused on driving and dishing. Larry, Julian, and I had played together many times before, so the chemistry we had off the court was on the court, too.

Julian was the best player among us, but he understood that the key to winning at basketball was playing together, getting guys to think not so much about scoring but about staying on the court. That was always Magic Johnson's credo. We had three players on the same team—us—who understood that team-play equals wins.

Our style rubbed off on the other two guys—one from Sacramento, the other from Santa Monica—and we ran until we couldn't run anymore. Actually, until Larry couldn't run anymore. In a rebound attempt, Larry came down on someone's foot under the basket and sprained his left ankle near the end of the fourth game. The swelling was too bad for him to continue.

45

He refused to go to the hospital, which I understood having had many sprained ankles myself as a football player in high school. Soak the ankle in Epsom salt, elevate it, ice it, and stay off it was the way to treat it. The problem was always staying off it because there always seemed to be something to do. And sure enough, we had a party to attend in El Segundo that night, one that could not be missed.

Totally unfazed, Larry announced while hopping on one foot into his apartment: "By tonight, I'll be on the dance floor."

After a shower, Larry soaked the ankle and in the living room elevated it under a small pillow. Julian and I washed away the sweat of basketball and got comfortable—he on the floor, me on the love seat.

In a way, the "ankle thing" was a blessing because it slowed us down long enough so Larry could study a script for a play he would audition for the next week.

"So what are you doing? Trying to memorize your lines?" I asked.

He promptly gave me a quick lesson in one phase of acting. "Actually," Larry said, "this is the first time I'm reading this script, so I'm reading it without interpreting it. After that, I'll read it again and begin the process of understanding the character, getting the essence of him, and finding where I can add layers to him. I'll formulate opinions of the script. And when you read or recite your lines, you have inner dialogue; you communicate to yourself what the lines mean to you. That's how it becomes authentic to you. Eventually, I memorize the script. And it has to be verbatim. Otherwise you do injustice to the writer."

Larry spoke with pride and passion about his craft. He talked the same way about anything that meant something to him: clothes, family, basketball, and, of course, women.

"Now, this is dangerous," I said. "It's bad enough you already have all this psychological approach in dealing with honies that gets them under a spell. Now you can ACT a certain way when you need to. That's dangerous."

"You know what?" Larry said, "I don't even have to act with women. But my training has taught me to understand the intonation of women's voices. I can interpret better now what a woman's tone or body language or facial expressions mean. Also, when I talk to women—or anyone, really—I can paint a picture in their head by using operative words. Imagery. I don't try to use my craft to manipulate women. That's like cheating. I can control that. But I am trained to interpret actions. So, if I get an advantage that way, I can't really help it."

Julian and I had seen Larry perform a role in the play "Purlie Victorious" at a small theater in Westwood nearly a year before. Talk about brimming with pride. He blew up the spot. Here was a kid from southeast D.C.—the part of town the government neglects—performing on stage in Tinsel Town. Gave us chills.

But it did not surprise us. The deal with where we grew up was this: if you got out of the neighborhood safely, you had big potential. The benefit of growing up in the inner city was that you leave it with book-sense from school, hopefully common sense, and definitely street sense from growing up around an assortment of elements. You were well-rounded, prepared to do battle in any arena.

That was another thing that made us so appealing to women. They wanted men who were men, who could talk intelligently about most any serious issue with a smart-ass white boy, turn to his left and deal with a drug dealer, cross the street and deal with a crackhead, and turn to his right and charm a woman. That was well-rounded, and that's who we were. I didn't have a college education, but I read as much as I could—newspapers, magazines, books—to stay on top of things.

I vowed to myself that I'd one day go college and get a degree. My thinking was that I wanted children one day, and I'd definitely stress the importance of education, higher education to them. But it just wouldn't seem right for me to push them in that direction when I hadn't done it myself.

"So, Laurence Fishbourne," I said to Larry, smiling, "how's the ankle? Are we going to have to leave you here tonight?"

"Stop tripping," he said. "I'm going to get my gear ready now. You know this is L.A., so we need to be at the Golden Tale by about 10. We start early out here."

We laughed as Larry limped his way around the apartment. He was also passionate about partying, and a sore ankle was not going to prevent him from getting his freak on.

"You bamas can laugh all you want," he said. "I'll be in the house. That's all that matters."

As Larry and I ironed our clothes, Julian decided to give Joanne another call. He hadn't talked to her since arriving Wednesday, and he said he really wanted to make sure she was all right. Again, however, he could not reach her, so he left her a voice mail message at work.

I wanted to use the phone to call Brianna, but Julian said, "Hold up. I need to check my messages at home. Give me a few minutes."

He received three calls: one from Joanne and two hang-ups. "I hate when people call and don't leave messages," Julian said. "But that's all right. I bought a caller ID box, so I'll find out who it was when I get home."

"It's about time you got one. I told you a long time ago to get one," I said. "You don't want to answer the phone when it's some other honey and Joanne is there. Now, can I get the phone now?"

Julian used the iron as I called Brianna. "What's up?" I said into the phone. "Julian and Larry are cool. Well, actually, Larry sprained his ankle when we played ball earlier today. He's walking around limping like your father did last week when he stubbed his toe on the bed."

"You're wrong for that," Brianna said, laughing.

"You doing all right?" I said.

"Yeah."

"You miss me?"

"You miss ME?" she said.

That irritated me. "You know, I can't get a straight answer out of you lately on anything."

"Ditto," Brianna said.

There was a moment of awkward silence. Not even 2,000 miles could quell the tension we'd had the last few weeks. I could feel a blowup coming so I decided I'd cut it short.

"Well," I finally said, "I just wanted to call and say hi, make sure you're all right."

Brianna was not letting me get away with that so easily. She was a tough one, a woman who was the oldest of four children. Her mother suffered a stroke when Brianna was fourteen and never fully recovered. So, Brianna assumed the role of mother to three as a teenager. She didn't have time or patience for games. And she usually said so—one way or another.

"Do you really care, Gregory?" she responded. "I don't feel like you really care. All I really know is that you care about money. And yourself. And Julian and Larry. That's it. And that's sad."

I was pissed off then. You know, the truth hurts. "It's sad you think that," I said. "You know, I call to say hi to you from California, and all you do is rag me. What's up with that?"

"Nothing," she said, and hung up.

I slammed down the phone. I was pissed, but I was not going to let it spoil my vacation. "I can't believe she hung up on me," I said. "But that's all right. Hey, I'm making drinks! Anybody want one? No? OK, I'll take two. C'mon let's go to this party. I need to have a good time tonight. I'm GONNA have a good time."

ELEVEN:

Aw Sukie Sukie Now

Julian

Because African-American men usually walked with a rhythm that exuded confidence—if not arrogance—Larry's limp was hardly noticeable to anyone but me and Greg. It just looked as if he put a little extra lean into his strut, which many men did with healthy ankles.

On the way to the party, I told the guys that I remembered reading in Vibe magazine where Toni Braxton said she found a black man's gait sexy. "I read that, too," said Greg, who had a nice buzz after two Absolutes and cranberries. "Man, I just don't get women. They get hooked on a man for all kind of wild reasons. They'll like you for the car you drive, the job you have. It's crazy. I met this girl when I went out one night, and, after about 30 minutes, she tells me she likes me because of the tie I was wearing. She was a tie freak. I didn't try, but she acted like if I wanted to take her home, she would have come because of my tie."

He shook his head. "As much as women don't understand me, I sure as hell don't understand them."

"She probably liked the tie but was attracted to you," I said, trying to make sense of a woman I did not know. And, really, that was funny because I couldn't make sense out of women I DID know.

"G, no man understands women," I said. "I could tell you one hundred instances when I've been confused or shocked by a woman's actions. You think they're thinking one thing and they're thinking another. I've stopped trying to figure them out. I just deal with them."

We cruised down the 405. "Hey, Julian," Larry said, "remember you told me about the woman you went out with one night a few years ago, and at dinner all she talked about was how men want sex immediately instead of trying to get to know a person?"

49

"Exactly," I said. "It was our first date. She basically told me, 'Don't have any ideas of getting me in the bed with you tonight.' I told myself it wasn't going to happen. Then she comes back to my apartment and attacks me, rips off my clothes, goes down on me, the whole nine. I couldn't believe it."

"What about the honey I met in New Orleans?" Larry said. "I think her name was Saundra. I met her at this club, Whispers. She's freaking me on the dance floor like crazy. I offer her a ride home, and she accepts it. She's rubbing on my leg as I drive, so I pull over into a parking lot. We get in the back seat and I power drive her—as you might say, Greg—for about 30 minutes. Then, we get near her house and she says, 'Let me out here, at the corner.' I said, 'I'll take you to your house.' She said, 'This is good. I don't want my husband to see me.' "

We laughed a good laugh. It was good for our psyches to point out women's manly, uh, attributes. Make that tendencies. Maybe it was a method to relieve some of the guilt we had for the things we did. I didn't know.

"When women start their men-bashing, they ignore women who do the same stuff men do," Greg said. "I mean, you can tell a woman that you're in a relationship, and if she wants to get with you, she'll do it, or at least try. So, if a man is messing around, the other woman has as much of a role in it as you do. That doesn't make men right or any less wrong. But women tend to forget a woman's part, too."

Those were the thoughts we carried into the party. From the fullness of the parking lot, it was evident we were at the right spot. And once we stepped through the doors, it was confirmed. Women everywhere. To the right and left and in front. Around the corner, at the bar, on the two dance floors.

There were two birthday parties in the club—one to the right of the entrance and the one we came to attend on the other side of the room. It was the birthday of one of my college friends who moved to L.A. after graduation to get into the record business. Billy Bryson was the public relations guy for an upstart recording company working out of the Beverly Center.

B.B., who turned thirty-five that day, promised a cornucopia of women. He delivered.

"What's up, boy?" Billy said in greeting me. "Glad you could make it."

Then he whispered into my ear. "Let me know which honey you want to meet, and I'll hook it up."

"Cool," I said, not that I needed his help. "Hey, meet my boys, Larry and Greg. Larry lives out here; you guys should hook up. Greg lives in Chicago."

"What's up?" Billy said. Then he showed us to a table. We said hello to everyone in his party area, about fifteen people at that point. Typical of Larry, he sat down for all of two minutes and then was off to roam the club.

Greg and I mingled with a few of B.B.'s friends, exchanged a few laughs. The music was pumping. I was waiting to hear anything old school to find my first dance partner of the night. Classic tunes never lose their bounce. Don't get me wrong, I like the new joints—if they're good—but oldies take you back. Greg was ready to scope out the club, so we excused ourselves from the table and took a walk.

There was much talent there; always was in L.A. As if the dee-jay and I were in cahoots, he played Frankie Beverly's "Before I Let Go" just as I introduced myself to a stunning woman in an apple green, chemise-style dress who stood up against the wall, away from the action. Her hair was jet black and pinned up, with a bang hanging down either side of her face. She had long, sexy earrings that accentuated her caramel complexion. Her makeup was neat, barely noticeable. She looked like a combination of Thelma from television sitcom *Good Times* and Sheryl Lee Ralph, which is to say incredible. The silk dress had a scoop neck in the front, revealing ample cleavage and a classy set of pearls. The dress was fitting, not tight. And she wore a sweet-smelling perfume, always a bonus.

She looked up at me with an expression that invited conversation. Women know how to attract a man's attention with their eyes. And they know how to say "bug off" without uttering a word. I did not get that from her. Just as I checked her out, she gave me the once-over. I wore a navy linen three-button suit, a cream linen shirt buttoned to the neck, and a pair of crocodile loafers I treated myself to. She was impressed. I could tell.

"That color looks nice on you," I said to the woman. Then I extended my hand. "How are you?"

She smiled, placed her hand on mine, and said, "I'm fine. And you?"

That was definitely an indication that she was at least interested—or had manners. When a man asked a new acquaintance all the questions and she just halfway answered or did not reciprocate, that was a telltale sign that she was not interested. But if she was cordial and asked questions, you had a shot.

"Good," I said, still holding her soft but cold hand. "I'm Julian Morgan."

"Nice to meet you. My name is Alexis Miller."

"Alexis, huh?," I said. "That name fits you. It's smooth, classy, kind of regal, you know?"

"You think so?" she asked. "Well, I like it, probably since I've had it all my life. But how can you tell that about me in 15 seconds?"

"Just by the way you're standing here. You're poised, understated. You give off an aura that you're a quality person, but that you don't think you're better than anyone. And you told me your name without me asking, which means you understand when someone introduces himself it's appropriate to introduce yourself. You'd be surprised how many women don't do or know that."

She raised her eye brows.

"I'm not psychic," I said, "but I'd guess that if you drink alcohol, you drink wine. Probably chardonnay."

"How did you know that?" she said, seemingly waiting on some deep response.

I paused for dramatic effect and said, "I guessed."

She delicately clutched my elbow and laughed. That was good, for a few reasons. She felt comfortable enough already to touch me. And she revealed a smile that seemed to illuminate the entire room.

I had been in the club less than an hour and already I had met someone I really felt good about. Usually, I'd be glad to meet an attractive woman, get her number, and then move on to meet more. Simple greed. But I did not feel greedy then. In fact, I was so captured by Alexis that I forgot about dancing.

"Alexis, you mind coming with me to the bar area so I can get us a drink? I'd rather not leave you standing here."

"Sure," she said.

I let her walk in front of me through the crowd, giving myself a rear vantage point of her figure. And it was booming: small waist; protruding hips; firm-looking, round ass; and strong legs. She wore high-heeled shoes that exposed her toes, revealing she'd recently had a pedicure. I could not find a flaw in this woman, and boy, did I search.

"When I introduced myself to you, I was looking to get on the dance floor," I said. Her eyes, brown and bright, alternated between my eyes and my mouth. She looked hard, as if she was searching for the truth in what I said. "But I'd actually like it better if we talked for a while."

"Well, I'd like to dance before the night's over," she said. "You came out to party, didn't you? But talking sounds nice, too."

We found a seat at the bar, which I gave to her, of course. She placed her Coach bag on the floor under her stool and crossed her legs. There was better lighting at the bar, and Alexis looked even more elegant.

For the next thirty minutes, we talked as if we had known each other for years. We made each other laugh. It was all so natural. She touched me on the arm occasionally. We danced three consecutive songs, and I found myself staring into her eyes quite a bit. She held my hand as we returned to the bar. Her hands were warm now, and they seemed to warm my entire body.

I concentrated on her so intently that I did not even notice anyone else in the club—other than Larry and Greg. She acknowledged her sister and girlfriend once, but basically we were locked in on each other.

TWELVE:

Party Over Here!

Larry

With my hands raised high above my head, I smoothly maneuvered on the dance floor with a woman who seemed less interested in dancing as she was in pushing her body against mine. There was no trace of an ankle injury, just as I had predicted. I moved confidently, fluidly. And my partner flowed in sync.

I had this way of picking out women who were vulnerable to my will. Some guys were gifted like that. I say "some guys" because I'm sure I couldn't have been the only one like that, although I didn't know of any others. At the risk of sounding conceited, virtually without any effort, I knew how to mesmerize a woman, have her hanging onto my every word.

And I was a closer—meaning I scored more often that not—because my style was persuasive, my words rhythmic, sometimes poetic. I learned way back in high school that women fell for that. They liked clever dialogue and words that made them feel good. I knew how to do it without sounding phony.

Before I even said a word, my dance partner was already captured by my rapture. It was evident in the way she looked up at me as we danced. She had goo-goo eyes. When the song ended, we left the floor, and I, without saying a word, directed her toward the bar where Julian and Alexis were.

The woman wore a black bodysuit that displayed her lean physique. She smiled a lot, almost too much, but that was better than women who were so stuck up they were sickening. I was stuck on myself, but I was not stuck up. Other than traffic, nothing was worse than a phony woman. The kind you asked to dance and she looked you up and down and then turned away without answering, or she'd answer rudely. The kind who wouldn't go some place because it was "too black," as if she were too good.

I never understood what happened to people that made them feel as if they were better or too good for someone else to give a simple, courteous response. Women wondered why they attended a party and men stood around and didn't ask them to dance. Many times it was because men did not want to go through the humiliation of rejection. To walk across the room and ask a woman to dance while she just stared at you and turned her head was embarrassing and frustrating.

It was inexcusable when men reacted angrily or disrespectfully to that rejection. But it was like this: as much as men went through to prove how macho we were, rejection hurt our feelings—feelings many women believed we did not even possess. Although it could be something as small as a dance, feelings and egos could be bruised. Weak men responded with nasty remarks like, "Why did you even come here? Take your ass home." A real man would simply say, "Thanks anyway," or say nothing and walk away.

All it would take for a stuck up woman to change her attitude would be to experience the other side of it, to ask a man to dance and get rejected in a mean-spirited fashion. She'd change in a heartbeat. But most women weren't "man" enough to ask for a dance.

But that did not apply to Shawna, an aerobics instructor who liked what she saw in me, wanted to shake her booty, and requested a dance. I liked her boldness. But such boldness also could be viewed as a weakness; a man would quickly take it as a come on, which was what I did in that case. But that was just me, my arrogance. It could have been that she just wanted to dance. I didn't know and really didn't care.

We made our way off the dance floor, through the crowd, and to the bar with Julian and this woman he seemed to be all into named Alexis. Yesterday, he was saying how committed he was—now look at him. At least I don't front.

After the introductions, I ordered drinks. Shawna smiled that perpetual smile, which was not lost on me. I was the ultimate opportunist.

"Your spirit is contagious," I said to her. "When you smile, it's like one of those lights on a lamp that gets brighter the more you turn the knob. Your smile gets brighter and brighter. And you know what? It makes everyone around you smile and feel good."

Then I smiled. And since we always looked to assist each other, Julian smiled, too, to validate my approach. Men worked together in dealing with women all the time, even when it was unnecessary. I remembered traveling with another set of friends—Dennis Roberts and

Nick Stevenson—to San Diego one weekend. Dennis and Nick met three women while we were dining on the boardwalk and told them this wild story about us visiting there to do research on opening another men's clothing store.

I came out of the bathroom and these ladies were sitting at our table. One of them said to me, "I think it's great you guys are in business together. Where are your other two stores?"

Although I had no idea what Dennis and Nick had told them, I did not miss a beat. "We have one in Pasadena and another in Manhattan Beach," I said. Women being women, they were impressed and could have been our sex partners the next night—if we wanted.

Usually, that type of shenanigans was unnecessary. But some men used all resources available, real or imagined. I was just being my usual self with Shawna. I used metaphors and analogies all the time, in any situation. By 1 a.m., she had written down on a napkin for me her home number, work number, pager number, car phone number, and mother's number. She might have written down her social security number, she was so 'pressed. I knew I had her.

It wasn't until then that Greg surfaced. He'd struck up a conversation with Marilyn Raines, a beautiful Continental flight attendant who lived in Newark, N.J. Greg was a breast man and Marilyn had a prominent set. Just as attractive to him, though, was that she was an avid reader, especially of African-American literature. That was Greg's business, his forte. So they both were excited about the conversation on authors and literature.

He brought her over to where we were and made the requisite introductions. It was smiles all around. Even the women seemed to get along, which really was an accomplishment since women usually had a problem doing that. That was another mystery of women that made me shake my head. Women could look at another woman and in an instant decide, "That bitch thinks she's cute," and treat her with disdain.

Jealousy had to be at the core of such foolishness. It also could have been that they felt threatened. Definitely women felt they were in competition with each other. I always viewed it as silly. I could get three groups of my male friends together who didn't know each other and they'd get along, laugh, play ball, and talk about honies as if they'd known each other forever. Get different factions of women together and it'd be a damned cat war. Crazy.

But obviously we had something good going because those

women were all so cool, probably because none of them felt threatened. I probably could have gotten with Shawna that night, but I'd already set up the booty call, so I put her off until the next night. Greg tried to get Marilyn to welcome him to her place that night, but she resisted, saying she had to return to her friend's house in Baldwin Hills because she had a 6 a.m. flight back East.

As for Julian, he seemed enthralled with Alexis. She said she was out with a girlfriend and her sister, who lived over by Fox Hills Mall. She was visiting from Orangeburg, S.C., which Julian found ironic because he had a cousin who lived there. Alexis grew up there, went away to college and medical school, and returned as a pediatrician to work in a community she knew needed her help. I could tell Julian found that commendable because he said it spoke for the kind of person she was.

When she left to go to the bathroom, Julian leaned over to me. "It's wild," he said, "but I haven't even thought about sex with this chick. Check this out: She gave me the number to her sister's place and I went to the phone in the lobby and left her a message."

"Saying what?" I said.

"I just told her that meeting her made my night," Julian said, "and that I wanted her to know that when she got in from the club. And I left your number. It's 818/555-1906, isn't it?"

"Yeah, that's it," I said. "But I can't believe you did that. That's a smooth move, though. I'll remember that one."

"But it wasn't even a move. It just came to me," Julian said.

When Alexis returned, the lights came on, indicating the club was closing, although it was just 1:25. We walked the ladies to their respective cars, gave them hugs, and promised to stay in touch.

When we got into my car, we took off our suit jackets and tossed them in the back seat with Greg.

"I like shorty Shawna," I said. "She's got pizzazz. Tomorrow, it's on."

"I'm telling you," Greg added. "Marilyn made me forget all about Brianna tripping."

"Yeah, I can relate," Julian said. "Not once did I even think about Joanne. This girl Alexis is legit, in every way. I don't know what I'm going to do with her. But I'm getting with her tomorrow, I know that."

Just yesterday the fool said he was ready to be a father. Today he doesn't know what to do with the baby's mama. All I could do was shake my head.

THIRTEEN:

Bang, Zoom!

Julian

A nice capper to a night out—besides getting some sex—was to fill up at breakfast. And so, we embarked on such a journey.

Larry turned right out of the parking lot toward Sepulveda Blvd. I was fumbling for the appropriate CD to play—something soothing but up-tempo. Greg was in the back, rambling about how many great looking women were at the club. This was like the old days, the feeling of camaraderie and closeness we shared after a night of pulling a few honies. When I felt like this, the air seemed thinner, even in thick-aired Los Angeles.

As we approached the green light, I glanced at the stars through the sunroof and gained a moment of serenity. Turns out, it was the last clear-headed moment I'd experience in my remaining days in L.A.

Larry flashed his blinker to turn right onto Sepulveda, but midway through the turn, the screeching sound of a speeding vehicle trying to stop rang through the cool night air. It was followed seconds later by the frightening and unforgettable sound of metal against metal.

That was the last thing I remembered for nearly two hours. A Suburban, traveling at what police later estimated to be 70 miles an hour in a 45-mile-an-hour zone, ran a red light and slammed right into Larry's vulnerable Pathfinder, knocking it onto the sidewalk, into an electrical pole and onto its side.

Only the grace of God prevented us from starring in funerals. Larry and Greg remained conscious throughout the accident but suffered painful injuries. It could have been worse, but we were sticklers for wearing seat belts, especially after the unfortunate deaths of basketball players Malik Sealy and Bobby Phils, and football player Derrick Thomas—all of whom were really good brothers.

Larry had a broken right wrist, a broken collar bone, and a dislocated ankle. Greg had bruised ribs and a separated shoulder. Both were sore all over but had no major cuts. I was knocked out on impact, sustaining a severe concussion, which is another way of saying I had the most excrutiating headache: a migraine times ten. Worse, it maintained its intensity for nearly two successive days.

My right arm was broken. The right side of my face was swollen and my neck was bruised from the impact of the airbag. Of course, I didn't realize any of this until I regained consciousness.

Before I did, I simply thought I slept the most peaceful sleep ever. I dreamed about walking into my first classroom as a college professor, at Framington State, a small community school about 30 miles outside Boston. I felt the nervous energy I had at the start and then the feeling of "I can do this" after completing that first class.

I dreamed about visiting my brother, Earl, in jail and the emptiness I felt each time I left him in that hellhole. Earl was not a bad guy; he was a good, bright guy who hung with bad, dumb guys who made awful, unlawful decisions. I guess, really, that made Earl pretty dumb to do that. He got five years for armed robbery and a series of other petty crimes. I cried inside each time I left him behind and wondered what I could have done to change his life's course.

I remembered dreaming about the time Larry, Greg, and I took three women to Atlantic City for a weekend. We swam, played pool, gambled, danced, talked—just had an incredible time. And I dreamed about my family watching me make the opening remarks at a Martin Luther King Jr. program in elementary school. They were the best dreams I'd ever had. Well, the wet dream I had that time wasn't bad, either.

But I came to realize these weren't dreams; it was a recap of part of my life. Had to be because any other dream I had usually was something weird in some way, not something that actually had happened. I didn't realize this, of course, until I awoke at Centinela Hospital near LAX.

Before I opened my eyes, I could feel my head pulsating like a thousand hangovers. Standing over me was a Dr. Wamer, whose expression was not exactly comforting.

"Glad you could join us," he said to me. "How do you feel?"

That's when it hit me that we were in an accident, a serious one. I was petrified.

I tried to sit up. "Where are Larry and Greg?" I said. "Are they all right?"

"They are being looked at by other doctors," Wamer said. "They got banged up pretty good, but they're all right. Or they will be."

That was a great relief. My throat was dry, as if I had swallowed dirt. My head rang and the room seemed to move from side to side.

One moment I could see Dr. Wamer and his yellow teeth, the next minute I could not. I was fading, but I wanted to know what happened.

"From what I understand, sir, a couple of kids from Palos Verdes crashed into the car you were in," the attending nurse said. "They were speeding in this big truck. Neither one of them got hurt."

"That figures," I said. "Hey, can I see Greg and Larry? What's wrong with them?"

"Listen, Mr. Morgan, don't worry about them," the doctor said. "They'll be fine. But we've got to run some tests on you."

"What? Tests?" I said. "What kinds of tests?"

"Tests to make sure your head injuries are superficial. We're going to give you a CT Scan shortly, which will determine if you received any brain damage whatsoever. You seem fine, sharp. But, you have to stay here a few days for observation. How does your head feel?"

"Bad, like the worse headache I've ever had. It's like someone's inside my head with a hammer."

"Is your vision blurry?"

"Yeah, a little. The room is moving from side to side, and you're fading in and out."

Dr. Wamer started writing. Then something important came to me. I sat up quickly and said, "Damn."

"What?" the doctor said, alarmed.

I remembered Alexis. If I had to stay at the hospital a few days, I wouldn't get to see her. I needed to call her.

"Where are my clothes?"

"You won't be needing them for a while, Mr. Morgan," Dr. Wamer said.

"I don't need the clothes, just something inside them."

"What?"

"A phone number."

"Mr. Morgan, that's going to have to wait."

As he spoke, I glanced down to my right, and I realized my arm was in a cast. "What's that, a broken arm? Damn. Anything else wrong with me?"

"You're going to be sore, if you're not already," the doctor said. "Your face is a little puffy and you have an abrasion on your neck from the air bag. But considering the wreck, you are blessed to be talking to me. For a long time, you were knocked out."

I heard him say that and then I fell asleep.

FOURTEEN:

On The Mend

Julian

Like most people, hospitals made me feel creepy. The smell bothered me and made my stomach turn. And the sound of all those machines was ominous. It was even more frightening to open my eyes and see gloomy-looking doctors standing over me. But that's what I faced when I awoke from my slumber.

Dr. Wamer was joined by a neurologist and a nurse. The doctors filled the air with technical talk that ultimately meant I would be fine, but that I'd experience headaches ranging in varying degrees of discomfort. And my equilibrium would be off a tad. Those symptoms would last for another day or so, I was told.

But I knew I was doing better already because my dick was hard. I don't remember the dream that put me in that state, but that was a positive sign to me. Hey, if *Ole Boy* was functioning, I couldn't have been too bad off.

Both Larry and Greg got their noggins banged too, but nothing serious. Their concerns were more on me as they hovered around my bed. The doctors left us to talk for a while.

"Damn, Ju, you all right?" Greg said, looking battered himself. "This shit is crazy. I can't believe this."

"What in the hell happened?" I said. "We were feeling good, rolling. This honey I met, man, I was looking forward to getting with her. I liked this woman. Then I look up and I'm in a hospital. What happened?"

Larry and Greg explained that two rich kids from Palos Verdes had some beers while cruising in "Daddy's" car, ran through the red light, and banged us up. The cops clamped them in handcuffs before whisking them away.

They described the scene as chaotic. Although they were in ex-

61

treme pain, they noticed I was knocked out, which gave them the scare of a lifetime. Greg said that was the most scared he'd been since Brianna told him she missed her period. Larry said he was more frightened than when he read for a supporting role in John Single-ton's movie, Shaft.

Glass covered the street and sidewalk. Although the Pathfinder was mangled, the stereo system still blared. Antifreeze poured from the busted radiator. Patrons from the club slowly rolled pass the scene and shook their heads. Women covered their eyes.

"It was a surreal thing," Larry said. "It was like everything was in slow motion. I was trippin'. We had to climb out of the car through the windshield. And you were just laying there . . . We thought you were dead."

"Nah, I'm here," I said. "I just hope you had insurance on that car."

"I did," Larry said. "And I'm getting a lawyer. These kids lived in Palos Verdes, which means "Mommy" and "Daddy" have money. They were drinking and ran a red light and hit us. And here we are all messed up and they are out on bail, walking around. But at the moment, I'm not really thinking about the money. But it will be ad-dressed."

Just about that time, the nurse returned to the room to check my chart. I must have been really dizzy when I saw her earlier because I didn't notice her virtues. The sister was cute—and genuinely con-cerned about all of our well being.

As she checked the chart, Larry checked out her body, which was a sight even in those confining, unimaginative nurse's outfits. And she had an innocent face, highlighted by deep dimples and thick eye brows.

"Excuse me," Larry said to her, "we're concerned about my friend here. Is he ever going to be able to think again? And is there any way to let some of that water out of his head?"

The nurse laughed. "Probably," she said.

"You're not Nurse Ratchet, are you?" I said.

"Not hardly," she said. "I'm Nurse Braxton. Or, you could call me Renee."

"Then Renee it is. I'm Larry Thompson. This is Greg Gibson."

"Nice to meet you," Renee said. "But I have to attend to Mr. Morgan now, so we'll see you guys later."

It was funny watching Larry with his shoulder wrapped, arm and ankle in a cast, sitting in a wheelchair, still trying to get his groove on. This man had no limitations and the ultimate confidence. He and Greg left, but I remember feeling that Larry was not yet done with Nurse Braxton.

I spent the next two days on my back in bed. When I was not sleep or undergoing a battery of precautionary tests, I daydreamed about all sorts of stuff. If this was going to happen to me, I was glad it did during the summer, when school was not in session. As a professor, I had perfect attendance with my classes and did not want to ruin that. A day missed was a teaching opportunity wasted. And there were no teaching opportunities to waste.

Finally, I spoke with Joanne, who was extremely upset at the news. She suggested she come to L.A. to lend support. I told her to stay in D.C. because I would be fine and see her in a few days. I didn't really want her to see me laid up like that. I felt out of control, vulnerable.

Also, I was not comfortable with women catering or fawning over me. I was probably too independent. Even when ladies tried to wait on me, it made me feel awkward. I had friends whose women or wives cooked dinner every day, served them, and then retrieved their plates after eating. I'd feel like I should be doing something to contribute.

Greg had no problem allowing Brianna to cater to his every whim. But he, too, insisted she stay in Chicago. Despite her frustrations with him, she was relieved her man was still here. The brush with death gave her renewed reason to be thankful she had a man who loved her and whom she loved. She wanted more—marriage—but that did not matter much at that moment, knowing Greg had endured an accident that could have taken his life.

Larry had a stream of women visitors roll through his place offering their services to make life easier for him. He accepted most of their help, particularly that of Monique Gadson, a stylish actress he met during an audition.

She seemed to have made more of a dent in Larry's psyche than any of the other five or six women he introduced us to during the trip. She did not say "How high?" when he said, "Jump," which made her different. She was not so enamored with him that she abandoned reason or pride.

He did not really go out of his way for her, not that I could tell, but he did express real interest in spending time with her beyond the bed.

I got to know Nurse Braxton a little before my release. Renee was from Oakland, loved jazz and got into nursing when she could not take advantage of a public relations degree she earned from San Diego State. But she loved her profession that she was in. And I surmised she did not have a man in her life since she did not mention one and indicated she had little time for socializing.

Finally, I passed enough tests for the doctors to grant me my release. I felt good but not quite right. There were occasional dizzy spells and headaches but nothing serious enough for me to stay there. I had one more day in L.A., and I definitely wanted to spend it at Larry's rather than a hospital.

When I got my clothes, Alexis' number was not there. I was disappointed. A great portion of my idle time at the hospital was recounting the time I spent with her at the Golden Tale and fantasizing about doing other things with her: a picnic, a movie, dancing, and most of all, conversing. Then I had no way to reach her.

My friend from college, B.B., picked me up and took me to Larry's apartment and then jetted to work. Larry saved a message Alexis left for me on the answering machine the night we met: "Hi, this is Alexis for Julian. I received your message this morning; it was a surprise and very sweet. You're something else. I'm glad we met, too. I look forward to dinner tonight. Call me. Bye."

She assumed I had the number. I met her sister but had no way of reaching her. Alexis said she was from South Carolina—Orangeburg—but she was not listed. I knew because I called South Carolina information.

So there was no reaching her, and that bothered me. But I tried to shrug it off as I spent my last hours with Larry and Greg, laughing and telling stories to keep each other's spirits up.

That was hardly the way we intended spending our final hours together in L.A. But considering how we escaped death or at least more serious injury, we definitely were grateful to just be breathing, even if it was the Los Angeles smog. Actually, it was amusing to see us sitting around Larry's place with much of our bodies wrapped in casts and bandages. We looked pretty sad. We took pictures to make sure we would not forget what happened, as if we would. Physically, we were beaten down. But mentally, just surviving was enough to keep us going.

So I really was not as dejected about my vacation being ruined as I might have been. But I did not have that accomplished feeling I usually have after hanging with Larry and Greg. I was tired, my head hurt, and I still was disappointed about losing contact with Alexis. But I was glad to be going home. Ditto for Greg.

FIFTEEN

Homeward Bound

Julian

I definitely had to be out of it because the beautiful sister sitting two rows in front of me on my flight back to D.C. did not faze me. I simply took a few Advils and slept, which was not easy with that cast on my arm.

When I got off the plane, I was surprised to see Joanne waiting for me at the gate. She usually just met me in the car outside baggage claim. But "I figured you'd need someone to push you in the wheelchair," she said as we embraced.

Joanne had that kind of wit, and I needed her warmth and sense of humor then. And I felt she needed me to reaffirm my commitment to supporting her through the pregnancy. To me, to do that meant to talk about it and not ignore it, to be matter-of-fact about it.

I said to her: "So how are you feeling? Want to stop at Dairy Queen? We can get some pickles and ice cream."

"No, I'm not having any cravings yet," she said, laughing. "And I hope I don't. When you crave for stuff, you probably eat more than you should, and I don't want to gain any more weight than I have to. I know you. If after the delivery I'm this fat person, you'll be looking somewhere else."

"That's not even funny," I said. "So what are you saying? I'm vain like that . . . I wouldn't do that."

That was the right thing to say, but not completely truthful. I'd been told that it is vain and immature, but I could not deny the reality that a woman's appearance was important to me. Very important. I was not attracted to skinny women or, uh, extra healthy women, either. What's worse was having a woman who ALLOWED her body to change so drastically that she was unappealing.

I'd been told that if I really cared about the woman, her size

65

would matter little. To that I said, "Bullshit." Part of the reason a woman attracted me was her physique. It was part of the package that made me feel good about her. A woman's smile was important to me, as well as her smarts and kindness and gentleness and charm and presence and wit and honesty and genuine nature.

If one of those elements were missing, it would not be the same. It would be like leaving out the yeast when baking bread; it wouldn't rise. I wouldn't bolt just because a honey threw on an extra 15 pounds. But I wouldn't like it, or be comfortable with it. Hey, if I grew a gut and the woman I was with made it clear I was unappealing to her because of it, how could I not understand her position? The gut wasn't there when we met. I'd just get one of those ab machines, eat less, do whatever it took to make myself appealing to her again. But a lot of women did not seem so prepared to make the same commitment to remain sexy.

If we just took care of our bodies, that would be a non-issue. But women had babies and used them as a convenient excuse to let their bodies go.

"So you're telling me it wouldn't matter if I got a little big after the baby came?" Joanne said.

"Would it matter to you if I got a little bigger?" I said. "Yes, but we don't have to worry about that because that's not happening—to either of us."

She gave me a "yeah, right" look and the conversation switched to the accident all the way from the airport to my southeast D.C. townhouse. My friends and even my students wondered why I refused to move to Maryland or northern Virginia or anywhere other than Southeast D.C. But my feeling was there was no need to. I loved Washington, D.C., and had a great allegiance to Southeast. One of my friends, Ricky Bat, convinced me on the conspiracy theory that the government wanted African-Americans to move to the suburbs so white folks could take over Washington, which was 75 percent black. I was not going to be a part of that kind of mess. D.C. was Chocolate City, and I aimed to do my part to keep it that way.

Joanne just shook her head when I talked like that. She was more black and white. She refused to even acknowledge life's gray areas, which bothered me at times because we lived more in the gray areas than anyplace else. Living comfortably there was another story.

"Look at your mail hanging out of that box. You didn't tell the mailman to hold your mail until you returned?" Joanne said as we rolled up my driveway.

"He told me to leave him a reminder in the box, and I did. I guess he started pounding mail in there and never saw my note," I said. "But it doesn't matter now. Let's just go in and chill."

That sounded good, but there were seventeen messages on the answering machine, so I had to go over them.

"Want something to drink?" Joanne said from the kitchen. I sat at the bar on a stool next to the answering machine and caller ID box.

"A nice, cold Heineken would be straight right about now," I said. "You can have some skim milk."

"Very funny," Joanne said. "Here's your beer."

The messages came from friends around the country. I wrote down the numbers and vowed to make the return calls—tomorrow. Just then, with a cold Heineken in one hand and the TV remote control in the other, I felt a sense of normalcy.

I could spend successive evenings at home alone just like that: swigging beer and flipping channels. Ah, life's great joys.

But Joanne was there, so I couldn't exactly live out that one, but it was still very nice to chill like that and have her head resting on my chest.

"I've missed you," I said to her. "When I was laid up in that hospital, I thought about how I could have been killed and how I would have never seen my child. And that you would not have me there to help raise it. It was a depressing thought in one sense, but inspiring in another. It made me realize I'm not just living for myself now. Not too long from now, there'll be a little person here with my genes looking for me to be a factor in his life. With that comes responsibility. I didn't really look at it that way before. So maybe God placed me in the hospital so I could have idle time to really think and understand the responsibility I have."

"You're a good man, Julian," Joanne said. Then she started crying.

I knew frequent crying could be a part of the emotional changes women went through when pregnant. Usually, Joanne was tough-minded and unfazed in times of duress. Rather unemotional, really. But that was twice she cried in about two weeks. Yep, she was pregnant.

It was about 9 p.m. when the phone rang. Greg called to see if I made it back safely. He was with Brianna at his downtown condo overlooking Michigan Avenue.

"My flight was cool; how was yours?" he said.

"All right, but I was uncomfortable," I said. "But I made it, so it doesn't matter. How's Brianna?"

"I'll let her tell you," Greg said.

"Hi, Julian," Brianna said into the phone. "Did that accident knock some of your boy's marbles loose? Let me tell you what he did: I pick him up from the airport and give him a big hug because I missed him and because I'm so glad he is not hurt worse than he is— or dead. And the first thing out of his mouth is not, 'I missed you, too.' Or 'Thanks for caring.' Or 'It's good to see you.' No, it's, 'Don't start with that wedding stuff.' He pissed me off to no end. That was the last thing on my mind. I'm just concerned about him. I know he told you that he told me to stop talking about the idea of getting married. Then HE brings it up. And the first time he's seen me in like six days? I'm sick of this."

"Brianna," I said, "calm down. You know how Greg is. He's feeling all beat up right now physically, and he just does not want any mental pressure. He was wrong to come out with it like that, I know. I also know he missed you while we were in L.A."

"Stop trying to look out for your boy, Julian," Brianna said. "He's tripping on this marriage thing so much that it's making me reconsider. I think that's what he wants."

"I'm not going to get into you guys' business; you all can handle that," I said. "I'll just say this: please don't overreact."

She breathed heavily into the phone. "I'll try not to," she said. "I'm going to put this crazy man back onto the phone. You take it easy until you feel better, OK?"

The next voice I heard was Greg's, and he was not his usual upbeat self. "Man, I'm going to lay back and get some rest," he said. "I'll call you again when I can talk. Right now, I've got an extra set of ears here."

"So are you going to your store anytime soon? You shouldn't, but I know you," I said.

"I'm probably just going to call down there every hour of every day," Greg said. "I've got some new merchandise coming in, and I need to brief my manager on that. But I'm not really up to doing much right now. But maybe that's jetlag."

"Maybe that's because you have bruised ribs and a separated shoulder," I said. "Man, just relax with your girl and enjoy life. Don't trip about anything."

"All right, black man," Greg said. "Get with you later. Peace."

SIXTEEN:

Moni's On the Money

Larry

For the first time in six days, my apartment was quiet, and I didn't like it. I was stir crazy. No company to me meant I was wasting time. I tried reading, but I got tired of that. And somebody ought to do something about cable TV. A hundred channels and most of the time hardly worth watching. So I decided renting a couple of movies from Blockbuster with Monique would be a nice evening.

I could have called on a number of women, but I wanted Monique. I did know that she might be busy since it was so last minute. But if I got her on the phone, I knew I had the game to convince her to come. It was all about confidence.

"Hi Monique, this is Larry. How are you?"

"Fine, Larry, how are YOU?"

"I'm cool, considering, but I wanted to know if you were interested in picking up a few movies and coming over. I know it's last minute, and if you have plans already, I understand. But . . ."

Monique jumped in. "It's ironic you called, because you were on my mind," she said. "I was studying for an audition I have in two days, and I need a break. I didn't have any plans, so I'll pick up a few movies and come by. One catch: I get to pick the movies."

"I can live with that," I said.

Despite my injuries, I got around enough to order pizza and get some drinks together before she got there. About an hour later, Monique arrived with "Donnie Brasco" and "When We Were Kings," the documentary about Muhammad Ali.

"You should be resting," Monique said. "I could have gotten some drinks together. Why is it men can't just sit down? You always have to show you're a man. What's up with the ego?"

"Actually, the question is: Why can't women understand when a man is trying to be considerate," I said. "Ego does not drive us in every facet of our lives at every moment. I knew you were picking up the movies, so I thought I'd do something. That's about being fair and considerate, not ego. But you have to feel like it's a man thing. I'm not taking for granted you're going to wait on me hand and foot."

Monique did not dare argue that reasoning. She simply put in "Kings." As we watched the documentary and munched on pizza, I told her of how significant a figure Muhammad Ali had been in my life, what Ali stood for as a man, a BLACK man.

"You probably just know him as a boxer," I said, "but when I was growing up, he was larger than life. He still is. This is a man who in the 1960s took black people's causes to the masses. He was direct, but eloquent. White people felt threatened by him, but because he was the heavyweight champion of the world, they could not ignore him.

"He pricked the country's conscience. Celebrities do not do that anymore. Really, he was just one of a few to ever to do it. Athletes today get the money and get on with their lives. They have their foundations and camps, but all of them combined don't equal what Ali did. He was the MAN."

When it was over, Monique was definitely enlightened. "That was excellent," she said. "I was aware that he was a great boxer and active in the '60s, but I had no idea that he was that deep. Someone told me I should see it, but I had no idea. I have even more respect for him now."

After a trip to the bathroom and kitchen, Monique put in "Donnie Brasco," a true story of an FBI agent infiltrating the New York mafia. As an actor, I loved the roles Johnny Depp, Al Pacino, and Michael Madsen played in depicting the Italian culture—their passion for food, the way they dressed and talked. They used the 'F' word—among other bad language—countless times, which struck a nerve with me because, as an actor, I frequently read the movie reviews in the paper.

"Now, this is interesting," I told Monique after the movie. "I really enjoyed that movie. I read about it, and all the critics called it great, which it was. But what's interesting is all the profanity in the movie. It didn't offend me, but it was there. I only say that because when Eddie Murphy, Richard Pryor, and Redd Foxx did 'Harlem Nights,' the critics could not get pass the language. All they wrote about was the heavy profanity. Well, as much as the 'F word' and profanity are a part of the Italian lifestyle, so is it with African-Americans or anyone else. But there's a double standard. And the only real way to convey to everyone a fair view of the movies is to have African-American movie critics. And we don't. Until we get that, we'll always see movies black people absolutely love—like 'Boomerang,' 'Five Heartbeats,' 'Get On the Bus,' 'Rosewood'—criticized by white critics for one thing or another because they simply do not understand our culture. And they don't want to."

Monique looked at me in a different way. I could tell. Before then, she kind of looked at me like she was attracted to me, like she wanted to get busy. I could tell by the things she said to me that she viewed me as a womanizer. At the audition when I met her, instead of rehearsing my lines, I walked across the room and hollered at her. I said, "Excuse me, miss, but you disturb me. Your presence disturbs me. Can I have sixty seconds of your time?"

I think she knew then that if I saw someone I wanted, I had no problem speaking up. And I parlayed those 60 seconds she gave me into so much more.

But after my brief commentary on movie critics, her eyes said something different to me. They showed that she saw the depth I seldom felt was necessary to show to other women. Until then, I hadn't shown her much emotion or that I really had much on my mind except small talk and sex. I could tell she liked the other parts of my personality that she saw.

And I felt differently about her, too. Maybe I just didn't notice before, but she seemed so sincere and pleasant. I knew she was a self-proclaimed free spirit, but it was not overbearing. I found myself thinking about seeing her again even as she sat right next to me.

"Larry, I can't stay much longer; I have to get up early," Monique said, standing up. "But I tell you, this has been a wonderful evening. I really enjoyed both movies. But the company was better. I learned a lot about you tonight, believe it or not. And I like what I learned."

"That's good," I said. "But there's a lot more to learn, too. If you want to."

"We'll see, I guess," she said, trying to hold on to some mystery. "We'll see."

"You notice I didn't even ask you what you learned about me?" I said. "I didn't because I already know. And I know because of how casual I've been with you, sort of like: I'm interested, but I'm not."

"Yeah, why's that?" Monique said.

"To be honest, I've been stretching myself lately, trying to work and act and maintain, at least, a little social life, that I haven't truly felt like myself. Now, with the accident, I'm forced to slow down and live my life and not microwave it. So, that's where I am."

"I hear you," Monique said. "I'm just wondering where I fit in with all of this."

"Well, what I like is that you seem to have the capacity to fit in anywhere: Friend, confidant, pal, buddy . . . lover. I'm sure you'd handle either of those quite well."

"Where do you WANT me to fit in?" she said.

"I have no preference because I see you as potentially a great friend. And because I'm very attracted to you, I see you as a great lover, too, to be frank," I said. I wanted her to leave with the idea that I wanted to sleep with her on her mind.

"Yes, but you did not come all the way across that room to meet me that day because I looked like I could be a good friend," Monique said.

I studied her face as she spoke. It was a slender face with high cheek bones. Her eyebrows were arched and she wore a thin eye liner. Her lips were just the right thickness and kissable with the reddish gloss. There was a mole directly in the middle of her chin. And she had a faint mustache if you looked hard enough. This face worked wonderfully with the short and reddish-dyed haircut she sported.

"You're right," I said. "I wasn't thinking about you as a friend then."

On that bad ankle, I stepped closer to her. While looking into her eyes, I placed my hands on both of her shoulders. She took that as an invitation to press her body against mine. I took that as an invitation to press my lips against hers. She took that as an invitation to slide her tongue into my mouth. I took that as an invitation to work my hands down her back and over her butt.

She took that as trouble, on two counts. One, she deciphered that my handiwork, so to speak, meant I wanted more on this night, which was too much. Two, it felt good to her. Monique gently pulled back. "Thanks for a good time," she said. "I'd better go, and you'd better get off that ankle and rest."

"Resting is not what's on my mind right now," I said.

"I won't even ask you what is," she said. "I'm afraid to know."

"Oh, I think you already know."

"I do, that's why I'm leaving."

I did not press the issue. Monique collected the videos and kissed me on the face. "I wish I could walk you to your car," I said.

"I'm fine. Just get some rest—and a cold shower," she said.

"I'll do both," I said, grinning. "Be safe. Let me know you made it home."

And then she was gone. It was nearly 12:30 a.m. She definitely had risen on my hit list. The next time, she was getting done. And I could tell that she had the same thing on her mind.

SEVENTEEN:

Mo Money, Mo Problems

Greg

I recovered quickly from my injuries from the car wreck over the few weeks since returning to Chicago, but Brianna and I did not. She followed my directive and did not talk anymore about getting married, and she continued the "no sex" moratorium, which I really hated because not only was I deprived, but it was like she used sex as a bargaining tool. That was not a new maneuver for women, but I still didn't like it.

We sat on the front porch of Brianna's house, on a warm, starry evening that would have been romantic at another time. Then she mustered the words she'd contemplated for weeks. I could tell something was on her mind. And when she called me over to her place to talk, I knew whatever it was, was coming out.

And from the seriousness on her face, I could tell that she was kind of reluctant about what she wanted to say. But Brianna was proud, someone who felt truth was the only recourse. I knew that look on her face. She was hoping to shock some sense into my head. But my mind was closed.

"Gregory, I love you," she began, "but this is not working for me. I've basically followed your lead throughout this entire relationship. I followed it because I trusted you and I actually was comfortable with the pace. But right now, after all we've shared and been through, I just don't see where you're leading us."

I tried to jump in; Brianna wasn't having it. "No, no, no. I don't want to hear it. I want YOU to hear ME. So, please, don't interrupt me. I don't know what you want out of this, so I have to take control of myself. You know, you tell me you love me and want to marry me and get me all happy and excited about it. And then you say don't talk about it, like I'm bugging you with it.

73

"At that same time, you want to function as husbands and wives do intimately. I'm sorry, Gregory, that just can't continue. We've invested a lot of time and emotion into each other, and if this is the limit, then we can't continue sleeping together. Every time we've ever been together, I gave you my body because I trusted you and felt we were on the same page. Right now, we're in different books."

I had no retort of any significance. I really did love her, but I didn't think I was ready for marriage. But the problem was I let us get so far into the relationship that it was hard to tell her that. It was an inexplicable feeling to be involved with someone, to really love someone, but not want to go the distance.

Why did I feel that way if I loved her? A couple of things. For one, I enjoyed the life I had, running my business, hanging out when I wanted without having to report to anybody. Brianna and I spent a lot of time together, but I had my space. Unlike a lot of people, I enjoyed spending time alone. My view of marriage would end that.

But mostly it was the financial part of it that was a major concern for me. Money consumed me. It was hard for me to separate women who were looking for someone to support them and women who were not.

I worked pretty damned hard, made many sacrifices, to get where I was. And I coveted my status. One night I talked to Larry and Julian about that on one of our many conference calls.

"Man, I worked for my dough, and the idea of now having to share it with someone bothers me," I told them. "How can someone come in who did not help me get what I have suddenly be entitled to half of it? Then you start talking about two months of your paycheck for a ring—no way. And then Brianna's talking about a wedding and reception that probably would cost about $20,000. And how much is a honeymoon? If you're trying to tell me money does not matter, you're tripping."

The closeness I had with my boys allowed us to spread the truth among each other, especially when our view was warped. And so, Julian and Larry jumped all over me.

"G, I think you're tripping," Julian said. "That's kind of what marriage is about—sharing. You know Brianna; she earns her own money. You think she wants your money? As for a ring, I agree that two months salary is too much. And a wedding can cost too much money. But the wedding is for the woman; it's her day, something she'll savor forever. If you love her, ask her to be reasonable on the costs, but don't let that be a factor in all this."

Larry then chimed in. "Yo, Greg. You know Brianna far better than me. But she doesn't seem to be the type of woman who you should be worried about like that. I know you felt like you were being pressured by her because she talked about getting married a lot. Again, you know her far better than I do, but you tell me if she was just excited about a wedding or trying to pressure you. Why would she pressure you when you two already agreed to get married?"

I started to answer, but Julian jumped in. "Hold up, G," he said, "but something just occurred to me. Marriages in your family have not worked out. Not your mom and dad, not your sister's, not your brother's. Not your uncle and aunt. Not your godmother's. Are you thinking about that?"

Julian surprised me with that. Usually I had a quick response to most anything, even it was just "Fuck you." But I couldn't get anything to come out.

"G," Julian said.

"Yeah. Well, Ju, that's a factor," I finally answered. "Marriages in my family just have not worked. I've seen how these people went from the wedding and being so in love and happy, to the divorce and being so bitter and hateful. It's incredible. If that can happen to them—and they were all good people—then it can happen to me. The history of my family says that we can't make it happen in a marriage. So why go through the wedding and honeymoon and spend all that money and then break up? I ain't going through all that."

"Greg, you can't think that other people's failures mean you will, too," Larry said. "If someone in your family gets a cold, does that mean you get a cold? No. This is not something you catch. And it's not hereditary either. A marriage is something YOU make flourish or fail. I know that much. You know they say you don't know what you have until you lose it."

And Brianna was gone now, making me officially single. I had not been that way in so long that I was not sure how to feel. In one sense, I was relieved to truly be out of a forthcoming marriage that I was not totally comfortable with. In another, I did not want to lose Brianna. It was a true paradox that it seemed only men could create. In still another sense, it was difficult to accept that I had hurt her.

"Brianna, I don't want us to lose contact, I don't want you to disappear," I said.

"Why, Gregory? Why? So you can keep up with what I'm doing with my life? If you really cared, you'd be in it. I want to be bitter with you. I want to tell you to screw yourself and those other nasty thoughts that are going through my mind right now. But that's through my mind. My heart says something else. And by not saying what's on my mind, I'm probably making the same mistake I've made with you for two years—following my heart. I'll just say that I hope you find whatever it is you're looking for that I lack, because all I've ever wanted was for you to be happy."

With that, she got up and walked into her house, the house she anticipated would be hers and mine, but was now more empty than ever. She refused to break down in front of me, to show her pain. But after locking the door, effectively locking out the man she loved, the emotion of it all engulfed her.

I watched through a window as she flopped down on the couch and poured tears onto a pillow until she fell asleep.

EIGHTEEN:

Sick Sense

Julian

The cast was off my arm and the weight work for the last couple weeks put some strength back into it. My headaches finally were gone. Well, the ones caused by the concussion, anyway. The headache of bills persisted: car note, credit cards, mortgage, insurance. I sometimes went to sleep with these nagging things on my mind and awoke with them there, too. Being a professor brought a certain amount of prestige, a great deal of satisfaction, but not a lot of pay.

On this morning, I awoke alone—Joanne had been working late and going home afterward for the last week. My thoughts were immediately on her as I stretched and glanced at my bedside clock. It was almost 9 o'clock, which was usually too early for me in the summer, but I had an 11 a.m. tee-time at the golf course, so I was eager to get the day started.

I'd avoided taking up golf for a few years because I felt it wasn't physical enough and was too time consuming and boring. Then I went out one day, and I was hooked. I knew it would be a good day because I'd hit the links, pick up a couple books from the post office that Greg sent, and go home and prepare an intimate dinner for Joanne.

After a week of not being with her, I wanted it to be a special night. Sex with her since the pregnancy had been better because we abandoned the condoms since the bun was already in the oven. And since we trusted each other, we did not consider the idea of transmitting a disease.

I played golf with Ricardo Ely, the Dean of Men at Bowie State; Kerry Mullins, the basketball coach; and Antonio Starks, a long-time maintenance man at the school. I shot a 102, which looked bad on paper, but was encouraging for me. In the previous eight times I played, I had not shot less than 112. This time, I got my first-ever birdie, and I pitched nicely out of the bunkers, which I often found.

We sat in the clubhouse afterward, chugging beers and discussing—what else?—women. I started to tell them about my impending fatherhood, but something told me to hold on to that bit of news a little longer. Women thought they were the only ones with intuition. Not so.

Plus, virtually any time a woman ever said to me that her instincts made her feel this way or that about something concerning me, it was wrong. Sometimes it was not even in the ballpark. Case in point: When I lived outside of Boston, I dated this woman from Atlanta long distance, and she asked if she could meet me in New York during a vacation I had planned with some buddies I went to school with. I told her, "It would be nice to see you, but, to be honest, we've planned this trip for a long time and we've planned for it to be the guys hanging out in the City."

Her response was, "So, what are you saying? You don't want me to come? Yeah, I bet it's you and the guys. Why don't you want me there? You probably have a woman you're already meeting there. I sense something is up with this. The way you've acted in the last few weeks has been different. You're so excited about this trip. Something is telling me in my gut that there's more to it than what you're telling me."

I was like, "What are you talking about? Because I'm looking forward to a weekend with my friends means I'm seeing another woman? Get out of here."

"Women can sense things like this," she said. So, we argued about that for about 10 minutes, argued about something she was clueless on. And that was just one of many times a woman's intuition stunk.

"Man, I've got to get home to the wife," Coach Mullins said, "before she starts 'sensing' that I was up to no good. You know how that is: whenever you really enjoy yourself without her, her senses tell her something's wrong. It's a trip."

We laughed, shook hands, and made another date to golf before departing. It was nearly five, so I missed the post office. But I stopped by to see my mom. As she gave me the 411 on the family news, I called to check my messages at home. There was one from a young Ph.D. candidate asking me about his dissertation and oral defense. He called periodically needing reassurance more than anything else. And there was one from Joanne saying she was sorry but that she had to get ahead on some work and would be in the office until about

9:30 and that she was going home afterward because she was already tired. Well, so much for the special night I planned.

Thank goodness I was already at mom's. I stayed and helped her with dinner, which was nice. We did not get to have many quiet moments together very often, so I savored that evening. At about nine, after we did the dishes, I gave her a big hug and kiss and made my way home. It was only about a twenty minute drive, but it seemed longer because I was sleepy, having stuffed myself as usual.

But it was a Saturday night, and I did not want to stay in and be alone again, so I thought I'd hit Takoma Station for some jazz or maybe the Foxtrappe to party. When I got to my place, I checked my messages again. Someone called and hung up without leaving a message, so I decided to put the caller ID to work. Turns out the number was my mom's, which was no surprise because she was not comfortable with answering services. She'd rather just call back.

But I checked the caller ID box to see what time Joanne called. Not that it mattered, but my instincts told me to do it. She called at 4:06, but the number she called from was not her office number, where she said she was, or her home number in Maryland. This number had a 703 area code, which meant northern Virginia. How could that be?

I replayed her message, during which she said, "Hi Julian, this is, well, you know who this is. I'm really sorry, but I'm swamped at work again. I just got here and I won't be able to leave until about 9:30. I know it's Saturday, but I have to do this. I know we had plans, but I'm already exhausted. Let's do it tomorrow, OK, after church. I'll meet you in front of the church before the eleven o'clock service. Well, I've got to get back to work. See you."

What was going on? I had seen that Virginia number before— when she left me a message when I was in L.A.—but I ignored it. Now here it was again. It was almost 9:30, so I called to see if Joanne was at work. I got her voice mail. I called her at home and got the answering machine.

I had no other option but to call the number. It had to be one of her sorority sisters, I thought. On the third ring, someone answered the phone. "Hello," the deep male voice said. I kind of froze.

"Hello," he repeated.

Finally I snapped out of it. "Hi, is Joanne there?" I said.

"Yes, just a minute," he said. If he knew it were me, he would have covered for her, but he figured it had to be someone she wanted to call her there. I heard her in the background say, "It's for me? Who could that be?"

Her instincts told her to not come to the phone, but she did not follow them the one time her instincts were right.

"Hello," she said.

"Joanne," I said. "What's happening? Where are you?"

She did not respond, which told me the unthinkable: the woman I was in love with, who was pregnant with my child, was seeing another man. I was standing when I made the call, but I had to sit because my knees got weak. The room started spinning. I couldn't see straight. It was as if I was drunk.

My stomach felt empty. Breathing was a chore. The phone trembled in my hand. No, this could not happen; only it did.

"Joanne, tell me something," I pleaded.

She said nothing.

"What is it, you can't talk right now?" I said.

"No," she finally answered calmly. "Can I call you later?"

"Call me later? For what? To tell me what, Joanne? I can't believe you. I can't believe you. I . . ." The words were hard to come by, so I just hung up on her.

I got up and tried to walk, but my legs were unsteady. I sat down on a barstool. I felt like I had no blood in my body. My head continued to spin. I just could not believe that the woman I trusted went out on me like that. I carried the phone to the couch and took a seat. Suddenly, I was hot and began to sweat. I prided myself on my ability to remain composed in heated situations, but this was beyond anything I'd ever experienced.

Women had gone through that kind of agony before—some, more than once—but I never expected it to happen to me. Especially considering the high regard I held for Joanne. As much pain as I was in, I did not cry outwardly. But I did on the inside. It actually gave me physical pain in my gut. "Shit," I said. Then I noticed that my mouth had gone dry.

My mind raced. How could this happen? Who was he? How long has this been going on? How could I be so stupid?

The problem with suspecting someone of being unfaithful was that everything they ever did came into question. So I asked myself all kinds of questions: When she said she was out with her sister that time, was she with him then? When I called her at midnight last week and her answering machine came on, she said she was asleep, but was she with him? And she had to be with him when I was in L.A.—the number was on the Caller ID. I felt like a fool. Even if all those other times she told the truth, how could I believe her about anything? Everything became questionable.

I was so glad that I had only told Larry and Greg—and the woman in L.A., Tara—about her being pregnant. Now I wondered how could that baby be mine when we used condoms. I don't recall one bursting. I had to shake my head to rid myself of those thoughts about a woman that I thought I knew and know I trusted.

The phone rang. The caller identified himself as Sam Burch, Joanne's former boyfriend she'd told me about not long after we met. "I want to talk to whoever just called my house," he said.

"That's me. What do you want?" I said.

"I called by using *star* 69. I'm just trying to figure what you said to my friend to make her leave here like she just did," Sam said.

"Listen, I don't know you, but Joanne and I have been dating for 10 months, and when your number appeared on my caller ID box, I called to check it out. What's the deal with you and her?"

He paused. "Well, we were engaged at one time, but now we're just kicking it."

"Kicking it?" I said. "For how long?"

"Man," he said, "I don't know you so I'm not talking about my relationship."

"Wait a *fucking* minute," I yelled into the phone. "That is a woman I've been dating for almost a year. She tells me she's pregnant with my baby. She leaves me a message from your house. I don't want to hear this shit. What's going on here?" I was amazed at how quickly I downplayed the relationship to protect my ego.

"She's pregnant? Wait a minute, I didn't know that. You're lying. She would have told me," he said.

"Have you been sleeping with her?" I said, knowing the answer.

"Yeah. I mean, that's none of your business."

"Hey, Sam, I'm telling you right now: Don't call my *motherfucking* house again."

Then I almost broke my fingers slamming down the phone.

NINETEEN:

More Bounce To The Ounce

Julian

I cursed to myself as I sat on the black leather couch. I was shocked, hurt, and embarrassed. I also was angry. None of those feelings dominated; they were all eating me up.

Here, I had gotten the Caller ID box so I could prevent awkward scenarios for Joanne (and me), and it turned out to be the thing that busted her shit wide open. Things have a way of working out.

The more I thought about it, the angrier I got. There was no way I would put my hands on her—I had no respect for any coward of a man who did that to a woman. But I wanted to make her feel my pain, to get back at her. Then it hit me: I would tell her about me and her sister, Donna.

If she knew that I slept with her sister, she'd grieve like I was, probably more because she'd feel doubly betrayed. Up to that point, it was my life's mission to make sure she did not ever find out about that. I could have prevented that fiasco, but I didn't, and it was something I was not proud of. I only told Greg and Larry about it, and I told them in a matter of fact way, not a boastful way. We went after women hardcore, but certain things were off limits to us, like pursuing a friend's lady or women at church or women in the same family. When I told them about it, they were like: "Damn, Ju. You need to stay away from her. Don't do it again."

That slip up with Donna haunted me each time I thought about it. But I was going to clear my conscience, at Joanne's expense, and then never speak another word to her.

About twenty minutes later, the doorbell rang. Having a guest was the last thing I needed then. But who would come to my house unannounced? It had to be Joanne.

I opened the door and just looked at her. She looked disheveled.

Her eyes were puffy, indicating that she'd been crying. I knew then that I could not follow through on those mean thoughts. That secret would have to remain just that. Hurting her then wouldn't have served any purpose.

"Please, Julian, can I come in?"

That was my cue to slam the door right in her face, but I didn't. Instead, I opened the door further and stepped aside so she could enter.

"I don't get you," I said. "Who are you? What kind of person are you? All this time I'm thinking we're doing well, and you're fucking around with this guy?"

"It's not what you think," she said.

"Oh, it's not? Listen, don't come in here and continue your lying. I know you're wondering how I even got his number to call back. Well, before I went to L.A., I bought a Caller ID box. But since you've been so busy in Virginia, you weren't here enough to even notice. So that's how I got the number."

"But . . . " she said.

"There are no 'buts,' " I interjected. "You left me a message from his house when I was on vacation. Today, you call with this elaborate lie about working on Saturday and being tired and going home afterward. All the while you were hanging with your boy. You're diabolical."

She could not say anything, so she cried. I gave her some tissue, but not a shoulder. Finally, Joanne spoke. I never anticipated anything she said so eagerly. I wanted to hear what she had to say to all of this. I wanted her to say something to make me feel better.

"I'm sorry. I know you're hurt, and I'm sorry. Sam and I always remained friends after we broke up last year. You don't know him. He begged me to come see him. And I did because he told me that he couldn't live without me, that he WOULDN'T live without me. He was unstable, and I was scared. So I went because I truly believed he'd do something to hurt himself. I didn't want that on my heart."

"But you didn't talk to me about it," I said. "Instead, you made up stories, you lied. You told me that was the worst thing I could do to you, and then you do it to me. And how long were you going to keep this up? He was holding you hostage with threats of suicide. You think he was ever going to let you walk away?"

She clasped her hands together and held them tightly. "I thought if I could talk to him while I was there with him," she said, "that he'd become rational and see that he had to move on with his life."

Anger took over then because it seemed she was too bright to be so stupid. To think I would buy those excuses was insulting to me. "How do you think being there with him was going to make him see he had to move on?" I said. "You just fed his appetite. You aren't stupid—you had to know this. Exactly how long was this going on anyway? It had to be since before I went to Los Angeles. I mean, according to him, you've been sleeping with him. Is that true?"

Once more she gave me that silence that spoke loudly. I just stared at her. Then I got that queasy, empty feeling again. I had to sit. I looked down at my chest and I could literally see my heart pounding.

"I'm waiting," I said sarcastically.

"Julian, I love you. You know that. I have no feelings for Sam. I was just trying to help him. I talked to his brother and his parents. I talked to his best friend. They all said I was the only one who could help him. They all tried to reason with him, but he wouldn't listen."

She talked about everything but my question, which gave me my answer. I had another question that was critical.

"So, Joanne, whose baby is it? I mean, we've always used condoms, and now you get pregnant just when you're sleeping with your old boyfriend? Please, tell me the truth."

"I only slept with him one time . . ."

"Oh, and that makes it all right?" I jumped in.

"I'm not saying it does. I'm saying I was not SLEEPING with him." She paused and her eyes welled up with tears. "Yes, I did sleep with him—one time. I can't explain what happened. I was trying to be a good friend to someone who really needed it. It was late, I was tired, and you were out of town somewhere, I think at your family reunion. I needed you, and you weren't there and . . ."

"Hold up! Now you're going to blame me for this? You've got some nerve."

"I'm not blaming you; I'm just telling you what was going on in my mind at the time. There's no excuse for it; I'll never try to defend it. I'm ashamed that it happened; I really am. And I'm scared."

"Scared? Why?"

"Because I don't want you to leave me. I love you. And I'm having a baby."

"Yeah, well that 'love you' stuff sounds pretty hollow right now. And you're having a baby all right, but it's not mine."

"Julian," she said. "Don't say that."

"Joanne, I'm going to say this and then you can go. We've never done anything without a condom. Never! I checked the condom each time and there was not a drop that got away, that I could tell. I knew that when you told me you were pregnant, but I just wouldn't even entertain you sleeping with someone else. I know better now. That is not my baby. It can't be. You slept with that guy without a condom. You knew him, and you believed he had not been with anyone else so you did it. I'm asking you now to be honest with me—if you're capable. Save some dignity and tell the truth. Be the woman I thought you were just one last time for me, please. I need you to be honest about this. You can't lie about something like this, Joanne."

She wiped her face and took a deep breath. Through the tears I could see the pain in her eyes. I actually felt sorry for her. I wanted to hug her as I did when her father died a few months back from prostate cancer. But the other emotions were more prevalent.

"I'm sorry, Julian. You're right," she said.

I knew I was right, but a chill still went over my body. What I had done to women in the past came back to bite me in the ass. I was so broken I didn't know what to do. I had played with women's emotions, unintentionally, but played with them nonetheless. I always regretted causing them pain, but I could never truly relate to how miserable they felt until just then.

I've heard of women catching their men in bed with other women and forgiving them and continuing the relationship. I was not built that way. Every time it was late and I didn't know exactly where Joanne was, I'd think she was up to no good. Every time I left town or she left town, I'd have that same feeling. That was no way to live.

And although I was not so keen at that point in my life to master the art of being an ideal mate in a relationship, I did know that with no trust there was only agony, one way or another. So I could not get past her poor judgment. I could not be with a woman who slept with another man while she supposedly was in love with me. And I damn sure couldn't deal with a woman who was pregnant by another man and got that way while she was dating me.

"Thank you for being honest about that, Joanne," I said calmly. "I really do appreciate that. But I don't know what else to say. And I don't think you should say anything either, really. There's nothing to say. You should just get in your car and go home. That guy Sam said he didn't know you're pregnant so I think you'd better tell him he's going to be a father. I'm sure he'll be happy. But there's nowhere we can go now. So, I think you should just leave."

Without resistance, thank goodness, Joanne wiped her face again, licked her dry lips, and slowly walked toward the door, head bowed. After stepping outside, she turned to look back at me with tears in her eyes. With tears in my eyes, I turned and closed the door.

TWENTY

Park It Right Here

Larry

In the following weeks, while Julian grieved in his own way, Monique and I got tighter. That night of video-watching was the start of something quite nice for us. I did not begrudge her for having a free spirit. Really, I celebrated it. And Monique basked in the security I showed and simply for not trying to change her.

"You're so different from any man I've ever dated," she said as we sat on a blanket at the park. "Most of them try to change me. I love nature, being outside and sometimes going against what is the norm. And I'm really still surprised that you kind of just roll with me."

"We are who we are," I said. "My mind is always open to learning, no matter what the source. I wouldn't want you to try to change me. And you know what: I wouldn't want to be with someone who was just like me—if that's even possible. How can you grow from that? I'm into growth."

And Monique was into pushing the envelope. I had told her about my dislike for women who smoked, that it was a complete turnoff without exception. The idea that it looked sexy—as some men thought—was something I did not agree with. And the smell it left on her clothes, in her hair, on her breath, and in MY clothes was intolerable. Still, the daring Monique dug deep into the picnic basket and pulled out, of all things, a cigar.

"Every now and then, I enjoy one of these," she said. "It's kind of liberating."

I just looked at her. I admired her daring, her freedom, so I just searched for the matches. Almost involuntarily, I lit the stogie for her.

I told her: "You're a trip. I really shouldn't be surprised, but I am. You don't seem to have any limits."

"Well, I wouldn't say that," Monique said. "There are definitely limits. But I live for today, for what makes me happy, what makes me feel good and content. That's what works for me."

Shit, I actually was envious of Monique's freewheeling yet controlled lifestyle. That was a paradox, but she pulled it off. She wanted more work in acting, as I did, but otherwise, she was doing what she wanted to do but not over-indulging in anything. Despite an appearance that I worked really hard to come off as extremely confident, I had less control of my life than anyone knew. I don't know if it was unconscious or not, but I always felt there were constraints in achieving the things I wanted. The little bit I had, I had to work hard for it.

So, what I did have, I was bound to protect. Just as I started to tell her that, Monique pointed the cigar toward me. I didn't want to take it, but I did. What the hell, I thought. I grabbed it. She stared intently as I slowly placed my lips around it and took several deep puffs.

"Wow, look at you," she said. "What do you think? It's smooth, isn't it? I dipped it in cognac last night and let it dry into the cigar. Can you taste it?"

"I don't know," I said. "Since this is my first one, I'm not sure how it should taste."

"Well, thanks for trying it," Monique said. "I know you didn't want to, but you did it anyway. For me. As for the taste, you'll acquire a taste for it—if you want to."

We sat there sharing the cigar and munching on grapes and shrimp cocktail as the sun turned from brilliant to orange before disappearing behind the downtown L.A. skyline. Usually, Los Angeles nights were on the cool side, sometimes even in August. But this night carried a warmth that was soothing, assuring.

I rested on my back with my hands clasped together behind my head, gazing into the dark blue sky highlighted by flickering stars. Monique sat to my left with her legs crossed, staring off toward the trees.

"It looks like we have the whole park to ourselves," Monique said, looking around. There were a few joggers in the distance, but that was it. And that was a cue for Monique to test my gumption and to feed her appetite for daring.

"Larry," she said seductively, "loosen your belt."

"What?" I said. I heard her, but I couldn't have heard her.

"I didn't stutter. You heard me," she said.

"I know I did, but I'm just wondering why you would want me to do that."

"Do you have to know everything?" she answered. "Just indulge me, please."

So I did. I sat up and took a look around; nobody was near. I loosened my belt and lowers the zipper, too. Monique did the rest.

"Lie back down," she said. "Just relax."

I did. She was so in control of the situation, so undaunted that if she had told me to jump into the lake, I might have done it. She gave the park another once over and then began to rub my chest. I closed my eyes and breathed heavily. She leaned over and softly kissed me on the lips. She then slowly worked her hands down my body, to my stomach and then my navel. A bulge quickly jumped up in my shorts, and Monique took aim on said bulge, gently rubbing it as it continued to grow.

Monique kept her hand in place but stopped stroking suddenly as two joggers approached. When they passed, she lifted her floral sundress and straddled me. I raised my hips, and in one motion slid down my shorts and underwear to my knees. Monique did not wear panties, so she was ready for a fantasy lovemaking session right there at the park, under the stars.

She reached deep into the picnic basket. I didn't say anything, but I looked at her thinking, 'What could she possibly want to eat NOW?' Turns out, she searched for a condom that she had packed. "You came prepared, huh?" I said to her, shaking my head.

"Ever since we decided on a picnic, I've been thinking about this," she said.

Who was I to prevent the fantasy? She stroked my manhood with one hand and used her teeth to rip the condom from its packet. Monique then slid the condom down my hardness. I was excited about how good her hands felt on my body, but more about the risk of it all. This was FUN.

Monique maneuvered so I could enter her throbbing, moist vagina. She closed her eyes and threw her head back and rode me as if I was a mechanical bull. Up and down, around and around, with no particular rhythm. Just going for it.

The blanket was hardly enough cushion to prevent my back from taking a beating on the ground, but I was so into the act that I was oblivious to the pain. Instead, I held firmly to her waist and enjoyed the ride.

Every so often I reached up to caress her breasts. But Monique was so wild that I mostly just held on. We enjoyed each other in the night air as if we were in the confines of a hotel room. This was far more exciting than our other encounters because it was in public. It was a thrill.

After several minutes, we achieved the ultimate: simultaneous climax. As the pleasure of it all burst inside her body, Monique gyrated as if electrocuted. I bit my bottom lip and thrust my waist toward the sky, shooting gism violently into the Trojan. In an instant, Monique collapsed onto my chest. I wrapped my arms around her and gently kissed her shoulder. For the next few minutes, we breathed heavily into each other's ear.

"Not that I feel like it or even want to, but maybe we should get up before someone comes by," I said, coming out of the semi-trance I was in.

"That was so good, Larry," Monique said. "I could go to sleep right here, just like this . . . But you're right."

We put ourselves back together. Monique rolled off me and lowered her dress. I took off the used condom and placed it into a sandwich bag Monique held open for me. She then handed me a moist towelette so I could wipe myself before pulling up my clothes. This woman covered every angle.

"You know what?" I said, "You are thorough."

"Well, I try," she said, smiling.

We packed the picnic basket and took a walk around the park, under the big, round lights over the walkway. A breeze developed and Monique asked for the warmth of my body. I think she just wanted me to hug her, because it was not cold. But I obliged, putting an arm around her.

"Man," I said, "and you called the cigar liberating. It was nothing compared to that. THAT was liberating."

She took a deep breath. "You're right."

We sat on a bench facing the lake in which ducks and swans waded and water shot up from a fountain.

"Hey, what's your day like tomorrow," she asked.

"What's tomorrow, Saturday?" I said. "Oh, I have an audition in Culver City at nine."

"Culver City? Me, too. You're reading for Creative Casting?" she said.

"Yep. What time are you going down there?"

"The same as you. Hey, wouldn't it be great if we both get parts?"

"Yeah," I said, "and we play opposite each other and have to do a love scene. That would be the easiest role I'll ever play."

We enjoyed a laugh and went back to Monique's place to engage in one of our favorite past times: video-watching. In this case, it was

"White Man's Burden." At the end of the movie, I offered my views on the flick, something I always did. "That was pretty good," I said, "but isn't it curious how white folks tried to ignore the symbolism of the movie as it reflects on racism? That movie was in the theaters about two weeks. They got it out of there like they were trying to sweep it under the rug."

Then I went home to go over my lines one final time before the audition.

Before I went to bed, I buzzed up Julian and Greg in a conference call to tell them about my night in the park. I did not leave out a single detail. Nothing.

"Right there in public, she was riding me," I said. "I think she wanted to be seen. I think she's an exhibitionist. But I ain't mad at her."

"Right there in the park?" Greg said. "Man, at this point, I'll just take a honey in the bed. Forget the erotic stuff."

TWENTY ONE:

Flipped the Script

Monique

L arry described going for an audition as taking an oral exam, only with much more pressure. "When you're talking about a role that really could change your life, you can't help but go into it with some anxiety," he said. "But in order to strike a chord with the casting agent, you have to fight through it and BE that character. Sometimes you know what they're looking for; sometimes you're not sure. It's hit or miss. That's what's scary."

He said he had his monologue down when he went to read before Yvonne Yeager, a big-time casting agent for Creative Casting. Yvonne was highly respected in her profession. She gained a reputation in the industry for locating untapped talent. Most anyone could see obvious ability, but Yvonne was keen on citing POTENTIAL.

That was something Larry and I kind of banked on since we had done strictly stage work, mostly in small-time theaters. The money and fame were in movies, and this casting call was for a film written by some hotshot young screenwriter out of New York. The director was looking to cast unknowns for leading roles. This was the opportunity Larry and I craved.

Sitting in that waiting room was like torture, observing all the other prospects. Larry said if you got caught up into checking out the candidates, trying to assess their chances, you could psyche yourself out. So, the power of concentration was important.

I was grateful to him because he shared with me much of what he learned from his time at the renowned American Conservatory Theater in San Francisco. Denzel had gone there, which was enough for me to know that good stuff was taught.

I had a year or two of acting lessons in West Los Angeles. I think I gained something from them—when the teacher wasn't trying to undress me with his eyes. But he was the last person on my mind when I went for the audition.

Larry performed his monologue and returned to the waiting room before I went in. He told me that he read in front of two men who flanked Yvonne Yeager. He said he quickly got over his anxiety and lost himself in the character. Yvonne—an attractive, well-kept woman in her late 30s, early 40s with blonde-dyed short hair a la Dennis Rodman—observed without expression, with her legs crossed. The two men were dressed in suits with open-collar shirts, Larry said, and wore thick-framed eyeglasses. They watched intently, but neither of them gave away their feelings.

"When I was finished," Larry said. "Yvonne said, 'That was very nice, uh . . . Larry.' She never really raised her head; she kept her head down at her clipboard to find my name. 'Very nice. We have your information, so we might be in touch. Thanks for coming out.'

"Just like that, it was over," Larry went on. "I think I blew it up, but you never know what they're thinking. It makes you feel kind of empty . . . But you just have to relax and do your thing. Break a leg."

Sometime later I had my audition. I played the role of a woman scorned, which I had experience in doing having dealt with some sorry-ass brothers in my past. Yvonne was very attentive, and I noticed her nodding her approval. There was a look in her eyes that made me think I had her.

That gave me more energy and confidence. By the time I was done, I had worked up a sweat—part from effort, part from nervousness, and part from excitement.

"Monique," Yvonne Yeager said to me, "that was very, very nice. I like the strength you showed, the emotion."

She then whispered something to the two men, who nodded their heads and then got up and went into an adjoining room. Yvonne rose from her seat and approached me. I didn't know what to think. "I really like you," Yvonne said. "You've got something . . . Are you available to read again and talk later this evening, around eight?"

"Sure, yes, definitely," I said. "Where do you want me to be?"

"Let me write down my address. Are you familiar with Malibu?" Yvonne said. "Call me at this number later for directions."

I was so excited that I did not ask any questions. I knew where Malibu was, but that was it. I hadn't spent any time there, but that did not matter. If I had to walk, I was going to be there. So, I took the small piece of paper, thanked Yvonne, and left.

"Larry," I said into the cellular phone, "Yvonne Yeager invited

me to her house tonight to read again; this time the writer and director are supposed to be there. I can't believe it. I mean, I've always
believed I'd get a break. It seems like it's here now, and now I can't
believe it."

"You'd better believe it," Larry said. "I'm happy for you."

It meant a lot to me that I could sense the sincerity in Larry's
voice. She did not take to him as well as she did me, and yet he was
genuinely happy for me. That wasn't typical of most men. Most men
would feel some sort of insecurity that would make them jealous. But
I didn't get that feeling from him at all.

At eight o'clock straightup, I pushed the doorbell to Yvonne
Yeager's ornate beachfront home. The front door was mostly glass, so
I could see straight through the house. I could see the ocean flowing
in the background.

"Boy, you're punctual," Yvonne said as she opened the door. "I
like that."

I stepped in and was awed by the house. It actually was intimi-
dating. I slowly looked around. There was a grand piano in the distance. It was white and elegant, which matched everything else in
Yvonne's high-ceiling home. There was marble at the entrance,
plush white carpet in the living room to the right, and a shining par-
quet floor leading to the rear of the house.

"This is beautiful, Miss Yeager," I said.

"Call me Yvonne. And thanks. I love it. Come on in here. I
made a pasta salad."

We walked back to the wide-open kitchen, which looked to
come out of *Better Homes and Gardens*. There was a white-countered
center isle that had copper pots and pans hanging above it—the
exact kind I envisioned for the home I always wanted. All the appli-
ances were white and hardly looked used. There was a fully stocked
bar just beyond the kitchen, toward the French doors that led to an
enormous deck that hung over the beach.

"It's a nice night—let's go out back," Yvonne said. She had made
two pasta salad dishes. She carried them outside on the deck and
asked me to sit. Yvonne went back inside to get two wineglasses with
gold trim and a bottle of Merlot.

At the candle-lit patio table, we ingested the food and sipped
wine as Yvonne told me of her expectations for the movie role. The
wine relaxed me, and I gave my open views of how I should play the
character. Moments later, the two men from the audition arrived
with the screenwriter and director, and I performed the monologue I

did earlier and another that required a different emotion. Yvonne Yeager and her colleagues were impressed. I could tell.

After the six of us discussed the movie and my role in it, the men congratulated me, gave me hugs, and left. Yvonne excused herself and returned to the deck a moment later with a lighter and two cigars. "This is sort of a celebratory smoke. Do you indulge?" Yvonne said.

"As a matter of fact, I do," I said, reaching for one. "I had one last night." After observing it, I added, "But not one this good."

Then we lit up. Yvonne pulled up two chairs, and we put our feet up. The ocean was dark, but the sound of it crashing onto the shore and the cigar relaxed me even more. I was on a high, having gotten official word that the movie role was mine. I WAS ON MY WAY. Yvonne opened another bottle of wine, and we conversed over the next hour about a variety of things, all the while enjoying the expensive stogies. I was impressed that a rich person could be so real.

"This is the life," I said. "This is living. I still can't believe I'm here."

"Let's go inside," Yvonne said, "to the den. It's more comfortable in there."

"Out here is great, but whatever you say," I said.

We made it to the sunken den, which had a big screen TV and a couch so cushiony that it almost swallowed me. There were pictures of Yvonne with an array of stars she cast who made it big. Immediately I envisioned a place in Yvonne's den for a photo of me.

Candles, on the ledge of the fireplace, provided light in the room. Yvonne flopped down next to me on the couch. She pushed a button on a remote control and mellow music eased out the Bose speakers. The whole scene was intoxicating, and I definitely was drunk.

"I think you're going to be great for the role," Yvonne said. "You're very talented. And better than that, I like you. You're grounded, but still adventurous. I can tell that. I liked you as soon as I saw you."

"Really," I said, blushing. "What did you like?"

Yvonne looked me in my eyes. "Your eyes," she said. "They're seductive. And your mouth. It's inviting."

"Huh? Wait a second," I said, trying to squirm away from Yvonne.

"Calm down," Yvonne said in a reassuring voice. "Calm down. I'm just telling you what I liked. That's all. You don't have to scoot away from me. I'm not going to bite you."

I did not have a reply, so I kept my mouth shut. But I was not so comfortable anymore. In fact, she blew my high. All the adrenaline

I had seemed to rush from my body. Yvonne Yeager, big-time casting agent that could change my life, was making a pass at me. Damn.

"Come here," Yvonne said calmly. "Listen, I'm not going to try to force you to do anything you don't want to do. But I have to admit that I find you very attractive. Don't be afraid of that. Don't run from that. I can be a good friend to you."

"Yeah, but what does that have to do with the role?" I said. "I mean, do I have it or not, and under what conditions?"

"Monique, the role is yours. This has nothing to do with the role. Your talent got you that role . . . This has everything to do with you."

That was reassuring, but it did not exactly calm me down. Yvonne then reached out and softly caressed my hand, which was slightly trembling. I wanted to pull away or to say something, but I couldn't move or get a word out.

"Relax," Yvonne said. "Listen, if you want to go, you can. But I'd like you to stay. I'm enjoying your being here."

My head was spinning. I wanted to get up, I really did, but I was transfixed on the couch. It seemed like me staying there relaxed Yvonne, made her think I wanted to be there. I stared at a candle and seemed to almost get hypnotized. Yvonne leaned over and softly kissed me on the lips.

I still couldn't move. Yvonne pulled back, and seemed to be looking at me for a reaction. Instead, I started to feel different, comfortable. It scared me that I liked her lips on mine. They were soft, gentle. I had women hit on me before, but I was repulsed by the thought of being with one. I was strictly dickly.

But my cousin from St. Petersburg, Florida, was gay, and she was open with me about her experience. She told me that a woman knew a woman's body better than a man, that if I just released I would be more pleased with a woman than I'd ever been with a man.

I thought about that, and the next thing I knew, I had placed my hand on Yvonne's thigh. Yvonne did not waste any time. She leaned over and kissed me again. This time, I kissed back.

We began rubbing each other's bodies. I was surprised that I liked the softness of her breasts. The only breasts I'd ever felt were my own, and they weren't that big. Hers were full and heavy, and her nipples were as big as thimbles. Touching them made me wet.

It was strange at first, touching a body as soft as mine. But I liked it. I actually liked it. After several moments, Yvonne rose from the couch and blew out the candles. Then she reached out for my hand, helped me up and led me to her lavish bedroom.

TWENTY TWO:

Gettin' My Groove On

Greg

L ife without Brianna gave me the freedom I was looking for. I
could come and go as I pleased, without having to worry about
somebody else worrying about what time I got in or anything. And,
most importantly, my money was secure. Yeah!

The only problem was, I didn't have shit to do with so much
time. I found myself at the store more than usual, which made my
employees a little uncomfortable. I was looking into opening up
another store, but that still did not consume a great deal of my time.
I already knew the ropes. I played a little more ball to stay in shape
and even got into jogging. But as for real excitement, I was hurting.
As much as I didn't want to admit it, not having Brianna left a major
void. She used to fill a lot of gaps in my life, and now she was gone.

I was in a rut without her, and I couldn't stay that way. My pride
wouldn't let me. So, I turned to my phone book. Although I had
been committed to Brianna for two years, I could not help myself
from meeting other women. And I was good about keeping in touch
with them over the phone for occasions just like the one I was in.

I skimmed the book and stopped at the number of Faye Westley,
a lawyer from Florida I met as she paid for a book in my store. I was
wary of her, though, because it was clear she was looking for a relationship; I sought a playmate. Also, I had an unwritten rule that dis-
allowed me from hitting on my customers as tempting as it was.
There were three reasons why: number one was I had to set an example for my staff; number two was she could be after my money; and
number three was—*she could be after my money*.

I passed on Faye and contemplated ringing Alisa Woodson, a
sweet, sexy secretary working at an architect's office. She showed
interest, but she had a boyfriend, and I was not up to competing for
someone's attention. I finally settled on Theresa Lackey, a big-booty

realtor I met through one of my employees a few months back.

Theresa was outgoing and funny, and she let me know soon after we met that she was very interested in me, despite my relationship with Brianna. In the previous two weeks, we had tried to contact each other, but played phone tag. It was nearly 4 p.m. on a Saturday, and I decided I'd call her and a leave message. To my surprise, however, Theresa answered the phone.

"Hi, uh, Theresa," I said. "This is Greg. I expected to be talking to your answering machine. What are you doing at home on a Saturday afternoon?"

"Oh, I'm just chilling," she said. "I'm surprised to hear from you. What are you up to?"

"Nothing, really. I'm calling to see what you're up to, if you'd like to hang out."

"What?" she said. "What happened? You're not on lockdown anymore?"

"That's cute," I said. "I never was on lockdown. I was just in a relationship."

"What do you mean, 'WAS'? Theresa said.

"Well, Brianna and I moved on," I said.

I could tell that got Theresa's attention. She had the hots for me from the first time we met, and now I was open season. That was the opportunity she coveted. And so, she proceeded with aggression.

"Well, Greg, I could say I'm sorry, but that would not be totally true," Theresa said. "I'm sorry if you're hurt behind it, but, well, I think you know I've been interested in really getting to know you."

"I didn't know for sure, but I guess I do now," I said. "So maybe we can get together in the near future and do a movie or something."

"What's up tonight? I mean, I'm free. If you are, we can get together tonight."

I couldn't believe what I heard. She said just what I wanted to hear. I wanted to get with her immediately, but I didn't want to come on too strong. But Theresa taking the initiative to set up a date played right into my desires. And it meant she was self-assured and not so hung up on protocol that she would let what she wanted pass. Men embraced the idea of women saying, "Let me take you to dinner," or "I'd like to see you tonight," or "Can I buy you a drink?"

A lot of women—and some men—feel a woman cannot be a lady if she asserted herself. So many women would rather let an opportunity pass than take the necessary steps to get what they wanted. A woman throwing herself on a man certainly would be viewed as too aggressive and improper. But to make the first move was not.

"All right," I said calmly. I didn't want to sound too anxious. "That'll work. Tonight is good."

We settled on seven. I found Theresa's place in Calumet City, about thirty minutes from downtown Chicago, despite her inaccurate directions. I rang the downstairs buzzer, and she buzzed me in. She waited for me at the top of the steps, looking thick in snug black capri pants that accentuated her plump butt and a colorful blouse that seemed to reflect light onto her face. It was clear she was trying to show me what she had.

She wore a wide smile and eyes that showed me her eagerness. I smiled too, but it was uncomfortable. This was my first time out with a woman on a real date since Brianna. I felt funny about it. And nervous.

"Well, Mr. Gibson," Theresa said. "Give me a hug."

We embraced, and I smelled the wonderful Prescriptives perfume she sprayed on her neck. "You look good," she said.

"Thanks. So do you," I answered. "And you smell good. What's that fragrance, Avon?"

We laughed. I thought I'd throw that out there because we both seemed a little awkward and needed something to ease the tensions. "Nah, it's Charlie," she answered.

We laughed some more and entered Theresa's cluttered but homey apartment. "This is my home. You're always welcomed. It's not much, and it gets a little junky at times, but it's home. It's clean and it's mine."

"I hear you," I said.

She grabbed her purse and turned off the lights, and we were out. On the way downstairs, Theresa offered to drive, which meant something to me. Even if she didn't mean it, it was considerate of her to offer. I looked at it like being out at dinner with a woman and she just sat back every time as I paid the bill. "She could offer something, the tip or anything," I'd think to myself. It was funny because I would want the money, but on the rare occasion it was offered I always refused. I just had the need to know that I wasn't being taken for granted, that I should pay all the time because I'm the man.

I told Theresa I didn't mind driving. I followed her suggestion to go downtown to the Hancock Building. We had pleasant conversation on the way there. She actually told me of her man troubles, which I took to be her way of letting me know that she was totally free of commitment. I didn't offer her any hope about us.

"I hear you," I said. That was my way of being standoffish without being standoffish.

We got to the Hancock Building and took the elevator up to the 96th floor. We took in the breathtaking view of the city.

The conversation ranged from relationships, to the Bulls, to travel, to food. I laughed freely, and that made me feel good about Theresa because it was something I really needed. I found her to be genuine, humorous, bright, and most importantly, levelheaded. And she had a booming body.

As I watched Theresa walk to the bathroom, I told myself she could be the one to help me get over Brianna. I felt Theresa was thinking the same thing. When she got into the bathroom, I was surprised to see Rhonda Stewart approaching me. She was a pre-Brianna honey I used to get with occasionally for steamy, late-night sex. It was like that's all she wanted.

She was like a dream to a single man. She was not concerned with being taken out to dinner or partying or the movies. All Rhonda wanted was sex and no commitment. When I saw her, I immediately wondered how I ever lost touch with her.

Then I remembered that she took a job with some new company in Omaha, Nebraska, as a conference planner.

"Hi, Greg," Rhonda said, her arms open wide, inviting a hug. "I haven't seen you in so long. You look good."

"Thanks, so do you," I said, looking her up and down. Indeed, Rhonda had kept herself up just fine. She was brown-skinned and tender, very nicely dressed. Her hair was as fly as usual. "What are you doing here?" I said.

She explained that she had moved back home with a new job just the previous week. She was out with her brother and sister-in-law, who were entertaining one of their out-of-town friends. As we talked for another few minutes or so, it was clear we were happy to see each other.

I wanted to get her number before Theresa returned, or give her mine, but it was too late. I could see her coming in the distance, so I quickly planted a seed I hoped Rhonda would nurture.

"You should come by my store on Huron," I said. "It's called Alpha Books and Cards."

"I heard you had your own business," she said. "I definitely will stop by there—on Monday."

"Cool," I said.

About that time, Theresa reached us. Immediately I introduced the women to each other. Rhonda extended her hand with a smile. Theresa gave a half-hearted shake with a "leave me and this man alone" look on her face.

Rhonda sensed Theresa was threatened, so she excused herself. But as a dig at Theresa, she gave me a long hug before switching off. Women can be devilish like that.

"Who was that?" Theresa said before Rhonda even reached her seat. She tried to sound casual about it, but I could tell she was upset. Or at least bothered.

"That's a friend of mine who I haven't seen in about two years," I said. "Why do you seem to be bothered?"

"Because I saw her over there earlier looking at us. Then I go to the bathroom and she's all in your face," Theresa said. "If she wanted to say hi to you, she could have come over while I was here."

I was a little alarmed by her response. She had a point, but we were on a first date and already she was trying to pull rank. That kind of insecurity was something Brianna never displayed; she was sure of herself, sure of US. No way would she let another woman speaking to me be a point of stress between us.

"It really doesn't matter, does it?" I said. I was calm, probably because I wanted some sex. Inside, however, I was burning. I thought to myself: "Who in the hell does she think she is? I haven't even hit the booty yet, and she's acting like *that*."

"Hey, Theresa, I'm here with you," I added, trying to be reassuring. "We're having a good time. That's all that matters, isn't it?"

"I'm sorry," she said. "I just don't like to be disrespected like that."

"I don't know if that was about disrespect or not," I said. "Maybe she didn't come over while you were here because she thought you might be offended. Maybe she just wanted to say hello and go back to her friends before you came to prevent the kind of drama that's happening right now. Whatever the case, let's just move on. All right?"

"All right," Theresa said. She looked at me from head to toe. It was a seductive look, which I was glad to see. But I was surprised that a moment after being upset, she had flipped the script. I had no idea what would come out of her mouth next.

"Since we're near your place, why don't we go there for a while? It's just 10:45. Maybe we can have a drink or something."

That surprised me, too. "'Or something' sounds good to me," I said, smiling. "Let's bounce."

Theresa took one last glare across the room at Rhonda, who was glaring back. Theresa then smiled and waved. She had me—and was going back to my place for "or something." It was exactly what I wanted.

TWENTY THREE:

It's Gettin' Kinda Hectic

Greg

Theresa accomplished her mission: she coaxed me into letting her stay the night. Not that it was difficult; I wanted her there, to satisfy my desires, which in my mind was the first step in moving on without Brianna.

Between the time we arrived at my Ontario Avenue condo and the time we left for the ride back to Calumet City, I got turned out. Theresa threw that thing on me viciously, passionately, and relentlessly.

She was insatiable. The drinks she had at the Hancock Building and the glass of wine at my crib erased her inhibitions—the few she had. After a sort of feeling-out process on the couch, she virtually attacked me. And I attacked back.

Over the next few weeks we had repeated interludes. Actually, they were more like sex sessions. There was very little, if any, romance involved. I'd drive out to her place or her to mine, and we would have some small talk, maybe a drink . . . and then it'd be on to the bedroom, the bathroom, the kitchen, the floor—wherever.

Although we were each other's "servicers"—that is, we serviced each other's sexual needs—I tried to make it clear to Theresa that there was no relationship beyond that. It was just about the booty. I did not want her to see anyone else, but I wasn't going to complain if she did. I just didn't want her to think that I was her man.

Maybe I was naive in thinking that I could have that woman's body as I did and she would not have any emotional attachment. I regularly tried to reinforce that we were "just friends" and not "together." She said she understood, but I wasn't sure if I believed her.

I mean, even though I was with Brianna, she pushed up on me hard. So with a chance to get at me, of course she said she was cool with us not being in a "relationship." She was not going to do or say anything to turn me away.

Meanwhile, I got with Theresa, but I still had Brianna on the brain. I missed her passion and strength and charm and wit. Theresa could not replace her. I talked to Larry about it, and he told me that maybe I should give her a call, see how she was doing. What harm could that do?

I had a date with a woman I met at a car wash—Claire McIntyre, a voluptuous Cook County sheriff—but I decided I'd call Brianna first to let her know I was thinking about her and to hear, if only for a moment, the soothing sound of her voice.

"Hey, Brianna, how are you?" I said.

"Fine . . . Who is this?" Brianna said, knowing it was me but not willing to let me know she still recognized my voice in an instant.

"This is Greg. I just wanted to call and say hello and to let you know you're thought about," I said.

"Oh, really?" Brianna answered. "Well, I'm surprised to hear that."

"You shouldn't be," I said. "You know I care about you."

That was the wrong thing to say. "Gregory," Brianna said with anger in her voice, "don't even go there. You care about me? Listen, let's not even do this. Why did you call me?"

"I told you why. What, you don't believe me?" I said.

"It doesn't really matter what I think or that you're thinking of me, as you claim," she said. "It doesn't matter."

"It does matter," I said. "But if you want to be bitter after two months, well, that's pretty sad."

"Yeah, so are you," Brianna said.

The next sound I heard was a dial tone.

That did not exactly go the way I planned. I was angry that Brianna still held animosity, but then again, what did I really expect? That she'd be so happy to hear from me after eight weeks that she'd melt at the sound of my voice? That she'd proclaim her love for me, ask me to come back to her? I had wrecked her life, so it would be some time—if ever—that she'd think of me without anger.

Still, I had to shake that stuff and meet Claire. I had told Theresa that I would be busy and unable to see her. I led her to believe it was work-related, although I did not say that it was. Definitely I didn't tell her I'd be out with a woman.

Claire and I agreed to meet at the Cotton Club. It was a Thursday night, a slow night, so I assumed I could be out without having to worry about being seen by anyone I didn't want seeing me.

I was anxious to see her because at the car wash she wore no makeup and baggie jeans, but still was attractive. Claire arrived at the club before I did. I noticed her immediately standing at the bar, wearing a white silk blouse, a long navy skirt, and a multi-colored neck-kerchief. She looked corporate but relaxed. I put on some black slacks, a black shirt and a four-button olive blazer.

We embraced, and I thought to myself that I was happy to be there; Claire was even more fine than I imagined. I led Claire to a table in the front section of the club, where a jazz band played mellow tunes.

We were in a corner, up against the red brick wall that lined the left side of the jazz room. A waiter lit the candle on the white-linen table and took drink orders. Claire was a direct woman, so she fired questions at me as if they came out of an Uzi:

Do you have a woman? What do you like in women? Are you a player? What's the most important quality that makes a good relationship? And on and on.

I was like, "Damn!" But it was our first time out, so I didn't make a big deal out of the interrogation. I just gave her short but direct answers. "I had a woman, but not anymore . . . I like a woman who is genuine and who has a good heart . . . A player? No, I'm not a player . . . Honesty has to be the most important part of a relationship, on both sides."

She seemed satisfied enough with my answers. The drinks came, and I proposed a toast. "To . . . the self-service car wash on 87th Avenue. Who would have thought it would be the place I'd meet such a nice woman?" I said. Claire offered a huge smile. We tapped glasses.

I was looking into Claire's eyes when I felt the presence of someone standing over me. I turned, looked up, and saw the angry face of none other than—Theresa. My heart skipped. I'd never been caught in that kind of crossfire before, and it was a crazy feeling. I tried to act like it was no big deal.

"Hey, Theresa, uh, how you doing?" I said. "This is, uh, Claire."

Theresa did not even look at her. There was an almost sinister look in her eyes. "I thought you had to work tonight," she said, standing over me.

"I didn't tell you that. I told you I was busy," I said.

I was embarrassed and nervous. Here I was on a first date with a nice woman and in came Theresa tripping. I was not sure how to handle the situation.

Theresa surely did. She pulled up a chair and sat down. Claire looked on in disbelief.

"Uh, Greg, what's up?" Claire said.

I tried to act like it was no biggie. "I don't know. What are you doing, Theresa?"

"We're all going to talk," she said. "You think I'm going to tolerate this?"

"Tolerate what?" I said in an angry voice. "Listen, I think we should talk over here, if you don't mind."

Theresa got up and stalked to the bar. I took a deep breath, shook my head and turned to Claire. Before I could say a word, she said, "I thought you said you didn't have a girlfriend."

"Claire, I promise, that is not my girlfriend. I don't have one. That woman is a friend of mine that I've dated lately, but we are not in a relationship. I can't believe she's tripping like this."

"Well, she is. I think I'm just going to go home. You need to handle your business because it's looking really stink right about now."

"Don't go," I said, although her leaving sounded like a good idea. I did not know how crazy Theresa would get, so I wanted to prevent a major scene. "Let me talk to her, find out what's up so we can go on with our night."

"Greg, I don't think so. She looks a little crazy to me. I grew up on the southside and I can defend myself, but I'm really not going to fight if I don't have to. So, why don't you call me later?"

And then she left, refusing my offer to walk her to her car. I then stormed over to Theresa, who was smiling. That made me even more incensed.

"What the fuck is your problem?" I said to her.

"Hey, Boo, it's all right," she said, trying to hug me.

I held her back. "Boo? Don't be smiling and acting like everything's fine. You've got a problem. Don't go around acting like you can control what I do or who I see."

That deranged look returned to Theresa's eyes. "If you have a right to fuck me, I have a right to do *whatever* I want," she yelled.

People near the bar heard her raised voice. It didn't matter to her. "How you gonna play me?" she added. "I gave you my body. I gave you whatever you wanted. Then you tell me you have to work and I find you here on a date with some bitch. Something told me to come here tonight. I was tired and I have to get up in the morning, but something told me to make the sacrifice and come to my co-worker's birthday party. And look what I find."

As she talked, I thought about Larry, who had told us of the time he had a woman at his house when another honey came over unannounced. He did not answer the door, and the second chick banged and banged until he did. She began screaming and ranting. Larry kept her from coming inside and tried a psychological approach in the hallway. He appealed to her pride. "Look at yourself," he said. "Don't disrespect yourself like this." It did not work. The woman was out of control.

I was desperate, and I couldn't think of anything else. Maybe Larry's approach would work for me. So, I said to Theresa: "Come on, now. You're a rational woman. Don't disrespect yourself like this."

Bad move. Like in Larry's case, Theresa got angrier. "I'll never disrespect myself. This is about YOU disrespecting ME. Who do you think you are a damned psychiatrist? You know what, I'm through with you."

She then walked toward the exit. About fifteen people witnessed the scene, so I went to the bathroom to regroup. I looked in the mirror and wondered what the hell had I done getting with this madwoman. The men's room attendant turned on the water in the faucet. I wet my hands and ran them over my face, which had humiliation, frustration, and confusion all over it.

I knew I had to get out of there. Maybe I could explain what happened to Claire, and she will accept my apology, and we could set another date. Maybe. When I got outside the door, I ran into a dude who was in the Army with me.

I didn't like Van Guilling, a sucker who tried to brag about anything at anytime. I stood there for a minute or two while he talked, but I was not even listening. I had no respect for Van. I had hooked him up with a female friend I had in Houston. The woman showed Van a nice time around the city because he was my so-called friend. Then Van said to her, "I like you. I hope you know Greg has a girlfriend in Chicago. I know he told you he doesn't, but he does. I thought you should know that."

That was fowl. Only a straight buster would do that to someone he's supposed to be down with. The woman in Houston was like a sister to me; I never got with her. She, of course, called and told me of how my "friend" played himself. Ever since, I had nothing to say to Van. I probably should have called him out on it and been done with it. But he wasn't even worth the energy.

Van rambled outside the bathroom about something he did or bought or whatever until I finally ended it. "Whatever Van," I said, and walked away.

Just as I reentered the jazz room, I heard someone call my name.

I looked to my right. In an instant, my face, shirt, and jacket were drenched. Theresa had thrown a vodka and cranberry right into my face.

I stumbled back into a crowd of people, wiping my eyes. A few guys prevented me from hitting the floor. I gathered myself and grabbed some napkins off the bar and wiped my face and clothes. I had never been that embarrassed. I wanted to just disappear. People pointed and held back laughter.

Suddenly, a bouncer stood over me, grabbed my arm, and asked me to leave the club. "You're asking ME to leave?" I said. "I got a drink thrown in MY face. I didn't do anything."

The wide body was hearing none of it. So, he grabbed me tighter by the elbow and led me to the front door. Outside, I looked to the left and saw a line of about twenty people waiting to get in, which was surprising because Thursday was usually a light night at the club. I quickly turned to the right so they could not see my drenched clothes. But to the right was Theresa, who I thought was gone. She still had that crazed look.

I stood there frozen for a second. Before I could think what to do, she slowly bent down and took off her three-inch-heeled pumps. She placed one shoe in either hand, heels upward. Then she took off running toward me, screaming. She swung the shoes toward my head like a ninja would some nunchakus, with intent to injure. I took a few blows on the arms, but I managed to get a hold on both her arms and shoved her toward the cars parked on Michigan Avenue. She fell back on a Honda, setting off its alarm.

The people in line looked on in disbelief, lots of them laughed. I wanted to help her up, but I instead decided I'd better just get out of there. So, I ran across the street to my car. I glanced back over my shoulder as I struggled to get the key in the door. Theresa was searching under the Honda for her shoes.

I got in my car and drove off, looking back in the rear view mirror to make sure she was not trailing me. Theresa had made me furious and embarrassed, but she also had scared me. I wasn't afraid of her. But I was afraid that I could hurt her if she confronted me again. It also struck me that I was going through that mess when I could have still had Brianna.

TWENTY FOUR:

A Blind Search

Julian

I was on the phone with Nicole Lamar when another call came in. I asked her to hold on. I clicked to the other line. It was Greg. And it was immediately evident something was up because he was not his usual boisterous, peppy self. He seemed broken, dejected, so I assumed it was woman problems.

I mean, if not job or money woes, what else could bring down a man? Greg was his own boss and had plenty of dough, so I knew a woman was involved. And I knew if he called me that late—it was about 1:30 a.m. in D.C.—he really wanted to talk. Needed to talk.

So, before he even got into the problem, I asked him to hold while I cleared the other line. I told Nicole that I'd get back with her. She was a beautiful, independent sister who sold cars—Saabs and Toyotas—in Maryland. Every so often we'd talk, usually really late at night. I was interested in her as more than a friend, but the friendship we developed was so strong neither of us wanted to risk it.

Instead, we had a platonic relationship that was important to us. I had given her a shoulder to cry on many times about busted relationships with men. She was a sounding board for me when that madness went down with Joanne. Nicole was almost one of the boys, except she had a soft, sweet voice, fat titties, and a juicy ass. Even though we did not get busy, I definitely noticed her physical attributes.

"Sorry, Nicole, but I've got to take this call from Greg," I said.

"OK. Tell him I said hello," she said. "Before you go, are we on to do a movie tomorrow?"

"Yeah," I said. "I'll call you at the office tomorrow. Goodnight."

"G, what's up?" I said after clicking back to Greg. "You all right?"

"Hell no," he said. "Remember that honey, Theresa, I told you

107

about—the one who was down for a sex-only hookup? Well she just flipped on me. I'm talking, she went off."

He went on to give me all the details. Greg paused enough for me to throw in a "Get outta here" or a "What?" or a "Stop lying." When he was done telling me the whole story, I could not help but laugh.

"G, stay away from that bitch. She's crazy."

Before I could get that out good, Greg had a call on his other line. I held on as he switched to it. After about a minute, he came back to me.

"That was that mad woman right there," he said. "Know what she said? This motherfucker said, 'It's not over.' I asked her what she meant, and she said, 'It ain't over. Watch your back.' "

"I know you don't want to hit her, but you've got to protect yourself," I said. "But tell me this: Could you see this in her? Did she give you any signs that she was a nutcase?"

"None," G said. "I'm telling you one of the things I liked about her was she was genuine and level-headed—seemingly. But you know, I'm just remembering this. The first time we went out, she acted kind of wild when I talked to this other chick. But I just kind of brushed it off. She got upset, but it was no big deal. But I guess we weren't having booty calls on the regular yet, either."

We talked about Theresa "the mad woman" for a few more minutes. I threw in some jokes to make Greg laugh, and soon he was laughing at himself and the situation. We tried to patch Larry in on a three-way, but he was not at home. "He's probably out with Monique," Greg said.

We finally got pass his chaos and switched the conversation to me. My chaos with Joanne was months behind me, but it still lingered some. I told Greg I had been out on a few dates, none that inspired a second get-together.

There was Shandra Crawford, who cooked dinner for me at the home she shared with a girlfriend. The food was all right, the conversation adequate, but the house was a wreck. I thought: How could there be magazines sprawled all over the coffee table, the trash-can overflowing, and her bed unmade when she knew she was having company?

Worse, the bathroom was a disaster. It smelled rank, with mold showing around the perimeter of the bathtub, which had a serious ring around it. Small roaches congregated on the bathroom floor as if they were at a convention. I was totally uncomfortable. It spoke significantly about the kind of person she was if her home was so unkept. It didn't have to pass the white-glove test, but DAMN. If cleanliness was next to Godliness, as I had been told, these women were bound for hell.

And on top of all that, Shandra's roommate, Terri—who dressed like she was out of a Luther "Luke" Campbell video—made passes at me every chance she got. I spent the last hour there thinking I would never return.

Then there was Monica Ross, who was so attractive under the lights at Republic Gardens, a black-owned single spot in northwest D.C., that I made myself available to see her the day after meeting her.

Well, the next day was a horror show. Those eyes that looked piercing at the club were bloodshot. The skin that looked so flawless at the club was acne-filled and discolored. The smile that was so warming at the club was crooked—and her teeth were gray. The hair? A weave. Even that nice-smelling perfume she wore at the club smelled like rubbing alcohol the next day. All I could do was shake my head.

What was it about the lighting in a club that made a hyena look like a princess? Maybe the few drinks I had contributed, too. But could I have been that bombed? I contemplated this as I let the sea dog into my house.

We had planned just a get-to-know meeting, but I cut that short by making up a lie about having to attend to a family emergency. She was polite and pleasant and said she understood that I had to leave after just fifteen minutes.

"But, I want a raincheck," she said as she left. I wanted to offer her a makeup kit.

And then there was Lakisha Jackson, a twenty-three year-old I met as she jogged around Anacostia Park. She suggested we meet at a party a friend of hers had at the Panorama Room, located about ten minutes from my house. To my dismay, she was dressed in classic hoochie gear—spandex aqua dress that barely covered her ass, bold fake-gold necklace, the works.

Plus, she knew practically every guy at the function, seemingly all intimately by the way they responded to her. She drank cognac straightup, about four shots in an hour. When we danced, she immediately turned her back on me and backed up against me. Then she invited another man to come over and dance with her, so we could sandwich her.

If all of that was not bad enough, she smoked cigarettes as if she were in a race. I had never and would never deal with a smoker, and this chick was a chimney. When she excused herself for a moment to say hello to a friend—a male, of course—I took my drink to the head and went home.

Lastly, there was Desiree Simmons. She seemed "real" cool. The conversation was straight. Then I went to her house, and she hit me with two pieces of news that I knew meant she was history.

One, she said her job was transferring her to Chesapeake, Virginia, but that she wanted to see me despite the distance. "I like you," she said. "Chesapeake is not that far, maybe three hours away."

Then she dropped the other bomb: She had a daughter, three.

So she had two of the three things working against her that I absolutely would not bend on: she was moving away, and she had a kid. All she had to do was smoke, for the hat trick.

I was totally against long-distance relationships, and I sure as hell would not deal with a woman with a child. It just was an automatic turnoff. She would always have a tie with the father, and I wasn't the type to deal with that kind of thing. If I were going to be with someone, she would be in D.C. and not a mother.

"So you're not the only one who's had it bad with women lately," I said to Greg.

"That's good to hear, sort of," he said. "I mean, I don't want you to have to go through that. At least you haven't been assaulted by one."

"No," I said, "just INSULTED."

We laughed and ended the conversation. "Peace," Greg said. "Watch your back," I said to him.

TWENTY FIVE:

By Any Means Necessary

Julian

Somehow I forgot to call Nicole about hanging out and catching a movie, so she left a message for me. "Oh, you can't call someone when you say you are, huh? What's up with that? Buzz me when you get this so I know what to do later. Bye, knucklehead."

I was so frustrated with the *knuckleheads* I had gone out with that I was about ready to give up on women altogether. I was serious about it, too. I was that frustrated. It was something that I NEVER even considered.

I mean, as long as I could remember it was almost like I was obsessed with women, with sex. Like a lot of men, I would go through drastic means to get into a lady's panties, measures I look back on now and just shake my head.

There was a time when I had just returned from playing ball, and on my way home I plotted how I would spend the evening—take a hot shower, order a pizza, return a few calls, then turn off the phone's ringer, and eat and fall asleep on the couch with the remote control in my hand. It was storming outside, so that was the ideal way to go.

But before I could turn off the phone, I received a call from Doris Douglas, a high school mate who gave me the booty back when I didn't really know what I was doing in bed. I talked with Doris occasionally, but we had not seen each other in years.

I don't know what got into her on this particular night, but she must have been horny. I was comfortable on the couch, with a slice of pizza in my hand, when she said, "I wish it weren't raining so badly outside because I wanted you to come over."

I sat up and placed the pizza back in the box. Although I was not very knowledgeable about sex the one time I slept with Doris, I do remember that she knew how to work that thang. There was no way

I was going to let an opportunity to get back in those drawers pass.

"Listen, Doris, you don't live that far from me," I said. "I was going to chill tonight, but if the invitation is open, I'd be glad to visit you. It's been too long anyway since we've seen each other."

So, I got up, shaved, got dressed, and fought through damn near a typhoon to get to the booty. And was it worth the hassle? Not really. But that did not prevent me from making other trips, like when I was zooted off four Long Islands but still swerved my way up 95 to Baltimore because Gloria Lackey returned my call and said she was hoping we'd get together on that Thursday night.

Never mind that I was drunk and that I had a faculty conference at nine the next morning back in the D.C. area. Never mind that I had never been to her house, so I had to find my way at 2 a.m. with directions written while intoxicated. Still, the booty was calling, and I was a slave to the booty.

And you know what? I found Gloria's place, despite the blurred vision and drunken stupor, and accomplished my mission. But when her alarm clock went off at six, I hardly felt like getting up to make the trek back home.

Still, the power of having sex was so pervasive that I didn't mind. What got old and ultimately changed my views on "getting with the honies" just for the sake of "getting with the honies" was the empty feeling of laying there next to the woman after I've finished my business. If I had my way, I would have gotten up, washed off my Johnson, gotten dressed, and left.

There was no connection with these sex exploits, no REAL fulfillment. Oh, the act itself was satisfying, for all I sought was the feeling of power I got from pleasing a woman—and I unloaded some backed up semen. But it was not lovemaking. I did not feel like I wanted to embrace those women afterward. Rather, I wanted to jet.

After dealing with the three knuckleheads of the last three weeks, I didn't want to BE AROUND women who did not move me much less sleep with them. I had never been so sour about women, and it bothered me.

If someone could measure a man's love of women, I was confident I'd register near the top. Their softness, their beauty, their grace, their bodies, their smell, their presence—I admired all that and more in women.

And now I felt like a needed a break from them. It all started with Joanne and her deceit. I knew what happened with her was not typical of women; in fact, it was atypical. Women by far were more honest than men, more faithful, more sincere, more everything involving truthfulness.

I just happened to run into one that had the veneer of a woman and the makeup of a man. And although I was disgusted with how Joanne played me, I still believed that she really did love me. I even believed she did not want that guy, Sam, and that she truly regretted her actions. Really, I believed everything she said. But I just could not forgive her.

So, I was excited about having a date with Nicole, my beautiful platonic friend. At least I could be around a woman again and feel good about the conversation. And with Nicole, I knew she'd always tell me the truth, sometimes even when I didn't want to hear it.

We ended up seeing *The Hurricaine* at the movies, which not only fulfilled our entertainment appetites, but also GAVE us an appetite. I was in such a good mood after the show that I decided to treat Nicole to dinner at Georgia Brown's, a black-owned restaurant in downtown D.C.

And, as usual, the meal was delightful and the conversation great. We discussed the movie and how it was as good as the book. I told Nicole of my disenchantment with women, which stunned her. She knew of my total love of women, so she immediately assessed that perhaps I should backup and spend some time alone.

"It sounds to me like you're trying so hard to rebound from Joanne that you've lost your patience and tolerance," she said. "You need to just cool out."

"You're probably right," I said. "But it's strange to feel this way."

"You just need to meet a nice woman—they're plenty of them out here—who doesn't have an agenda, who isn't crazy, and who doesn't mind cleaning her place. That's not too difficult. You used to meet good women all the time. You used to have a problem deciding which GOOD woman to choose from."

"Boy, how times have changed," I said.

TWENTY-SIX:

Moni In the Middle

Monique

The visit to Malibu was far more interesting than I ever envisioned. I went there hoping to earn a part in a new movie. I left the next morning with the job AND the discovery of another side of my sexuality.

The thought of being with another woman repulsed me before Yvonne Yeager invited me to her house. Before the sun came up, I rested in Yvonne's huge, soft bed with my eyes open, staring at the sheer white covering hanging over and around it.

I was amazed that I enjoyed the softness of Yvonne's hands and the delicate way she kissed my neck and shoulders. It was clear Yvonne knew what parts of a woman's body needed attention. She made all the right moves to please me in a way that I did not think was possible by a woman. Even Yvonne's perfume calmed me. This was such a contrast for me. I mean, I enjoyed the roughness of a man's hands and his manly smell and handling of me. I enjoyed the hardness of a man, the friction involved with passionate sex.

I looked over at the still-sleeping Yvonne and shook my head. I thought: Yvonne knew what she was doing last night. She seduced me without my even knowing it. She arranged the romantic setting and had the wine and cigars to relax me, loosen my inhibitions. But why me? What did I give off that she knew I would go for her advance?

Over breakfast we had a serious talk.

"Yvonne," I said, "this is VERY different for me. I've never expected to ever be interested in a woman. I still really don't know how this happened. I don't regret that it happened, though. I just don't know exactly what to say about it."

"Well," Yvonne jumped in, "you really don't have to say anything. First, I want to tell you something very important. And that is that I've never met someone and, just like that, kissed her and spent the night with her. Never. And I really can't pinpoint exactly why I wanted that with you. But you caught my attention at the audition yesterday, and when I left there, I was just looking forward to your coming here."

"My problem is this," I said. "I have this guy I've been dating lately. You actually met him yesterday; he read at the audition, too. Anyway, I love men. And to be frank, I love having sex with him. It's so different from what we did last night. But I'm an honest person, so I'll tell you that although I enjoy men, I had a great time with you. I really enjoyed it."

In other words, I was confused as hell. I wanted Larry and Yvonne. Yvonne told me there was no pressure on me to feel as if I were in a relationship. She advised me to not tell Larry about my night with a woman.

"But if you feel like you must, let him know I'm not trying to threaten what you guys have," Yvonne said. "I know you had a life before last night. But I do want to see you more."

"I want to see you more, too," I said. "But I also want to see Larry. But I have to tell him about us, if you don't mind. I'll ask him to keep it to himself—I trust that he will. But he has to be told. That's just how I am."

Yvonne reluctantly agreed. And as a caveat, she told me that she'd find a role for Larry in the movie she was casting if he'd accept our relationship and continued to see me. I couldn't believe she'd accept that kind of arrangement, but that's what she said. I think she believed that she'd win me over.

"I don't know if that'll work or offend him," I said. "But I guess I'll see."

Later that evening, I invited Larry to my place for dinner. I figured I'd try the same tactic on him that Yvonne used on me. And so, I set a romantic mood, with candles all around, the smooth sound of a Jean Luc Ponty CD floating through the air, which went well with the aroma of roasted chicken, asparagus, and mashed potatoes.

I had a bottle of Remy Martin and a cigar. Larry passed on the cigar, but he enjoyed the congac. And as a topper, I wore a short, sexy black dress.

"I see you're in a great mood," Larry said. "What's up with you?"

"I just wanted to cook you dinner, have a nice evening," I said. "And I wanted to tell you about my visit to Yvonne Yeager's house. It was very interesting. But let's eat and relax first."

We dined and drank. And when I returned from the bathroom, I found Larry sitting on the couch, his pants down by his ankles, sporting an erection. I was startled, but I quickly got over that and got up on it.

I didn't wear panties, so I just raised my dress and slowly walked over to Larry and straddled him. We worked out each other for the next several minutes, ending up on the floor.

"I did not have this in mind when I asked you over," I said.

"You should have," Larry asked.

"I'm not complaining," I said. "But I did want to talk to you about something, about Yvonne Yeager."

We cleaned ourselves up and sat on the couch. Larry asked me to lean back on him as he put his arm around me. For Larry, this was not rare—it was UNHEARD of. He basically was Mr. Unaffectionate. Holding hands, hugging, they usually were out of the question for Larry. "What's the point?" he had told me when I tried to cusp his hand once. "We're together. Everyone can see that. No need in holding hands."

For him to initiate a show of affection was a big deal, a big step. He told me that he had never experienced love but for him to want to cuddle with me meant his feelings were more than casual. Much more.

"So what happened there? How was Yvonne Yeager up close and personal?" Larry said as he rubbed my arms.

I took a deep breath. I had been practicing in my head how I'd tell Larry about my lesbian encounter. But with the time at hand, all my prepared words, I forgot.

"Well, a lot happened," I began. "Yvonne was great. She was very real, very, uh, very positive, and just cool. She had food and drinks and a cigar for me. We sat out on her deck and just talked and enjoyed a cool breeze. It was . . ."

"It sounds as if you were on a date," Larry said, laughing.

He meant it as a joke, but he was right on point. And he gave me the opening I needed because I wasn't sure where I was going with my story.

"Well, Larry," I said, "that's kind of what it turned out to be."

Larry stopped moving his hands on my arm. He leaned around me so he could see my face. He immediately thought the writer or director tried to get with me.

"What do you mean?" he said.

It was difficult for me to actually say.

"Well, I mean the whole night was set up like a date," I said. "I did read again for the director and writer, and it went well, as you know, since they gave me the part. But when they left, Yvonne and I just chilled."

"So what's the date part?" Larry said.

"That's just it. The date part was me and . . . Yvonne."

Larry softly pushed me away. He sat up on the edge of the couch. His face was strained. He heard me, but he couldn't have heard me.

"What?" he said.

"Yvonne likes me," I said flatly. "I mean she REALLY likes me."

Larry said, "'Like you' like, 'attracted to you?'"

"Yeah," I said. "She likes me like a lover."

"Hold up. How can she like you like a lover when she hasn't been with you like that?" Larry said, still not getting the picture.

I was hoping Larry would understand without me having to say it. But he either genuinely did not catch on or he knew what I meant but wanted to hear me say it. That way, there'd be nothing left for interpretation. When people start assuming, they usually assume for the worst.

Finally, I came with it directly. "Larry, I have been with Yvonne."

Larry sat there dumbfounded. I actually felt better having said it. I wasn't really embarrassed by the experience, but I was nervous about what he'd think or say.

I said: "She came on to me, and I ended up spending the night with her. I don't know how you'll take this. I've never thought of myself as bisexual. I never had any attraction to women. But something with her just clicked. I told her that I was seeing you and that I wanted to continue seeing you."

"What?" Larry said. "You want to continue seeing me? Come on now. You just told me that you were with another woman. Why would you want to deal with me? What's there for me?"

"A lot, if you just open your mind," I said. "I know you like me. And I know you love acting. This is a case where you can have me AND get the shot you need for your career."

"What are you talking about?" Larry asked.

"Well, Yvonne said that she'd cast you in the movie if you kind of agreed to continue seeing me while I see her, too," I said. It sounded so crazy that I paused to make sure I said it right.

"Please don't take that as a bribe or something," I added. "It's just that she's really, uh, interested in me, and she knows I'm really interested in you. And she liked the way you read at the audition. She hadn't made up her mind about who she was going to cast in the part you read for. But she will if you agree.

"Listen, I know you'd like to get the role on your own merits. But you probably would have gotten it anyway. You're a good actor. She recognizes that. But in this business, in this town, we all need a break any way we can get it. This is yours and mine."

"So that's why you went with this lesbian thing with her? To jump-start your career?" asked Larry. It sounded like he was hoping that was my reason. But I couldn't lie to him.

"Well, no," I said. "She and the writer and director gave me the role before anything with me and Yvonne happened. I don't know why I went with it. Maybe it was there inside me all along and she just brought it out. I don't know."

Larry looked at me. I had done it again, surprised him when he thought I could not. He remembered telling me during our erotic picnic that I had "no limits." I dismissed that notion then, but this latest deal left no doubt in Larry's mind.

Now, my free spirit nature that he liked put him in a quandary. Could he stay with a woman he liked knowing he would basically compete for her time with a woman? Could he let her go knowing that she was a ticket to the acting break he desired for so long?

It was a moral dilemma, one he certainly could not make on his own. He told me how he shared all of his business with his two boys, so I knew he'd consult them about what to do.

"Monique," he said, "this shit is deep. I don't want to seem like I'm putting you on hold, but I've got to put you on hold. It's good to know you still want to be involved with me, that you didn't just play me for a woman. That's some consolation, a little consolation. But let me think about it."

I nodded my head. He gathered himself and went into the bathroom. I heard him say, "What the *fuck* is going on in this world?"

TWENTY SEVEN:

Go With The Flow

Larry

On my ride home, I wondered how I should tell my boys about Monique's venture to the other side. There was no doubt I would tell them. If I'd ever kept something from Julian and Greg, I couldn't remember. This wouldn't be easy, though.

I was torn between being troubled with dealing with a bisexual woman and my career being launched by my involvement with a dike. I said dike because when the three of us talked about a man being bisexual, we dismissed it. In our minds, he was a fag. No in between. So the same had to apply to Monique.

With this deal, I was not fooling myself. I knew that it was a decision that really was about my ego and ambition. No one I knew was more confident in his ability to get a honey and keep her than me. So, my ego was on trial in this one. How could a man who had boasted he could "turn a lesbian straight" if given the chance, now have one of his honies tell him she wanted a woman?

Not me. But it was me.

I had put a lot of time, energy, and effort into learning the craft of acting, and I wanted to see it pay off. I'd performed in local theaters in front of gatherings as small as thirty people and as large as two hundred, on a good night. But I was not someone who decided to jump into something without a plan. So, I went to and graduated from San Francisco's renowned American Conservatory Theater.

That was no poo-butt training. Denzel went there. Danny Glover. Kevin Spacey. I took the necessary route to earn a chance to do something big, but I had not received a break. And in L.A., more so than anywhere, you needed a break to really show your ability. And a break translated into knowing someone who was making the decisions.

So, how could I pass up on the chance Yvonne Yeager was offering, ego or no ego?

Thankfully, when I got home, Greg and Julian were in place. I needed them to help me sort through my dilemma. I was sure they expected it to be just another of our frequent catch-up calls. But I made it clear from the start that I had something significant to share.

After the usual greetings, I said: "Fellas, I need to tell you some wild shit." Then I let them have it. I told them that I'd really started to care about Monique, which was wild enough considering only a few times in my life I had cared enough about a woman to say I cared.

Then I told them that Monique spent the night with Yvonne Yeager, told them the honey I was involved with went AC-DC on me, told them she wanted to continue seeing me while seeing Yvonne too, told them a part in the movie was in it for me.

Of course, they were thrown. "You're bull-shitting," Julian said. "Hold up. Let me get this straight. You're telling us that Monique fucked—or whatever it is two women do—the casting agent and wants to see both of you? And if you agree, you get a role in a movie? This shit is unreal."

"No, it's real," I said.

"L," Julian said, "well maybe you should just go with the flow. You're not in love with her, are you? So just do what you have to do to get the part in the movie and move on. Shit, maybe they'll invite you to bed with both of them. We've turned some tricks in our day, but not that one."

"You know I thought about that," I said. "But it's deeper than that. It's like, what if SHE makes a decision down the road and decides to kick me to the curb? I've never worried about that before because I know where I stack up against a man. There's so many busters out here who don't know how to treat a woman that they make me look even better than I am. I ain't mad at 'em; it's a fact.

"But there are different dynamics stacking up against a woman, especially a woman with power."

Greg was quiet up to that point, which meant an eruption was coming soon. He always had an opinion and was always brutally honest.

"Fuck the bullshit, Larry," Greg said. "This is a chance for you to get some big-time Benjamins. A movie? How can you let that go? That's what you've been working for. You've got bills to pay, don't you? Let them do whatever two women do together—probably tease each other to death without a dick—and get what you need for your

career. You told us how hard it is to get a break out there not knowing the right people. Well, now you know the right people. Hey, it's
up to you; it's your career. But how can you let a chance to get paid
pass like that?"

I absorbed their words, but I could not make a decision then.
Greg and Julian brought up how Kevin Garnett bust the Knicks' ass
again, which lightened the mood. I engaged in the conversation for
a moment, but the matter at hand was foremost on my mind. That's
how I was. When something mattered to me, I was totally focused on
that. That's how I could quickly learn the lines of a script and interpret them. And if something was heavy on my mind, I'd wrestle with
it until it was resolved. I was an intense thinker and worrier—totally opposite of Julian—to the point where I'd get a fever blister
around my nose or a knot on the back of my head when I was especially burdened.

"I'm going to talk to her tomorrow and see how that goes and
make a decision," I said. "Straight up: I don't know what I'm going
to do. I don't know what to do. But I don't like shit to just linger. So,
I'll be calling again."

With that, we ended the phone call. The next day, I met Monique
at the same park where we enjoyed each other on a blanket. We sat on
a bench this time. Monique did not hide her uneasiness. She fiddled
with her hands and could not sit still. I was antsy, too, but only on the
inside. A rule of mine was to not show emotion in my actions, to be
completely blase. I seemed calm, in control. But I wasn't.

I began by telling Monique that I cared about her, and that was
why the situation bothered me. Then I lied. "It really doesn't matter
that it's a woman or a man," I said.

"But this *is* a woman, and it *is* different," Monique said. "At the
risk of sounding like I'm begging or trying to convince you, I'll say
this: Yvonne cannot do for me what you can do. You're a man. I need
a man."

Not that Monique pleaded such a strong case, but I finally gave
in to my desires in acting, while squashing my ego. "I don't know
how we're going to do it, but I guess we'll find out," I said. "This is
going to be a trip."

"Thank you, Larry," she said. "Thanks for having an open mind
about this. We'll make it work."

Monique then gave me a hug and invited me to a cocktail party
the next night at Nuclear Nuance, a trendy spot on Melrose Avenue
in Beverly Hills. She sold it as an opportunity for us—the three of

us—to develop a calm over our unusual sexual triangle. I wasn't hot on it, but I agreed, mostly because I saw it as a chance to ask Yvonne about my role in the flick.

I convinced myself that I was comfortable with the arrangement, that I could drink and chat with my girl and my girl's girl and hardly feel uncomfortable. I'd never used acting in relationships before, but this was a chance for me to play a role I never imagined.

And the acting began just as I arrived at the place, when I spotted Yvonne and Monique at a table, both resplendent in elegant black dresses. Immediately, my mind started fucking with me. "Did they dress together and decide to match?" I thought to myself. An uneasy feeling came over my stomach.

"Did Yvonne buy that dress for her?" said a little voice in my head. Finally, I got past that and went over to them.

"You two look nice," I said to the ladies. I hugged Monique and shook Yvonne's hand before taking a seat. "It's nice to see you again, Miss Yeager."

"Ah, come on now. Call me Yvonne," she said.

I thought: "There's a lot of shit I'd like to call you." But I played it cool.

Yvonne then called over a waiter, who took drink orders. She left a tip and proposed a toast. That little voice in my head chimed in again: "Who does she think she is, the man? She's doing all the things a man normally does. Is she trying to show me up?"

I knew then that the arrangement was going to be harder than I ever thought. After a few moments of awkward conversation, Monique excused herself and went to the bathroom. I didn't think she really had to go. I think she figured—hoped—that if I spent a few moments alone with Yvonne that we would absorb each other's personas and start the process of actually liking each other. As soon as she was out of sight, Yvonne slid over one seat, next to me.

"I think it's big of you to come here," Yvonne said. "I'm not in competition with you. I'm really not. I want you to know that. I want us to get along. We just have the same taste in women."

I did not know how to take that, so I didn't respond, in fear of saying something I'd regret. I just shook my head up and down. When Monique returned, I told her I wanted to talk to her before the night was over, but that I would mingle among the crowd. Sitting there with them was not going to work.

"Why are you leaving?" she said, although she knew the answer.

"I'll be back," I said.

While away, I decided I needed to take Monique away from the crowd later, spend a little quiet time with her, see where her head was, where MY head was. Before I could get back to her table, however, I ran into a couple of women I met at a party a few months back. Although I wanted to make arrangements to get with one of them in the future, I let it pass because I was not sure if Monique— or Yvonne—was watching. This was different. In the past I was not blatantly disrespectful, but I would hardly let a prospect get away without at least getting her number or giving up mine. And, thinking about it, sometimes I WAS disrespectful.

This time, I chatted with them briefly and excused myself. From a distance, I watched Monique and Yvonne whisper into each other's ear. They were smiling, happy. It gave me a creepy feeling.

One of Yvonne's many fans—probably actors kissing up to her— ventured to the table. One guy persuaded her to get up and meet some other folks. I saw that as a chance to make my bid on Monique's time after the function.

So, I smoothly strolled to her table, and stood to her left side. I leaned over and whispered in her ear, "Is there any way possible to force time to click off the clock quicker? I have some special plans for you this evening that I'd like to get on with."

Instead of blushing, Monique sort of frowned. She raised from her seat and looked into my eyes.

She said, "Larry, I'm sorry, but . . . I already made plans with Yvonne. She . . ."

I jumped in. "You don't have to explain. I see what's up."

"No, Larry," Monique said. "I want you to come with us."

"What are you, tripping?" I said. I was insulted and my ego had taken all the abuse it was going to in this crazy setup. It came to me right then that I was trying to make it happen because of one reason and one reason only: the movie. Oh, I did like Monique, cared about her. But if the movie role was not in the equation, she would have been history about three seconds after she told me she slept with Yvonne. No doubt about that.

So, in the anger that engulfed me, I disregarded my acting desire. There'd be other opportunities, somehow, some way, I decided. But I knew that no role was better than playing the role of a sucker between two lesbians.

"Monique," I said, "I'm not dealing with this. It seems like you've made a choice. I can't play this game. It's too much. So, have a nice life."

Before Monique could answer, I turned and walked away. I heard her call my name, but I did not stop. There was nothing she could say that would make a difference.

Just as I stepped outside, I ran into a fairly attractive honey wearing too much perfume standing in front of the club. I walked toward her and asked for "sixty seconds" of her time.

She gave me whatever time I wanted. And although my interest in the woman was not that great, I got her number and asked about getting with her later that evening. She was down. I needed that. That was a test to see if I had not lost my edge while dealing with Monique and Yvonne. Getting that woman's number was like therapy for my bruised ego.

When we finished talking, I walked to my new jeep with my chest out and a strut in my step I had lost ever since I learned of Monique's new desires. My ego was in place, and that was something to feel good about.

TWENTY EIGHT:

Accentuate The Positive

Greg

After a few weeks of watching my back for Theresa—who showed she was capable of acting like a fool—I finally felt like she had gotten over me. That was a relief because her performance that Thursday night left me wondering—afraid almost—that I'd have to get physical with her to protect myself.

Although her reaction was crazy, I spent a lot of that time wondering what I contributed to Theresa's frustrations. And in being honest with myself, I came to the conclusion that I had not handled things as well as I could have. I admitted that I took cold advantage of her in trying to get over Brianna.

Although there was no reason for Theresa to go as far as throwing a drink in my face and attacking me, she did have the right to be pissed off with me—even if I kept reinforcing that we were not in a "relationship."

It was called the having-your-cake-and-eat-it-too syndrome. It was not a fair way to deal with a woman, but it was a common practice, a common goal of men. Realizing all this, I softened my position on Theresa and actually contemplated, for a few days, calling her to apologize for my role in that night.

Then I decided to leave well enough alone. She had not called me, so why conjure up unpleasant memories? But just when I thought I'd never hear from Theresa again, she called me one afternoon while I was working in my bookstore. We had just gotten a huge shipment of books, and I was stocking shelves just like everyone else.

I told one of my employees to put her on hold and took the call in my office in the back.

"Theresa? I'm surprised to hear from you. What's up? You called to threaten me again?"

I didn't mean to go there, but it just came out.

"Greg," she said, "thanks for taking my call. I want to apologize to you for what happened, well, you know. I'm really sorry. I've never done anything like that before. But I was feeling so good about us and then to see you with that woman, I just lost it. But that's no excuse. I know you don't want to have anything to do with me now, and I understand that. But I hope you can find it in your heart to forgive me."

I was relieved to hear Theresa speak as if she had some sense. "I forgive you, Theresa, but I'd like you to forgive me, too," I said.

"For what?"

"For not being honest with you about what I was doing that night. For not making you feel secure when we did get a chance to talk about it at the bar."

We had a pleasant conversation for the next several minutes. We even laughed a few times. "You don't have to answer this," Theresa said, "but whatever happened with that woman. She was cute."

"Yeah, well, nothing happened," I said. "I called her later that night and tried to explain things to her, but she was sort of standoffish, so I let it go. She didn't seem to believe me, which I understood, but that still bothered me. It's like women don't believe men are capable of being honest. Anyway, we never spoke again after that night."

"I'm sorry," Theresa said. There was silence. I asked her if everything was all right.

"Yeah, I guess," she said. "Since that night, I've been kind of down. Not only because of what happened, but just my life. It's a mess, really. I can't keep a man. I'm not happy with my job. My mother and I get into it constantly. It's just that nothing's going right for me right now. I'm sort of depressed."

Suddenly, I felt the need to help a woman who weeks before had humiliated me in front of a laughing audience AND who had tried to physically harm me. Not that I was a psychologist, that I could offer a professional opinion. But she seemed so vulnerable, so in need of encouraging words. So, I tried to help.

"I don't know exactly what's bothering you so much, but that doesn't really matter," I said. "I do know that sometimes we get burdened with so much that we don't realize all the things in our life that we should be thankful for. If we did that, we'd feel a lot better when hard times hit."

I went on. "I want you to try something. I want you, at the end of every day, when you come home from work and kick off your shoes, to get a pen and paper and write down the things in your life that you are thankful for on that day. For example: 'I'm thankful that I woke up this morning. I'm thankful that my girlfriend called to say she had a healthy baby. I'm thankful that I made it to work and back safely. I'm thankful that my father loves me unconditionally.' That kind of stuff. Everything.

"You do that everyday, and I think you'll feel so much better about yourself and your life because happiness is not always about having a big house or a nice car or money. It's more about understanding and appreciating what you have and who you are. You're a nice woman, Theresa. You have a lot to offer to your friends, to men, to your job, to your family, to yourself. Don't lose sight of that. It would be sad that you forget all that because some things aren't the way you'd like them to be right now."

"But, that's easier said than done," Theresa said.

"OK, the first thing you have to do is eliminate the negative attitude," I answered. "To everything I say positive, you add 'but ...' To me, it's like the old half-empty, half-full theory. There are two ways of looking at everything. For instance, if your mother said to you that she wished you spent more time with the family, you could take that as her complaining that you disowned them or that she missed you and would like to see you more. It's all in how you look at it.

"That's where you have to change. Just thinking back on our conversations now—I didn't really take notice then—but a lot of times you found the bad in a situation instead of the good. Negative thinking can almost become a habit, and I think that's probably what you've gotten into."

"How do you know all this stuff?" she said. "Did you study psychology in the military?"

I laughed. "Nah," I said. "I learned about writing down daily what you're thankful for from an episode on Oprah. I saw the follow-up show months later, when people came back to say that doing it changed their lives. I've tried it; it works. As for negative/positive thinking, that's just how I feel about things. I've had my times when I've fallen into ruts. But it's much better to find the positive in a given situation. I'm not saying to not deal with something that is negative. Just don't dwell on it."

We talked for another forty minutes about many issues. By the time we hung up, Theresa's voice was livelier and her spirit bright. She vowed to write down daily the things she was thankful for, starting that night. She promised to look at situations from a positive standpoint more so than negative.

And she asked me if we could be friends. "I mean, just friends," Theresa said. "You know, an occasional talk here and there. I can't say I have too many true friends. They don't come along that often."

"You're right about that," I said. "Sure, we're friends. We'll talk soon. Be good."

When I hung up the phone, I had felt good about talking to her, about helping someone who needed it. At least I hoped I helped her. It was the best I felt about anything in a while.

I reviewed the words I shared with Theresa and got stuck on a few of them: "Happiness is not always about having a big house or a nice car or money."

"Money," I said out loud.

My passion for money, my lust for it, my obsession with it, pushed the woman I loved out of my life. I was going to clear six figures this year—not bad for a guy with no college degree who was not an athlete or entertainer—but that was not enough. I set goals. First it was to travel abroad—on Uncle Sam via the army. Then it was to watch the money grow that I so diligently saved and invested wisely but conservatively. And then it was to find a city away from D.C. that I could make home.

If I had taken heed of my own words to Theresa, I would not have allowed loot to come between me and Brianna. Brianna was everything I sought in a woman. Thinking about it, I had no legitimate complaints or concerns about her. But I shunned it because of insecurities about money. If I had seen the positive side in her wanting to discuss the wedding and wanting an engagement ring and having a grand ceremony with a romantic honeymoon to follow, I would not have been in the back of my store with a grim social future.

For the first time, I found myself at fault in our breakup. I thought: She probably talked about the wedding because she was excited about becoming my wife. She wanted an engagement ring because it was an outward show that she had someone who loved her and would be her husband. She wanted a church wedding because she believed weddings should take place in God's house under His domain, and she wanted all the people we cared about to share the occasion. She wanted a honeymoon because it was an opportunity to privately express love and affection and happiness with one another before beginning a life together.

Suddenly, Brianna's actions seemed all so reasonable to me. And I was certain, after thinking about it, that my thoughts on finances were unreasonable. Brianna never once talked about sharing my assets, about bank accounts. She was making $50,000 annually—before the end-of-year bonus. In fact, throughout the two years we were together, she paid for various activities we experienced although I clearly had more money. Hell, Brianna took me to New Orleans for my 32nd birthday, an all-expense paid deal—plane ticket, hotel, food.

"What the hell was I thinking?" I thought.

At that moment, I missed Brianna more than ever. I realized it should not have had to take losing her and dealing with other women to see she was a special person. But in reality, that's what happened.

Immediately, I knew I had made a mistake that I might or would always regret. I knew that somehow, some way, I was going to make Brianna understand how I was trippin' and how much I needed her in my life, how I checked my *baggage*.

There had to be room in her heart to forgive me. I was going to win her back. But I knew it wouldn't be easy. She talked about protecting her heart, about me not hurting her. Yet, I did.

So I knew I would have to come with a strong game to make headway with her. And I knew I would have to have a tough skin. She would be extra difficult to make sure I was sincere.

But being relentless would be easy because I was motivated by the heart only. I'd pursued women in the past out of lust. But this was a comeback attempt generated by love. There was a huge difference.

And it was so ironic how I got to that place of realization. Were it not for Theresa's borderline depression, I might not ever had spoken the words about ultimate happiness, which applied to me as much as her. That talk with Theresa made me see how much *baggage* I was carrying around and that I now had to unload it.

Funny how things happened. Now came the hard part: Getting Brianna to trust me again.

TWENTY NINE:

Back In The Mix

Greg

Although it was scary trying to get back into Brianna's life, it was also exciting. Not too many times does a man truly know what he wants in a mate. Sometimes, it was right there for him to see right away. Sometimes, it took some drama to get to that point. Sometimes it never happened. I felt fortunate to know, to truly *know* that Brianna was the only woman I wanted.

And I had a distinct advantage in getting close to her again because I knew her so well. But because she was bitter about what transpired, I had to proceed with caution.

I'd never given a woman that much thought before. Usually, I'd just go with whatever moved me. But then I'd never felt like this before. I felt like Brianna was a good woman, but I learned something about myself in the several weeks we were apart—I needed her. I'd never, ever felt like I needed a woman before.

I might have felt like I wanted a woman for sex purposes or just to kill some time with, but not to be a part of me. I spent last night reminiscing about me and Brianna and I realized the only unrestrained laughter and joy and fun I had with a woman was with her.

Julian used to talk about women not "accepting prosperity," meaning they would have a good man and not appreciate him. They'd always want more time, more this, more that. And I realized that I did not accept the prosperity that came with Brianna in my life. I took her for granted.

I contemplated many approaches to reinserting myself in Brianna's life, but, instead of calling to talk or asking for a dinner date or sending flowers, I went through a pile of photos Brianna and I took together over two years.

I searched for the perfect picture that would make Brianna smile and feel good. I wanted it to strike an emotional chord with her. It took about fifteen minutes, but I found one that I settled on. It was the first anniversary of our meeting in front of the library where we met.

She wore an Angela Davis tee shirt and jeans. I wore a Hugo Boss polo shirt and jeans. We went there as a way of honoring the place where we met, before taking in a movie. Brianna asked a passerby to take a picture of us in front of the building. She smiled the brightest smile, staring into the camera lens. With my arm around her, I stared at Brianna, which showed how captivated I was by her. The picture was perfectly clear, and it captured the happiness we felt.

She had called that one of her favorite pictures of us together. I had promised to get a duplicate for her but never did. And since I loved it so much, I refused to give her the original. That definitely was the photo to send to Brianna then.

The other thing about that photo was that it was taken on the first day that we ever talked about getting married. It was after the movie in the car on the way to dinner. She said: "Did you think we'd last this long?"

I said, "You know what? I did. I knew a year ago that we'd be good together. I could just feel it. Let me tell you: You're stuck with me now."

"For how long?" she said.

"Until you're tired of me," I said.

"What if I never get tired of you?" she said.

"Then I guess that means we will be married one day," I answered.

I remember her getting quiet for a few seconds. "Don't say stuff to me you don't mean," she finally said. "Don't play with me like that."

"I'm not playing," I said.

Ever since then, she'd bring up marriage, subtly at first and then blatantly. But I was the one who first planted the seed in her head. I never realized that before. She simply ran with the ball that I put into play.

Knowing that made me really careful about how I let her know I wanted her back. I addressed an envelope, put a stamp on it, folded a blank sheet of paper around the photo, and placed it inside. At first I was going to write a short letter. But I decided I would just send the picture. The photo would be statement enough. At least I hoped so.

I dropped it in the mailbox before the 5 p.m. pickup and hoped for a response from Brianna in a day or so.

In the interim, I plotted my next move. This one would be more direct but still not very strong. The night I mailed the letter, I thought about all the things I knew about Brianna, little things that would let her know I remained in tune with her despite the breakup. Little things that would let her know I really had to be thinking about her to remember something so minor.

And so, I thought about the perfect next move until I fell asleep. But at nearly three in the morning it hit me, and I sat up in the bed as if awakened by a bad dream.

"That's it," I said aloud. Brianna had given me a box of candles one year for Christmas. "Not to create a romantic mood, either, Gregory," she said. "Sometimes when you come home and want to relax, just turn off the lights and your phone, light one of these candles in your room, and rest in your bed. Just think about me and relax."

Brianna was into meditation. She studied it and practiced it daily. It was a level of concentration I could not reach. She gave me the candles to help me at least wind down.

At 3 a.m., I scrambled around my condo until I found the right box. I found one of the scented candles and placed it inside. Then I got a book of matches from the pile I had collected from restaurants around Chicago and placed it in the box, too. No accompanying card or letter. I hoped that message was clear: light the candle and think about ME.

I was so pumped about things that I could did not go back to sleep for another two hours. My mind raced. I wanted to stay ahead of the game, to think of more ways to let Brianna know how much she meant to me, to show her that I had realized my mistakes and wanted to correct them.

Finally I slowed myself down and decided I'd wait until I heard from her until I moved on something else.

But I felt good that I had my next move already packaged and ready to be mailed.

THIRTY:

How Ya Like Me Now?

Brianna

I couldn't believe Gregory had the *audacity* to call me a few weeks ago and act like nothing had happened between us. At the very least, he acted as if I was supposed to get all wet just from hearing his voice.

It wasn't like that. Not at all. I was still angry that he forced me to end our relationship. That's exactly what he did. I couldn't take the way he treated me, the way he made me feel small about our future. It was as if I were some kind of burden. I put up with it for a long time, probably too long. That's what I convinced myself, anyway.

In reality, though, I missed Gregory like crazy. I missed the passion we had, the open friendship, the way we'd play "Scrabble" at night and then showered together before bed. I missed him saying, "Bri, you know you're my ace." Those words made me feel so good. And I missed him just being there. I felt safe with him.

So, with all that in mind, I began to question whether I did the right thing in ending the relationship. Maybe he would have come around. Maybe I did pressure him about marriage without being aware of it.

Those thoughts floated through my mind every time I ran across a man—for lack of a better word—who tried to use completely unimaginative game with me. Which was often. So were the guys who stared at my body while "talking" to me. Or a guy who perpetrated being a big shot.

I told my close friend, Alicia, that I had forgotten how bad it was out there for a single woman.

"There is not a lot to choose from," I said to her. "And what's worse about it for me is that a few months ago I thought I was safe from this single-life stuff. Let me stop. Thinking about it makes me want to choke Gregory."

The morning after seeing Alicia, I checked my mailbox and found the usual assortment of junk mail, a credit card bill and a letter with no return address. The handwriting looked familiar, but I could not place it. When I went back into the house to the kitchen, I opened the letter.

I unfolded the sheet of paper, and what looked like a photo fell to the floor, face down. I looked at the paper, but it was blank. I bent down and picked up the picture, turning it over while still squatting. When I saw it, a chill went through my body.

Slowly I rose and put a hand on the counter to hold my balance. But I kept my eyes on the photo. I immediately knew the only person who could have sent it was Gregory. I could only smile. And tears came to my eyes.

I recalled that day of the photo, how happy I was that I had a man who made me feel like a woman. I thought: "For a year I asked that man to get me a copy of this picture, and he sends it to me now."

Then another thought clicked into me head: "He wants me back."

My smile grew as wide as the room. I pressed the photo up against my heart, which was beating rapidly. I wanted him back, too. That one picture and knowing he wanted me back opened up all my emotions. During our time apart, I would not allow myself to think we'd ever be back together. That was the safe way of thinking, the way to protect my heart that had already been battered.

Even with my feelings quickly resurfacing, I was apprehensive about throwing myself right back into his arms. I decided that if he really wanted me back, he would have to earn it. He'd have to show that he was committed to planning a future with me without reservations. He'd have to show that his heart was in it. And he definitely had to show that his lust for money was secondary to his love for me.

A day after I received the photo, Gregory called. I was not home, so he left me a voice mail message:

"Hi, Bri, this is Greg. I hope you're doing well. I was calling to say hello and let you know you're thought of and to see what you think of the mail you should have received yesterday. So when you get a chance, give me a call, please. Talk to you later."

I was even more excited and happy after hearing the message, but I was not sure if I should call right away. I thought I'd wait a short while to cause him some anxiety before finding out what he had to say.

To confirm if that was the right approach, I called Alicia for advice, which turned out to be a bad idea. Alicia was my hairdresser who became my so-called friend, but she mostly was envious of me. Also, she had the potential for backstabbing. I knew that, but I still kept her as my so-called friend. She never had anything good to say about Greg, although he made me happy.

And instead of feeling badly that Greg and I broke up, Alicia was glad. It was the old "misery loves company" situation. Each guy Alicia dealt with lasted long enough to sleep with her and get tired of her negative disposition—and then jet.

She had no use for a good man, and would not have known what to do with one if she had one. For her, the womanizer, lying types were attractive. It was sad because she was attractive and bright when she was not trying to find the negative in a given situation.

Here's an example: When I told her that I had taken Gregory to New Orleans for his 32nd birthday, instead of hoping that she'd one day have a man she was moved to treat similarly, Alicia took the opposite bent.

"No you didn't, girl," she said to me. "Has he ever taken you on a surprise trip? He has his own business. He's making good cheese. And you're spending money on him like that? Girrrl, he don't appreciate that kind of thing. That's how men are. He be playin' you."

I sort of dismissed Alicia's take on the trip, but her words did remain in the back of my mind. My family was puzzled why a woman like me, who had myself together, not only accepted but also sought advice from a "friend" who never had my best interest at heart. If I could see Gregory's misgivings about being engaged and getting married, why couldn't I see through Alicia's envious stands?

Somehow I did not. And so, when it was time for help in what to do in response to Greg's mail and message, I buzzed up Alicia. I told her about the picture and the phone call, and Alicia jumped right into her usual negative position.

"Oh, so now he wants you back, huh?" she said. "Greg is slick. He's trying to appeal to your emotions. But you've got to see through that, girl. All these months and now he's got you on his mind? Yeah, right. This probably means he's horny. Girl, you do what you think is best, but I wouldn't trust him."

"No, Alicia, Greg's not like that," I said. "I know him. He's not motivated by sex like that. Anyway, I just want to know what I should do. Should I call him or just wait for him to call me again?"

"I can tell you want to call him," Alicia said. "But I say let him wait. You shouldn't just run back to him because he sent you some picture and left you a message. If he's really serious, he'll call again."

Alicia interjected some other negative stuff, enough to finally jar me into a long overdue reality.

"Wait a minute, Alicia," I said. "I asked you if I should call him or not. That's all. Why do you always have to be negative about Gregory? He's never done anything to you."

"Nah, I'm just sayin'. I'm trying to look out for you, girl. That's all," Alicia said.

"Well, Alicia, this is important to me. I don't need any negative input."

"I ain't trying to be negative. I'm telling you this on the real," Alicia said.

Since I read her, Alicia let up on her negativity. "Brianna," she said, "you have to do what you think is best. Not what I think. But if you ask me my opinion, I'll give it to you. You my girl."

Over the next several minutes, we plotted my course of action— or non-action— as it would turn out. If Gregory Gibson wanted Brianna Harewood, he'd have to really show it. I would not call him; to call, Alicia and I reasoned, would have been too accepting too soon. And if he did call again, I would not act so happy to hear from him; it would show weakness.

Knowing Gregory, I knew that after a few days he'd wonder, "Why hasn't this girl called me?" He wouldn't want to call me, because he never liked to put pressure on people. But more than anything, he did not like things left unresolved. He liked to have his head clear, so I knew that he'd call again.

Two more days passed, and I knew Gregory was getting discouraged. And so was I, to be honest. I began to think that he decided since I didn't call him back or respond to the picture that he said, "Hey, forget about it."

That thought scared me because I did want my man back. But then it also made me realize that if he gave up that quickly, then he didn't really want me back. And that scared me, too.

But I was with Gregory when he went through the process of opening his bookstore. I saw how committed he was to doing the research in running a business, how on point he was at filing the necessary papers on time, how he spent every available moment working with the architect on the store's layout, how he fought with publishers and distributors to extend his credit, how he put in long hours, how he did most of the handiwork himself, even installing the security alarm.

All that told me that if he wanted something he would do whatever it took to get it. And I just knew, in my heart, that he wanted me. And my mother told me something about men that I'll never forget. She said, "A man actually is more emotional than a woman when it comes to love. I don't care how much he's into his work, if there's a woman he really, truly loves, he'll go after her."

Like all daughters and mothers, we had our differences. But I believed the things about life my mother taught me. So, although doubt crept in at times, I believed Gregory would call again.

But before he did, he got called on by the most unlikely of people. I couldn't believe it when Alicia told me she went to Gregory's place. I didn't show my anger—not at first. I wanted to get the whole story from her first, find out how much damage she did.

"It looked like he was about to leave when I got there," Alicia said. "He was surprised because I didn't buzz him from downstairs; someone was leaving as I got to the front door. So, I just rang his doorbell.

"He opened the door and was stunned when he saw me standing there. He said, 'Hey, what's up?'

"And I said, 'Hi, Greg. I've been talking to Brianna, and I thought I should talk to you, too. Can I come in—or is it a bad time?'

"He let me in, but I could tell he didn't like me being there," Alicia said.

I didn't like her being there, either. I was so pissed I could have screamed. But I wanted to hear the rest—I thought.

THIRTY ONE:

Kickin' The Knowledge

Julian

When Greg told me of his realization that he needed Brianna and only Brianna, I was happy for him. I always felt like he had not handled her concerns the right way, but I also respected that he knew what was best for him. Hey, I was on the outside looking in.

I just hoped that too much time had not elapsed and that Brianna had the capacity to forgive and let him back into her life. At that point in my life, it was good to be excited about something. My post-Joanne attempts at finding a woman were futile and frustrating.

It got to the point where my students started looking better and better to me. Shit, some of them were already women—physically. I told Nicole—my sexy platonic friend who had men trouble as badly as I had women trouble—about Shelanda Coleman, a thick-bodied junior from Hagerstown, Md., who had all but set the booty out for me with her homework.

Shelanda would wait after all the students left the classroom to ask some innocuous question. She'd come during my office hours to ask about why she received a certain grade on a project, what courses she should take, if she should change her major, the pros and cons of living off campus—anything to spend some extra time with me.

I was not hip to the game from the start. It took me a while to see where she was coming from. And, to be honest, it was difficult for me to resist her flirtatious overtures, but when I thought about the types of scandal I could be involved in—hell no! I wasn't about to throw away everything I worked so hard for. In fact, there were some fine sista-professors and adjunct lecturers, and I wasn't going to go there with them so students were out.

Still, like a lot of men, it was hard for me to read when a woman made an advance or tried to express interest. Yeah, a brick wall had to fall on my head for me to really know.

That was so because women were quite adept at sending mixed signals. To wit: There was this big-tittie, big-ass woman who used to frequent the Classics Nightclub in Camp Springs, Md. She always wore little leather skirts and bopped around the club basically arousing every man's attention in the place.

One night I was determined to find out who this woman was. Greg and I stood at the upper bar near the bathrooms, sipping on Ice Teas when she approached. She stopped near the tables in front of us and made serious eye contact with me. Then she smiled. Greg nudged me. "You got her," he said.

So, I bolted from the bar and politely addressed her. "Excuse me, Miss. How are you?"

She looked me up and down and turned and walked away. Deflated, I virtually crawled back to the bar. Greg asked, "What happened?"

"Nothing," I said. "That motherfucker just looked me up and down and walked away. I asked her how she was doing and she didn't even answer me."

She destroyed my whole night. I felt like everyone in the club saw what happened, so how could I approach another honey? I was glued to the bar, I was so embarrassed. I damn near pissed on myself because I was too ashamed to go to the bathroom. But I kept ordering drinks. By the time the club closed, my kidney damn near burst. I actually let out a few sprinkles on myself.

"How can she give you the eye like that and then don't even speak to you?" Greg said.

I didn't answer. He knew I was shell-shocked, so he did like any good brother would do. "Fuck that bitch, shorty. Let's party," he said.

What was so wild about it was that about three months later, I saw her again, at the same club. I looked at her and turned my head. Later I saw an old classmate, Nadine, who said she had a friend who wanted to meet me. Yep, it was Miss Stuck Up. I couldn't believe it.

After the introductions, I just looked at her. She said, "Have we met before?"

I said, "Come on, who you playing?"

"Huh?" she said.

"I stepped to you a few months ago, right here. I asked you how you were and you looked at me and walked away," I said. "So you don't remember that, huh?"

Of course, she said she didn't, but I didn't believe her. "I wouldn't do that," she said.

"Yeah, OK," I said with a smirk on my face. "Nice meeting you." Then I turned and walked away.

"You probably did the right thing in that case," my friend Nicole assured me. "But men usually don't have a good sense about when a woman is interested. That case was an exception. Women are very subtle. If she has respect for herself, she's not going to be very overt. Say you're out somewhere, at a club or a play or the gym. If you notice a woman and she gives you extended eye contact, she's trying to tell you something.

"If you make eye contact with her several times, she's probably trying to tell you something. But most of you prehistoric men don't get that kind of hint. There was this guy I saw at a Congressional Black Caucus seminar. Gorgeous. Strong. Um, um, um. I gave him the extended eye several times. He was about 15 feet away. I smiled at him. Do you know that fool just stood there looking at me? He didn't move, didn't say a word. Nothing. Finally I said: 'If he's too stupid to recognize I was flirting with him, he's too stupid for me to deal with.' So I left."

I jumped in there. "But Nicole," I said, "he probably had some other woman flirt with him and he approached her and she looked at him like he was crazy. Once it happens, it's hard to make that move again."

"It's hard because there are enough women out there who will come right up to you and just introduce themselves. For every woman who tries to get men to hold on to chivalry, there is another one who just tears it down."

We were sitting in the living room of Nicole's apartment in Temple Hills, Md., right outside D.C. As she talked, I looked deep into her eyes. I studied her mouth. She was such an attractive woman: high cheek bones, deep dimples, walnut complexion. Why in the world was my buddy manless?

Because we developed such a strong, close, and reliable friendship—the only such one that I had with a woman—I could feel comfortable telling her most anything on my mind. Because she was a little down about her man prospects and because I wanted her to know what was on my mind, I just blurted it out.

"You're beautiful, Nicole. I don't know how you would have man troubles. You should know that whatever problems you're having with men is not a reflection on you. You've got the total package. If you weren't my buddy, I'd step to you so correctly."

She smiled. "You must really know me because I definitely needed to hear something like that. Thank you. You know how I feel about you, Julian. I know you're a good man with a good heart. I also know you've dogged some women, too. But I don't know a woman other than me good enough for you—and I know a lot of women.

"Let's be open about us," she continued. "Can I tell you something? Sometimes I wonder what we'd be like if we were different kind of friends. You know I love you in a sister-brother kind of way. But do you wonder still about how it would be if we dated?"

She surprised me with that one. We had been buddies since high school. We took many classes together in the 10th grade, including driver's education. I helped her learn the rules of the road and she helped me in math. Our friendship grew from there.

When we went to separate colleges, we wrote each other letters regularly. We told of each other's experiences. I even introduced her to a guy once who I thought she'd like; she didn't. She knew my family; hell, she was part of my family. And it came to be that we'd call on each other for support or advice or just the opposite-sex opinion in relationship matters. She was my homie.

"I try not to wonder about us in that way, but it's hard, especially when I see us both between relationships," I admitted. "It's hard because I know what kind of person you are and that you deserve the best. But it's also easy because I value your friendship like I value Larry's and Greg's. It's different because they are my boys. We're like brothers. But as wonderful as you are as a woman, I just couldn't jeopardize not having you as the friend that you've been to me. You're my girl!"

"Thanks. I feel the same way, Julian," Nicole said, tearing up.

To loosen things back up, I said, "But if you want to let me hit the booty a couple times, we can talk about it."

We both laughed a good laugh. I hugged her—yeah she was sooo soft—and whispered, "You know I love you, Nicole."

"I love you, too, waterhead."

We spent the rest of the evening laughing to The Chris Rock Show and trying to figure out what we would do about our plights. She suggested we call Larry and Greg on a three-way to see what was up with them, but neither was at home.

"See, it's easy for me to just be by myself because I'm not a man. I don't need sex to exist," Nicole said.

"What? Ah, come on. You think men HAVE to have sex? What are we, animals?" I said in mock disgust.

"Well, yeah," she said, laughing. "Nah, but men can't sit around without sex and go on with their lives. You guys will plot to find that next piece of ass. And if it takes too long, you start having anxiety attacks."

"Girl, you tripping."

"So when's the last time you had sex, Julian?"

"What? OK, let me think. Uh, probably a month."

"Stop lying! You got with SOMEBODY, I know. Don't you know I know you? You've told me how you are, that sex is important to you. So now you haven't had sex in a whole month? Listen, since the day you lost your virginity—how old were you then, nine?—you haven't gone thirty days without sex. No way."

"So you think I'm a sex fiend? Girl, let me tell you. It's been that long. And that was with this chick who I used to bang back in college. I wasn't tripping on it. But she kind of offered it, so I did what I had to do."

"How do you 'kind of offer' sex, Julian?" Nicole said.

"Like this: You invite a man over to your crib after 11 p.m. You open the door wearing a robe. You have on no clothes under that robe. Then you invite the man to your bedroom. That's how you 'kind of offer' sex."

"Oh," Nicole said sheepishly.

THIRTY TWO:

My Girl Saturday

Julian

I left Nicole standing in her doorway, laughing and shaking her head. But I promised to take her out dancing the next night, Saturday, which would be a first for me. I had never gone out with a beautiful woman who was a friend, who I had no ambition to get into bed.

She liked to go to the Foxtrappe, which usually had an adult, up-scale, well-dressed crowd. Really, she liked the deejay, who kept the party pumping—and she liked to dance. But I kind of anticipated the "date" with her for one reason: Any time I'd ever been out with a woman, other women would make advances—some subtle, some blatant. Or they'd pay me serious attention.

Why that happened, I had no idea. Greg, Larry, and I talked about that many times. Each of us had been out with a woman, minding our business, when another woman would make a play. It was like: because we were with someone attractive, the women were interested in us. Like, "He must have something going on since she's with him," it seemed they thought. And then they'd give us the eye all night. It was a trip.

So, my going out with Nicole to the Foxtrappe would certainly draw attention from women. She was 5-foot-8 and thick, with dark hair down to her shoulders, a wonderful set of white teeth and a nice set of breasts. Nicole seemed to think she was on display all the time, the sexy way she dressed no matter what the occasion.

Even if it were just going to the mall, she wore jeans and a blouse that snuggly fit to accentuate her figure. So I really anticipated what she'd rock to go dancing at her favorite spot.

Since I knew she'd attract attention, I knew I'd better come correct, too. That was no problem since clothes were a passion of mine.

At least three times a year I'd drive from D.C. to Cleveland—a seven-hour trip—just to shop at the Hugo Boss outlet. I didn't mind getting on the highway; actually, I enjoyed the solitude long drives afforded me. And I loved to shop.

So I had Boss gear for days, and on this night I pulled out a three-button black crepe wool suit and a black silk shirt. I loved black, could wear it everyday. Nicole drove to my house because she wanted to spend the night and go to church in my neighborhood in the morning.

When I answered the door, she stood there flashing a smile that would move any heart and a body that could make any outfit look sexy. In this case, she had a sexy outfit AND her sexy body. The skirt was black velvet, above the knees, revealing her shapely legs. The blouse was sheer black, with a black and gold bustier underneath. She smelled of Bijan. She was tight.

"Hey, girl, you're looking fly," I said. "Enter."

"Look at you, in all black, huh?" Nicole said. "The mortician look. I like it."

We sat at the counter-bar and had a glass of Moet before leaving for the club. On the way, I told her about my theory on men getting attention when they were out with attractive women. She confirmed my beliefs.

"Women notice men with other women," Nicole said. "You know why? We're always checking out each other; we're always in competition. And if a woman we think has her stuff in order is with a man, we're curious about him. It's not like we want to get with him, necessarily. But you can't help but notice him."

"Well, you're going to get me a lot of attention tonight," I said, "because you're looking tight—as always."

"So you're using me to meet women?"

"Don't even try it. Going out was YOUR idea, not mine. I'm just going to take advantage of it."

Just as I suspected, I was like Tupac with Nicole at the club: all eyez were on me. I couldn't help but laugh about it. I milked it to the hilt, too. I posted up with her in the upstairs lobby near the restrooms, where most everyone traveled at one time or another. At times I put my arm around her and whispered into her ear.

"So you're not using me now, huh?" Nicole said. "And you know what else you're doing? You're cramping my groove. Why don't you buy us a drink and then go check out the club? Here's some money. I'm going to chill right here for a while. But don't be too long because I want to dance."

I made my way through the crowd and to the bar near the seating area, away from the dance floor. On the way, I ran into a few buddies I knew. We kicked it for a while. Each of them asked me who I was with, and when I told them Nicole, each wanted me to hook them up. "She's out by the bathrooms, sitting down. Looking good, too, in all black," I said. "Shoot your shot."

They all did—and missed. I ordered drinks for Nicole and myself at the bar. As the bartender mixed the cocktails, I checked out the club. The dance floor was packed. All the tables were full of well-dressed folk out to get their groove on.

I bobbed my head to the music. I was really pumped about the prospects for the night. The women outnumbered the men, by probably 4-to-1. Yeah, I was going to pull someone. Hopefully someone with her shit together.

I brought Nicole her drink. She was talking with some guy wearing glasses and a bow tie. A Steve Erkel type. I handed her the Slow Gin Fizz. She smiled and introduced me to the geek. "This is my boyfriend, Julian. Are you ready to dance, honey?"

All I could do was smile. She used me to get away from the bow tie, which was cool. "Come on, sexy," I said. "Hey, thanks for keeping my girl company for me," I said to the guy.

Nicole tugged on my jacket. "You would go overboard with it, wouldn't you?"

"Just be glad I saved you. You owe me."

We danced a few songs and laughed at some of the people. When we left the dance floor, she made the requisite trip women make after a few dances—to the bathroom. I told her to meet me in an hour in the lobby, and we could decide then how much longer we'd stay. I walked over to the poolroom, which was beyond the dance floor.

There was a woman playing pool, bent over with her considerable ass pointing right at me. It was familiar ass, but I couldn't pinpoint it. When she made the shot and stood upright, she turned toward me. I knew that ass, all right. It was Donna Copeland, the sister of my ex-girlfriend who gave me the booty a few months back.

She was bitter about me cutting off what she wanted to be a relationship, and I wondered how she felt after so much time—and knowing I had ended things with her sister, Joanne. I had not seen her since that afternoon at Joanne's apartment. Didn't want to see her, either.

"Julian. Hi. What's been up?" Donna said. "You been hiding?"

"Nah, just busy, I guess," I said. "How are you? How's your sister?"

"I'm fine. Joanne, she's at that table right there. Go say hello."

I had not seen Joanne since that evening at my home. She called and left a few messages, none of which I returned. I had gotten over the pain I felt from her unfaithfulness; time really did heal. I still cared about her in a way. I did not want her back in my life, but I did think about her and wondered how she and that guy were doing, how she'd look as her stomach grew.

So I walked over to the table. She saw me coming, and we made eye contact from 20 feet away. When I got to her, she stood up, wanting to hug me. I wanted to hug her, too, but I was not sure if I should have. So I just smiled at her.

I looked at her closely. She was wearing a slinky—and I do mean *slinky*—little black dress. There was no sign of her being pregnant. She looked as lovely as ever. Whoever else sat at the table with her was gone to the dance floor, the bathroom, somewhere, because she was all alone.

"Hi, Julian," she said. "Have a seat. I can't believe you're here. I was thinking about you."

We spent the next forty minutes or so talking. She apologized again for her actions. "I hope you realize now that the things I did were not like me," she said. "We all make mistakes. I regret that one every day. Every day."

"I think about it from time to time. I can't lie about that. But you know what, Joanne?" I said. "That's not what I think about when I think about you. Not all the time. We had a lot of good times together. That's really what I hold onto. I know you're a good person. But what happened, happened, and I know me. I could never forget that it did. And I could never trust that it wouldn't happen again. Some people get over things better than others. I wouldn't be able to be with you and live with any real inner peace."

I know that my behavior was no better—my sleeping with her sister and all. I also know that they say what's good for the goose is good for the gander. *But not for this gander*!

"I was really hurt by what happened, but I know it was my fault," she said. "It still bothers me that our relationship ended because of something I did. But I can't blame you for the way you feel. I know if it were reversed, I'd feel the exact same way."

We caught up with each other's families and even danced together. Nicole was on the dance floor a few feet away, and she did a double-take when she saw my dance partner. She made her way over beside us and gave Joanne a hug.

"I should have known you were here if Julian was here," Joanne said. "I can't believe Larry and Greg aren't here, too."

I checked her out thoroughly as we danced. She should have been about four months pregnant, but there was no sign of a protruding stomach. I wanted to ask her about it—and about Sam, her old boyfriend. But I didn't.

However, Joanne noticed me zooming in on her stomach. When we left the dance floor and she returned from the restroom, she told me some significant news. "I know you're wondering about the baby," she said. "Well, I thought about it and thought about it. But everything around my being pregnant was wrong. I did not love Sam. And the way he was acting, I didn't want to have to be around him forever because of a child . . . So, I did what I had to do."

An abortion. I did not know what to say. That never even entered my mind. "Man, I'm sorry, Joanne. I had no idea," I said. "How did your friend take it?"

"I have to admit that I lied to him," she said. "I told him you said I was pregnant just to get him upset. He believed me, so he never knew I was pregnant. Then, three days later I went to the doctor and had it done. It has eaten me up, but I couldn't bring a child into this world with a father I had no feelings for. Plus, he wasn't stable.

"I remembered everything you said to me the last time I saw you. The only way to get rid of him was to get rid of him. He WAS holding me hostage. I stopped taking his calls. It was scary for a minute, because that fool stalked me for about three days. I mean, Julian, it was scary. I called the police, and he still would show up on my job. Then one day he just stopped. It's been two weeks since he stopped. So, I'm all right now—I hope."

"Me, too. That sounded crazy. Anyway, I'm glad I saw you tonight," I said. "I think we should keep in touch occasionally, you know?"

She agreed. Nicole came over and joined us. It was about 1:30 then, and she was ready to go. I was, too. It was a good night for me, a different kind of good night than I expected. I renewed a friendship with someone who at one time meant a lot to me. There was a great reward in that. And before Nicole and I left, Joanne stood up and we hugged.

THIRTY THREE:

Act Like Ya Know

Larry

Julian called to tell me about running into Joanne, and we ended up talking mostly about my exciting news. Despite my leaving Yvonne and Monique to do their thing, Yvonne hooked me up with a part in the movie.

It was a smaller role than the one I auditioned for, but it was a job, one that put me on location in New York. Yvonne was no fool. She got me in the movie, but she made certain I would not be anywhere near where Monique did her work. It was like a boss recommending his secretary's boyfriend who also worked for the company gets transferred to Inskter, Michigan, or some other obscure company location.

In my case, I got New York, which was ideal because Julian got into his Alfa Romeo and drove up to hang out with me in the City.

Over three days, we did the New York thing something fierce: the Shark Bar, Jezebel's, Soul Cafe, Justine's, Chez Josephine, Cafe Beulah. A couple of my partners, Roland and Al, threw one of their huge parties following a New York Knicks-Los Angeles Lakers game, which was a must-attend event.

The function was hype, not only because there were quality-looking women all over, but because Julian and I ran into some buddies who grew up with us, guys who were cool but who we had lost touch with. As soon as we got into the party, we ran into Rob Brown and Clifton Parker, a couple of New York sportswriters we had not seen since the Million Man March in D.C.

Rob and Cliff were two of the many brothers I cited to women who claimed "all men cheat." I couldn't name myself, so I named them. Those two definitely appreciated the beauty of women, but they were committed to being faithful to their wives.

They did not know it, but they were shining examples and inspirations for me and my crew because the stability they had was not something we thought about very much. We were more into floating, seeing what was out there. But Rob and Cliff gave us hope that it COULD be done. We just did not know how.

There were other brothers who lived totally different from them. Like Tony Wyche, who was at the party with a nice little honey from the Bronx. Tony was married and that woman was not his wife. He was out there as much or more than single guys. That night, when the chick he sported went to find a friend, Tony went into his regular monologue. It was usual for him to brag about getting with a honey.

"Yo, we're just getting here because I had to get a quick shot first. You see how sexy she is," he said to me. "I drove over to Jersey, near the George Washington Bridge. It was a trip. I got her dress up and my drawers down, over on her side of the car hitting it. Next thing I know, I see a light. Yo, it's the POLICE, shining a flashlight on my ass. He knocked on the window. I rolled it down. He said, 'Mister, I suggest you pull up your pants and go home.'

"I couldn't believe he didn't bust us. But that was enough for me to say, 'Let me get to the party.' "

It should have been enough to say, "Let me go home." Instead, Tony went to the South Street Seaport. He told Julian he saw a honey he wanted me to meet and then left to go get her.

"That boy is still wild," I said to Julian. "He's got a beautiful wife and family, but still out here running hoes."

"You know how that is," Julian said. "Brothers can have what we think is the bomb at home, but not be satisfied. I've seen it too many times."

Tony came back with Tonya Taylor. He had no idea that Julian had known Tonya for years, known her very well, very intimately. Tonya was very outspoken about many issues, and she carried her outspokenness to the bedroom. I recall Julian telling me about dating her not long after moving back to D.C. from the Boston area.

Julian said it turned her on to talk nasty and for him to talk dirty to her. Said it was a must during sex.

"Her talk excited me like crazy," Julian said. "It made me hit it harder, try to drive right through her."

What I liked about Tonya was that she liked phone sex—even though she didn't do it with me. I remember Julian telling me and Greg that she'd say stuff like: "Guess what I'm wearing. Just a white tank top. I'm in the bed; wish you were here, too. My nipples are hard thinking about what we'd be doing if you were here. Just thinking about you inside me has me so wet."

And on and on. We were so tight that Julian even admitted to masturbating while listening to Tonya over the phone.

"After a minute or so," Julian said, "I'd hear her scream out. She had no shame, only pride."

I thought of all that when Tony brought over Tonya to Julian. I know he did, too.

"Hey, Julian, what are you doing here?" she asked.

"Just hanging out with my boy. He's here working on a movie. How've you been?" he said. I was surprised Julian got out a coherent sentence. He looked at her, but his mind was on getting with her back to the hotel. I've seen that look on Julian's face before.

"Good, great," she said. "Guess what: I'm getting married."

The erection in Julian's mind deflated in an instant. But him being so quick to adjust to whatever, Julian put on a quick happy face.

"What? Congratulations," he said. "When? And who's your fiancée."

She went on to tell Julian who and where, but I watched him closely. He did not pay much attention to her. After a few more minutes of mundane conversation, she finally left. "Damn, whoever got her has a serious sex life in front of him," Julian said to me.

The quest was to find another Tonya Taylor, and maybe I did. I met a couple of other honies who looked good, but whose conversation or personality did not move me. I got some numbers that maybe I'd call so that when I came back to New York I'd have something to do. Julian did the same.

We rolled out of the party at about 1 because I had to be on location at 7, so I needed some rest. Julian did, too, since he was getting on the road back to D.C. when he woke up.

***

Julian

Larry and I talked about getting together in a month or so, maybe in Chicago with Greg. On my ride down the New Jersey Turnpike, I thought about my sad plight. As happy as I was with myself—my job, my family, and my friends—I was down about the women I had in my life. Well, not exactly down, but I definitely did not expect to be thirty-three years old and without a woman in my life that I felt good about.

I turned down the radio as I drove so I could concentrate on all the honies of my past. In most cases I felt like each one of them brought admirable qualities. But they all also fell short of my desires in one way or another. Funny thing was, I didn't truly know what my desires were. I kind of floated from one relationship to another with no purpose, no order. As sharp as I thought I was, I was immature in reality. I enjoyed a woman for the moment, but not truly for what they were or who they were.

So, I never worried about not having a woman in my life. I knew guys—and women—who felt like they always had to be in a relationship, that being single somehow meant something negative. For me, it was important to have women, but not to be in a relationship. I was not any good at relationships because I didn't know how to be good at it. I actually needed a woman to help me understand what it took. But she would have to be subtly effective, not overbearingly pushy.

In other words, she did not need to be a control freak. In the few instances I felt good about a woman before we got really into the relationship, it would come over her to "label" what we had. I didn't get that. Why, if everything was going well, categorize something that's running smoothly?

I called it the "Can't Stand Prosperity" syndrome. Too many times I'd heard of women instead of enjoying a man's company and time, virtually forcing a "label" on things. Inevitably, the man felt like the woman was pressing herself on him and what they had, which usually caused friction in a situation that flowed so nicely.

I had been through that a few times, and it bothered me to think about it as I crossed the Delaware Memorial Bridge because the women's actions stunted our possible growth. But a real problem within myself also occurred to me: I had never looked at a woman as more than a sex object. If she appealed to me, my mind wondered how I could get her in bed. It was like a sickness. No matter what circumstances I met one, I could not—DID not—avoid imagining her in bed.

It was interesting that once I got with a woman, she expressed the same thoughts, that she had visions of giving me her body from the beginning. That thought made me smile to myself. That thought stroked my substantial ego.

I got a little tired behind the wheel as the lines on the highway became hypnotic. So I pulled over at the Maryland House rest area to buy a Pepsi to refresh for the stretch run to the District.

The car that exited in front of me had South Carolina tags. The frame around the license plate read: "Alumni, South Carolina State." The words sparked my memory. It hit me immediately that

South Carolina State was in Orangeburg, S.C. It was where my older cousin, James Warren, who was more like my big brother, worked as a chef.

And it came to me immediately that Orangeburg was where the woman who captivated my imagination in L.A. lived and worked. Alexis Miller. For the first few months after the Los Angeles trip, I could hardly keep her out of my mind. She was a beauty, but I remembered how I felt talking to her. She was the ONLY attractive woman I met and had more interest in who she was than how I could sleep with her.

I started feeling frustrated all over again because I lost her sister's L.A. phone number during the car accident. I wanted to reach her so badly, even after all that time. I pulled into a parking space, turned off the car and sat there daydreaming.

She had to be disappointed, I thought, that I never called her after such a natural and pleasant conversation we had that night at the Golden Tale. I recalled the apple green dress she wore, the way she looked up at me, the sound of her voice, the softness of her cold hands, the confidence she exuded, the dangling pearl earrings she wore. I even recalled her scent. It was almost as if I actually smelled it right then.

I made a vow to myself right there in the car. I had to find that woman. Somehow.

THIRTY FOUR:

Food For Thought

Larry

My first movie experience was not what I hoped it would be, but I still was all right with it. I knew my thirty-second dialogue could end up on the editing room floor, but I absorbed the experience, got paid, spent a week in New York, and cleared my head about Monique and Yvonne.

I was certain that I did right by letting them do their lesbian thing without me complicating things. I thought: Why deal with a triangle when there were so many eligible women out there?

However, I did call Monique when I got back to L.A. to tell her how the shoot went in New York and to thank her for her role in convincing Yvonne to assign me the job. She sounded genuinely happy for me and went on to tell me how difficult it had been for her on the set in her first major movie role.

Neither one of us brought up Yvonne Yeager during the talk. Why ask questions we knew might produce uncomfortable answers? We ended the fifteen-minute conversation with Monique telling me, "When we're finished shooting, let's get together for lunch or something."

"We'll see," I said diplomatically. I should have said, "No way," but I thought she was just being nice.

When I hung up, it hit me that for the first time in a long time I did not have someone who felt like she was my girl, or who I felt obligated to spend even a little time with. It was a Tuesday, and I had the rest of the week off from the bank because the shoot in New York went quicker than the director and producer initially expected.

The feeling of total freedom was welcomed. I actually did not know what to do with five days free of work or auditions—and no honies worth calling Julian and Greg about. In other words, I was

153

bored. So I chilled in bed, watching *The Young and The Restless*, *The Bold and The Beautiful*, and *As The World Turns*. When the last soap opera went off, it was 3 p.m., and time to eat.

I went to the kitchen, but I only had a bottle of ketchup, some packets of soy sauce, and a jug of water. That was it. Oh, there were some frozen string beans in the freezer and some white potatoes in the refrigerator, but that was it. The cabinets were lined with dishes and a few sauces.

So, although I did not feel like interrupting a day I planned to spend in bed, I got up to go to Ralph's, the local grocery store. On the way, I thought about how peaceful it was to be on vacation with no responsibilities, to not have my phone ringing with some woman trying to get with me. I had eased away from most of the women I used to get with. Those thoughts vanished when I pulled up at a traffic light next to a woman with a long ponytail in a drop top Sebring. Larry the Lover emerged immediately.

"How are you today?" I asked the woman. "How does the sun feel on your face?"

"Good, real good," she said, smiling.

"I bet," I said. "Hey, I'm going to the grocery store. Would you like to help me shop? I'll buy you some suntan lotion."

The woman laughed. "I can't—I've got some place to be," she said. "But maybe I'll see you around."

"I hate to leave it on a maybe when we can be certain," I answered. "My name is Larry."

"Larry, my name is Lisa. Lisa Tisdale. I live in Studio City, and I'm listed in the phone book. So, you should call information and get my number and give me a call, OK?"

"I'll do that," I said.

The light changed, and as she drove off I wondered if she looked as good out of the car as she did in it. One thing for sure: I knew I'd find out. She could be the start of a new stable of women for me. I definitely had gotten bored with all the others, to the point where I just stopped calling them. Getting a new crew would spark excitement in my life.

Every now and again I liked to reload, so to speak. Most women just did not hold my interest for the long haul. I could deal with most of them enough to hit the ass, which I looked at as much a benefit for them as it was for me.

"Women give up this energy like their bodies mean more than men's bodies," I told Greg and Julian once. "I've had women say to me, 'But I gave you my body. I don't take that lightly.' You know what I said to them? 'I don't take my body lightly or share it lightly, either. My body means a lot to me, too. So we gave each other something we both consider precious.' "

When I arrived at the grocery store, I ran into a few of my buddies I played ball with in Santa Monica. We kicked it in the parking lot about nothing substantial and watched women come and go.

I heard one of the guys ask me a question, but my attention was taken by this woman in cutoff jean shorts heading for the store's entrance. Her body alone caught my eye, but I also thought that she looked familiar. Of course, I had to find out.

"Yo," I told the fellas, "I think I know that woman. I've got to go, but I'll get with you at the gym."

I grabbed a grocery cart and went into the store. But I did not see her. So, starting from the left, I checked every aisle. Finally, I spotted her. She was in Aisle 7, looking over frozen vegetables, when I approached.

"You know, fresh vegetables are much better for you than frozen," I said to her.

She looked up and saw my smiling face. "What are you, a nutritionist?" she said.

"Nah, but I read a lot," I said. "Please don't take this as a come-on line, but you look very familiar. I know you from somewhere."

"How come I don't feel the same way?" the woman said skeptically.

"I don't know. Let's see. When you go out, where do you go?"

"I don't go out."

"I'm telling you, I've seen you before. We've met. Where do you work?"

"Why?"

"I'm really not trying to invade your privacy, as it may seem. It's just that I KNOW I've met you before, and it's bothering me that I can't remember from where."

"Well, while you think about that, I'm going to finish my shopping."

Clearly she did not know me if she thought that would be the end of my pursuit. Her walking away from me just added to my fire and desire to get to know her. So, I followed her. As she looked over pastas, I made a recommendation.

"Try this linguine right here," I said. "It takes 11 minutes to cook, and it's firm and won't stick together."

"What are you, a chef?" she said.

"Nah, but I like to cook. I've kind of learned by trial and error," I said.

"I thought you came in to shop. Your basket is empty," she pointed out.

"I know," I responded. "I'm going to get to it—eventually. Right now I think you need my help. You don't shop much, do you?"

"Do you go around following women in grocery stores all the time?" she said sarcastically.

"No, not at all." I wanted to assure her, but if I was too adamant it would seem phony. So I left it at that. "But I know you from somewhere. And I think if I talk to you something might click and let me know how I know you."

"You're a trip."

"Just go ahead and shop. I won't disturb you. But let me just tell you this: my name is Larry Thompson."

She looked up at me, her brown eyes barely visible through her slits. It was almost as if she was squinting, but she wasn't. There was a certain seduction about her. "I know that name from somewhere," she said.

"See. We know each other from somewhere; I'm telling you," I said.

And so, we shopped up and down the aisles. I picked up a few items—trout, chicken, spinach, juices, sodas, napkins, bacon, eggs, and bread. The woman placed in her cart plums, oranges, apples, wheat bread, skinless chicken breast strips, apple juice, turkey bacon, and spring water.

She loosened up a bit, and we talked in general along the way about the beautiful fall weather, the increased prices at the store, and the wild little kids running around ignoring their parents. When we checked out, I walked the lady to her car. I was thoroughly impressed with her charming personality. I wanted to see her again, to remember where I had met her.

"OK," I said at her car. "Looking at the things you bought, this is what I learned about you. One, you don't cook a lot. You buy just enough to get you through a certain amount of days. So, you either spend a lot of time at a boyfriend's house—you're not married, I checked your ring finger—or you do a job where you work a lot of hours and you work through the dinner hours. And whatever your job is, you have to deal with people most of the time. Also, you're very health conscious. No pork, no sodas, no skin on the chicken.

And you're very cautious, kind of private—you haven't even told me your name. There's probably more I could tell you, but I don't want to keep you here too long."

The woman looked at me and smiled. I helped her place her bags in the trunk and closed it. Then she folded her arms and slowly nodded her head. "You're good, Larry," she finally said. "I must admit, you're good. You were on point on some things."

"What things?" I said.

"Well, I am into staying healthy, eating right," she answered. "I don't spend a lot of time at home because of work—no boyfriend—and I work when most people are at home eating. And on my job, I do deal with people most of the time. I'm a nurse. My name is Renee."

"A nurse? What hospital?" I said.

"Centinela."

And then it clicked for me. "I knew I had met you," I said, smiling. "Think back about three months ago. My two buddies and I were in a car accident. I was in a wheelchair in my boy's room, Julian Morgan. He had been unconscious. I introduced myself to you. I even remembered what I asked you. I asked if my boy would ever be able to think again and if you could get some of that water out of his head."

"I remember. I can't believe it, but I remember," she said. "Well, it's good to see that you're doing better. How are your friends?"

"They're great. They are not going to believe it when I tell them I ran into you. It's a small world," I said. "I feel vindicated—and relieved. If we left without me remembering how I knew you, it would have driven me crazy."

"Yeah, I'm like that, too," she nodded.

We talked another ten minutes or so. All the while, I thought about how I could broach the subject of seeing her again. Finally, I just came with it.

"Well, Renee, I don't want to be selfish. I could keep you here all day, talking. But I won't do that. I would, though, like to see you again. Maybe we can have lunch."

"I don't know, Larry. I don't have that much free time," she said. "I'm in a nurse's sorority, an officer, which takes up a lot of my time. And I try to work out almost everyday—when I'm not too tired. And I also go home to Oakland to visit my folks a lot."

That was all well and good, but it was not the answer I wanted to hear. "I understand that," I said. "I don't want a lot of time, really. Maybe we could just meet on your dinner break one night or maybe I could go shopping with you again."

I liked Renee—her wit and presence and conversation—and was not about to let her go without shooting all my game.

I felt like Renee found me interesting, too. We had a nice conversation. I made her laugh, feel comfortable.

"All right," she said finally. "What about tomorrow evening, about 6:30? Let me write down my number. Do you mind driving?"

"Not at all," I said.

"Good," Renee said, "because I hate to drive. You said you're on vacation, right? OK. I'm off tomorrow, so call me during the day, and I'll tell you how to get to my place. I'll meet you outside and we can go from there."

"Great," I said. "What would you like to do? Dinner? A movie?"

"I have something in mind, but it's a secret. You like secrets, don't you?"

"If I didn't, I do now," I said eagerly.

THIRTY FIVE:

Hallelujah!

Larry

When I had a date with a sister who excited me, I'd spend much of the day preparing for it. Not in front of the mirror, but in my mind I'd sort of visualize how it should go. That's what I did anticipating my evening with Renee. My mind was consumed with it pretty much from the moment I woke up.

I called Renee at 1 p.m. to confirm the date and get directions to her place. It was a brief conversation, but very pleasant, so much so that it raised my anticipation into the stratosphere.

I knew after hanging up that I had to be proper when I pulled up to get her. I already had a haircut, but I went back to the barbershop to get my fade freshened. On the way home, I stopped to get the jeep hand-washed and waxed. At least three times I tried on outfits, settled on one, and then changed my mind. Finally, at about 5:30, I decided on some gear that would be appropriate for a nice dinner out, a movie, or whatever: a flowing pair of tan slacks with a cream silk shirt, a brown three-button blazer, and a pair of brown cap-toed shoes.

I admit that I admired myself in front of the full-length mirror in my bedroom for several minutes. It had been a long time since a woman moved me to such narcissism. Usually I did not need any motivation; no one admired *me* more than *me*.

In this case, however, it was all about making sure I was right for Renee. I felt good about her agreeing to a date when I was far from my best. When I met her, I had thrown on a pair of shorts and a tee shirt and had not given my hair much attention before departing to the grocery store. Renee would see another me, at least physically—one I was confident she would be impressed with.

Renee lived just fifteen minutes from me, which had me thinking in advance about the convenience of seeing her in the future. When 6:10 came, I headed to the car. I knew I'd be early, but it was important for me to be on time. I wanted to show promptness. I actually smiled to myself as that thought came to my mind. Usually, time was less significant to me as it should have been, but with Renee, I was motivated to show punctuality.

When 6:30 came, I was in front of Renee's building, listening to jazz. Even the music had to be right for this woman. I stared off toward the 101 Freeway when I heard a tap on the passenger side window.

I pushed a button that unlocked the door. "Hey, how are you?" Renee asked.

"Good," I said, sitting up. "You snuck up on me. How're you?"

"I'm fine," she said, revealing her captivating smile. "It's good to see that you're on time. You're punctual, huh?"

"If you only knew. Promptness has not been one of my strong points. But I've been working on it lately. And I knew I couldn't be late for picking you up. I didn't want to waste a minute."

Renee smiled. She was stunning. When I first saw her months ago, she was attractive, but was at work and not at her best in that nurse's uniform. Ditto for the grocery store trip, although she did reveal a tight, shapely body. But she was casually elegant sitting in my "replacement" jeep. She wore a long navy blue skirt, a navy blouse, and a navy and rust vest.

Her makeup was neat and flattering to her high cheekbones. She had her hair curled in some configuration that complimented all her features. It did not go unnoticed.

"You look great," I said, starting up the car.

"Thanks. So do you," Renee answered.

I pulled out onto the street before asking about where we were going. When I did inquire, she just offered directions. "Are you hungry?" she said. When I answered "yes," Renee said, "Too bad, because we're not going to eat."

I was amused. I had no idea what she had planned, but I could tell that it meant a lot to her. And it really did not matter to me. I was versatile, could function in almost any setting. Mostly, I was just glad to be with her.

"OK," she said, "turn right into this parking lot right here."

I followed her direction, but I was confused. We were in the parking lot of Macedonia Baptist Church. Renee could sense my confusion. She opened her purse and pulled out a Bible.

"Have you been to Bible study lately?" she said.

"No. Actually, I've never been. But I guess there's a first time for everything," I said. Then I smiled. She had gotten me. Of all the scenarios that I envisioned with Renee, attending Bible study with her was not one of them. If I had a lifetime to guess what she had planned, I never would have come up with that.

"You're not an Atheist, are you?" she said.

"Nah. I, to be honest, haven't been to church in a while. But I do believe in God. I pray—not as much as I should, but I do pray and acknowledge Him. So, I won't get struck by lightning entering a church—at least I hope not," I said smiling.

"Well, this is how I spend my Wednesday evenings," Renee explained. "I'm a Christian. It's important for me to have an understanding of His word. And even though it'll be something different for you, I think if you have an open mind, you'll get a lot out of it. You'll feel good leaving the church."

I nodded my head. It was hardly the evening I anticipated, but I did not mind Renee's surprise at all. I really didn't. "Let's do it," I said.

Inside the church, Renee introduced me around. It was clear she was a faithful attendee and well liked. The church was small, quaint, with a lit cross hanging over the pulpit. There were only seventeen students, including me, for the study session.

The pastor opened things with a prayer as we all held hands. Renee's hand was small and soft and I made sure to hold on to it a few seconds after everyone said "Amen."

She dug into her purse and pulled out another Bible, this one for me. Reverend Neva Davis, a diminutive man with a strong, authoritative voice, resumed the discussion from the previous week, which was about God's goodness and mercy.

For nearly twenty minutes, the Reverend cited chapters in the Bible and initiated dialogue centering on God's love for the world and the wonderment and significance of His mercy. I paid close attention because I did not want to seem unknowledgeable if a time came for me to interject. Also, the conversation interested me.

A year earlier, I had serious issues that I seldom addressed, questions that ate at me every time I thought about it. This forum seemed like the place to get some answers. My cousin and her husband lost their baby after three months. Sudden Infant Death Syndrome. There was a pain that dug deep inside me when that tragedy happened, something that took a lot out of me and my entire family.

The death made me question how God—the Almighty—could let something like that happen to an innocent, sweet child. It came to my mind immediately when I learned the group was studying the Lord's mercy. Anytime I ever talked about the tragedy, I'd get choked up, and this case was no exception.

I really planned to just listen and learn, but I couldn't hold back. So, I said: "Can I ask a question? I don't want you to get the wrong idea, because I do believe in God. I haven't been to church like I should and I don't pray enough, but I know where my blessing come from. But I don't understand when a three-month old child like my cousin's dies for no apparent reason and God allows it. I know it's like I'm questioning God, Reverend Davis, but it's something I just can't comprehend. And it's bothered me for a long time. I mean, where's the mercy for my family?"

Renee looked closely at me. I could see her out of the corner of my eye. It was like she sensed the pain in my words and saw it in my eyes. I glanced at her and quickly turned away. I did not want her to see what she already had detected. Most men preferred slamming their hand in a car door over showing pain, much less tears. I considered myself a man's man, and I viewed displays of emotion as a weakness. So, as much as it hurt me to rekindle the anguish of my cousin's death, I did my best to not show it.

"My brother," the minister began, "you struggle with this because you cannot look at it with a Christian's heart. In times of sorrow, you praise God. Praise His heavenly name and thank Him for being merciful. As a Christian, we understand and KNOW that God is never wrong, never makes a false step. We know this because we believe. This is called faith. Unwavering faith. And faith is at the core of a Christian's life. It gives us strength. When something happens and God doesn't intervene as you THINK He should, don't question Him. He knows what is best, what is right. That is how we live our life."

Reverend Davis went on to quote some Bible scriptures as illustrations and had me write down some others to read at my leisure. "I understand what you're saying, and you're right," I said. "It is difficult for me to see it completely the way you do. But I'll keep trying, and I'll read the Scriptures you gave me."

At the end of the study session, the group held hands as Reverend Davis led a final prayer. In it, he asked God to give me "the vision he needs to see life in a Christian way." Renee's hand tightened around mine then.

"I hope we see you again, Brother Larry," the pastor said.

I glanced at Renee and smiled. "Thanks for having me. I enjoyed it," I said. "And I'm sure I'll be back."

We chatted with some of the people as we made our way out of the church and into the parking lot. As I opened the car door for Renee, she said, "Did you really enjoy it?"

"You think I'd lie to a man of God? Sure I enjoyed it. Just as you said, I feel better now than I did going in."

"Well, I'm glad. And I was glad that you got involved, too. That was great. Anyway, are you hungry?"

"What, is that a trick question?"

"Not this time. I know a nice Italian restaurant not too far away. You interested?"

"Just tell me how to get there."

She did, and we enjoyed the pasta, talked, and laughed. I took a moment to savor a refreshing conversation with a woman in which there was no sexual tension or innuendo. The talked flowed. It was effortless. There was a contentment about Renee. She was happy. Lots of people professed to be happy and then went on to complain about their job or bills or whatever.

She had bills like everyone else, but she was unfazed by life's little troubles. The joy of being a Christian seeped through her pores. She had an element we all desired: inner peace.

"You know, Renee," I said to her in front of her apartment, "I've never dated a Christian before. Shoot, some women I've dated may have been the anti-Christ."

We both laughed. "Really," I added, "I had a great time. I would never have guessed we'd go to church, but it was great. I'm really glad I met you again. I hope that we can get together again soon."

Renee opened her arms and invited a hug. We embraced, and I closed my eyes. "You feel like you belong in my arms," I whispered into her ear.

"Really?" she said. "Maybe so."

I held the Bible she gave me at the church. When I tried to return it to her, she refused.

"Keep it and READ it," she said. "But don't forget to bring it with you Sunday for church service. You can pick me up at about 10:30, if you're available."

"It's a date," I said.

THIRTY SIX

Lighting Up The Candle

Greg

Not hearing from Brianna was killing me, so I decided I'd go ahead and mail the candle. But before I could leave, my doorbell rang, which was surprising because visitors had to go through the doorman downstairs to get into the building.

When I opened the door, I was stunned to see Alicia, Mouth Almighty, standing there.

"What's up?" I said.

"Hi, Greg," she said. "I've been talking to Brianna, and I thought I should talk to you, too. Can I come in—or is it a bad time?"

So there was Alicia, Brianna's confidant and a notorious meddler, standing in my living room. She had never warmed up to me, never acted like we were friends. She didn't do anything malicious, but I was perceptive. I could tell when someone didn't like me. I just kept my distance from her because I knew about her rep for getting deep into other people's business.

"Have a seat," I said to her.

Alicia sat on the couch and looked around. With a rep like hers, I wasn't sure if she was looking to see if the place was clean or if she was searching to see if a woman had been there. Not that it was any of her business, but that never bothered her before.

"What's up?"

She took a deep breath, trying to look as if whatever she had to say was not easy. Phony best described Alicia.

"Well, Greg, I've been talking with Brianna, and . . . well, I don't want to see my girlfriend hurt anymore by you," she said. "It's been months since you guys broke up, and she's finally getting her life back together. You sent her that picture last week, and it really upset her."

"Wait a second," I interrupted. "What business of that is yours?

Why do you think it's your responsibility to come here—unannounced—and tell me what Brianna is feeling? I know she didn't send you. So why don't you just let me and Brianna deal with each other and mind your own damned business?"

"Oh, I know you ain't gettin' nasty with me," Alicia fired back. "See, I told her to leave your ass alone a long time ago. But she didn't listen and she got hurt. I don't want you hurting my girl anymore."

"Yeah, I bet you did tell her to leave me alone. But why? So she could be miserable like you?" I snapped back. I was pissed, and when that happened, I went for the jugular. "Misery loves company and I know you're miserable. You can't keep a man, so you want her to be lonely like you."

Meanwhile Alicia was really clownin': finger waggin', eyes and neck rollin', and one hand on hip in an I-dare-you stance. I continued. "If you were really her friend, you would be supportive. But you're always hatin' all the time. I know you. I know how you are. You're triflin', and you want everyone else to be triflin'. You're life ain't complete unless there's drama."

Alicia got up and stormed over toward me as I stood by the window overlooking Ontario Avenue. She pointed her finger toward my face, which I quickly knocked down.

"Don't touch me. Don't let me have to call my *maaan* to kick yo' ass," she said.

"Don't you ever put your finger in my face," I shot back. "And 'my *maaan*'? What '*maaan*'? You ain't got no man. Stop frontin'.'"

She yelled. "You're the one miserable, with yo' cheap ass. You got your own *biiizness*, and you a tight-ass. And you made Brianna miserable. You can say what you want about me, but that's the deal. Nigga, you ain't WHOA."

"You know what," I said, "Just get the fuck out. Don't you have a job? Go to work or something. Just get out of here! But understand this: I will deal with Brianna as I feel and whenever I feel. So you just go back to being your miserable, lonely self."

"Yeah, we'll see," she said and slammed the door.

I was fuming. I thought about calling Brianna to see if she put Alicia up to visiting me, but then I thought better of it. That was not her style. Brianna was always straightup. She would not send that bitch to me to speak for her.

The only good that came out of Alicia's visit was that it made me even more determined to get to Brianna. So, after enough time passed for Alicia to be gone, I grabbed the boxed candle and went to the post office.

As I stood in the line, my impatience started to get the best of me. I wanted Brianna to have the candle right then. At that moment, it hit me. I got out of line and drove to Brianna's house. I knew she'd be at work, so I ran no risk of her being there. I placed the box at her front door.

When I pulled away in my car, I felt good knowing she'd receive it that evening after work. And I was hopeful that she'd call me to initiate conversation. Until then, I decided to go to the store to pass some time and occupy my mind. I couldn't just sit around at home waiting for the phone to ring. I wouldn't play myself like that.

It took a while, but six finally came, and I headed home. I knew Brianna's schedule; she'd be home no later than 6:30, if she did not stop somewhere along the way. I wanted to be at the crib in case she called as soon as she found the candle.

***

Brianna

I got home at 6:20. I pulled up in the driveway on the right side of the house, parked in the detached garage in the back and entered the house through the kitchen door.

As I always did, I dropped my keys on the counter and started undressing as I headed straight for the answering machine. There were two messages, but one I felt compelled to return immediately. It was Alicia, and she seemed upset.

I took off my blazer and kicked off my pumps and pushed #4 to speed dial Alicia's number. She answered the phone on the first ring—a busy body like her felt someone might hang up if she did not answer quickly, and she could not stand to miss a call. It could be some juicy gossip.

"Girl, what's wrong?" I said to her. "I got your message."

"Bri, I'm all right now, but I was a little upset earlier," she said. "I did something I probably shouldn't have done."

"You didn't sleep with that guy you met last week, did you? Please tell me you didn't—not already," I said.

"Well, I did, but that's not what I was upset about," Alicia said. "I went to see Greg today."

"Greg who?" I said. "My Greg?"

"He's not your Greg anymore, is he?" Alicia said.

"You know what I mean. Why did you go see him?"

"Well, I was thinking about him trying to get back in your life, and I could see you were already falling, and I don't want to see you hurt by him again," Alicia said. "So I went over there and told him that. I told him that you've moved on with your life and to leave you alone."

"Alicia, you're my girl, but you had no right to do that," I said. "I told you he sent me the picture because I share stuff with you. But I don't want you to get in my business on that level. You shouldn't WANT to be in someone else's business like that. You know I know how to handle Gregory, how to deal with him. And even if I didn't, you don't go talking to him about me or for me."

"I'm sorry, Bri, but it's hard to sit back and watch you make another mistake," Alicia said.

"I didn't make a mistake the first time. See, you don't get that," I said. "Because it didn't work out doesn't mean it was a mistake. Gregory's a great person. Sometimes it doesn't work out, but that doesn't mean it's a mistake. It just means it didn't work out."

Alicia asked me to hold on so she could answer a call on the other line. I said I would, but then hung up. I was so pissed that Alicia overstepped her boundaries that I started sweating. I had to get a glass of water and sit down. And knowing Alicia, I assumed she said some things that would make Gregory say, "Forget it" and move on. Alicia could be that persuasive, that much of a nuisance.

So, I started feeling a little down. I thought that by not calling him and then Alicia going to his place, I had blown it. I started questioning myself. I thought that maybe if I had explained to Gregory that his money was not an issue with me and that the things that did matter we had to compromise on, maybe we could have worked it out and still have been together.

Then I thought that my ending the relationship should have shocked him into a reality: that the money had far less importance without the woman he once said was "out of his dreams." That's what he told me, that I was "out of his dreams."

As much as Gregory acknowledged my character, he still was so attached to money that he was blinded. And indirectly he basically put me in the category of the countless hoochies men encountered who were all about their money. But I knew money could change people—or at least alter them in a way that they were so protective of it that anything else was secondary. And I truly believe that's how Gregory was struck.

Worse, I didn't know if I could make him see how money had changed him. Shit, I wasn't sure if I should make him see it.

Greg was levelheaded and smart, and should have been able to see it without anyone's help. I was hardly conceited, but I understood that I brought a lot to the relationship. Then I thought: if Gregory could not see me for who I was, then we needed to be apart.

I went back and forth with my emotions on what to do about the man I still loved. Oh yeah, Greg was still in my heart, still my "Gregory." And that was scary because I was not sure if that would ever change.

Finally, when it was clear Alicia was not going to call back, I took a shower to wash away the day and freshen for the night. My appetite, which disappeared when Greg and I broke up, had finally returned. But on this night, I simply toasted a bagel and had an orange.

I sat at the dining room table enjoying my "dinner" and skimming the newspaper when I realized I had not gotten my mail. So after eating, I went to the mailbox, which hung on the front of the house, next to the door.

When I opened the door and stepped out, I kicked something on the ground. I picked it up and retrieved the mail from the box and went back inside.

The box was strange because it had no return address and no postage. Someone had to bring it to my door. As a woman who lived alone, that gave me a little concern. I quickly put the safety latch on the front door and hurried to the kitchen door in the back and did the same.

I then went back to the box. I shook it. I was an avid reader, so I was quite aware of the Unabomber, who at random sent bombs to people's homes. I actually was nervous to the point where my palms got sweaty.

Finally, curiosity got the best of me. I got a knife and slowly, delicately cut the tape across the top of the box. The two sides popped up, and I actually jumped back. Since a bomb did not go off, I took a deep breath. But I still did not feel safe.

So, I slowly leaned over the box as I slowly pulled back the sides. I saw newspaper and finally decided that my curiosity was just going to have to kill me. I abandoned all the caution and pulled the contents out and placed them on the kitchen counter.

I fought through the newspaper and finally got to the candle and the matches. I was not only relieved, but Gregory immediately popped into my mind and heart. I held the candle and smiled. I raised it to my nose and took a healthy whiff. The jasmine fragrance was refreshing.

It was one of the candles I sent him and told him to burn as he relaxed and thought about me. In receiving the candle, I got the message from Greg. He wanted me to think about him. And what I thought was: "Who is helping him come up with these thoughtful ways of communicating with me?"

Greg had not exactly been Mr. Romance in our two years together. He was not cold and impersonal, but he allowed me to set the moods, plan our activities. Always. So, for him to tantalize me as he had, made me smile and feel so warm inside.

If he solicited someone's help, I did not care. If he did, it meant that he really cared and wanted to make sure he did it right because it was important to him. If he did it on his own, it meant he really cared and gave it some real thought.

I ignored the other mail and took the candle and matches into my bedroom. I placed it on the nightstand, turned off the phone and the lights, and lit the candle. Then I laid down on the bed and clutched a pillow, closed my eyes, and thought about Gregory.

For the first time in a long time, my heart felt full, lively.

THIRTY SEVEN

Starting Over

Greg

My heart pounded. When 8 o'clock came and I did not hear from Brianna, I got nervous and started thinking all kinds of negative thoughts: "Maybe she just does not want to be bothered with me. Maybe Alicia was telling the truth, that she has moved on with her life."

Whatever went down with her, I was determined to find out. The waiting game was hardly one I liked to play, and it was one I no longer wanted to endure. So, I went to the fridge and broke open a Heineken. I finished it in five big gulps and let out a resounding "Ahhh!"

Then I went into my bedroom and lit one of the candles like the one I sent Brianna and turned out the lights. Then I dialed Brianna's number. It had been a long time since a conversation with a woman frightened me, but this one gave me the jitters.

I knew that it would crush me if Brianna was still trippin' or not receptive. In many ways, I was not sure how I would go on if she said she was not interested in getting back with me. I never prepared myself for failure, only success.

If I had to get over Brianna's rejection, I would. What choice would I have? But I learned something about myself when the realization hit me that my lust for money pushed away the woman I felt was my soulmate.

It was a thought that NEVER entered my mind. Well, maybe it did, but I was too stubborn or too afraid to admit it. I was in NEED of a woman. In need of Brianna.

All my adult life, the women I dealt with were hardly given a second thought when I gave them the boot. I did not NEED them. Shit, sometimes I didn't even WANT them. They were gone and that was that. I did not look back. Usually I said, "I don't know how I dealt with her for so long. I should have been left her."

But I never felt that way with Brianna. There was never any closure because my heart was always open to her. I said one thing and did one thing, but it was all to convince myself that I was better off without her. Stupid.

I lost Brianna and gained a lesson that was costly: to side with money over love was a mistake. A mistake that I knew could mean the ultimate pain.

It wasn't until the second ring of Brianna's phone that I realized I did not know what I'd say to her if she answered. My heart pounded more. By the fourth ring I thought she was not home and that I'd get her answering machine.

And I did. As her outgoing message played, I thought of what to say. But before the beep came, I heard Brianna pick up the phone.

"Hello," she said. I heard her, but her answering machine message was still playing. "Hold on a minute," she said, turning off the machine.

"Hello?" she said into the phone.

"Hi, Brianna. This is Greg. Greg Gibson," I said.

***

Brianna

My heart started racing. I had made up my mind to call him as I relaxed to the burning candle he sent me. But there he was on the phone; I was caught off guard.

"Hi, Gregory. How are you?" I said.

"I'm OK," he said. "I hope you're not busy because I want to talk to you, see how you're doing."

"Just a minute," I said, "I have to blow out this candle."

I was clever like that. I wanted Gregory to know I received and burned the candle, but I did not want to come out and say it. Greg was sharp, so I knew he picked up on my subtle message.

But I did not blow out the candle. It relaxed me. I returned to the phone.

"I'm back. No, I'm not busy Greg. What's up?"

I wanted to sound casual, to not sound pressed. I knew it was a game, sort of. It would have been simpler to just say, "Thank you for the picture and the candle. I'm so glad to know that you thought of me like that."

Yet, I couldn't possibly play myself like that. After all that we'd gone through, the last thing I was willing to do was put my feelings out there to be walked over. Not again.

"You know, I have all this stuff on my mind, and I really don't know where to begin," he said.

"Why not at the beginning?" I said.

"The beginning would make this a long story," Greg said.

"I have time," I answered.

"Cool," he said. "Well, the real beginning was more than two years ago, when I met this woman at the library. I got to know her, fell in love with her, and planned to marry her."

"So what happened?" I said, going with the program. I liked it when Gregory talked about me without mentioning me by name, like I did not know the story. I found it to be cute, clever, which was different for him because he was usually as direct as men come.

"Well, I kind of messed things up. Not kind of, I did mess things up," Greg continued. "There is such a thing as not accepting prosperity. I did not embrace you or us as I should have. I did not cherish the one thing I've learned was more important to me than anything.

"There are some evils that make people look at things in a different way when it should be so clear to them. Money is one of them. I never, ever looked at money as being the root of all evil, as people say. But it definitely can be. I didn't do anything crazy to get money. I just cherished it to a point where I made it my end-all and be-all. And you know what: In the end, that money bought me some of the things I really liked or wanted, but it did not bring me the one thing I really LOVED and NEEDED."

"Needed? You told me many times you didn't need anything or anyone," I said.

"Well, I love and need you," Gregory said.

I felt a chill run through my body. He was always expressive, but he had never been so eloquent, never spoken with that much thought and feeling.

"Gregory," I said, "I received the picture you sent last week. It made me think of you so much. It made me remember how good I used to feel about us. And the candle today, it was just so perfect. I lit it and laid here and went to sleep, thinking about you. And the things you just said, it's great to hear."

"But . . ." Greg said.

"But I need to know what is different now," I said. "I mean, I can already see that you've changed some. Just the picture and the candle, they were so thoughtful. I'm not saying you're not a thoughtful person because you are. But in the last several months, it seemed like you kind of got relaxed with us. You didn't seem to put any thought into the relationship.

"So that makes me want to ask you something: Did someone help you? Did someone tell you what to say? I bet it was Larry and Julian. You guys probably did one of your three-way calls and hooked it up."

I said that in a way that let Gregory know I was joking, but he left nothing to chance.

"Nah, I got some help, but it wasn't from them," he said. "It was my heart. When I was without you, it was hollow. I tried to fill it, but I couldn't. When I thought I'd never have you again, my heart ached. And when I knew that I had to have you back, my heart raced. Right now, it's pounding. Can you hear it?"

"I'm not sure if it's your heart I hear or mine," I said.

"Brianna, you asked me what is different now, and I want to tell you," he said. "The first difference is the only difference, and that is that my heart controls everything in my involvement with you. When you answered the phone, the words just started coming out of my mouth, out of my heart. If I sat down and tried to write something I thought you'd want to hear, it'd be a mess. When I sent you the picture, it was something that just came to me.

"Same with the candle. Same with anything that I'll ever do with you. Since we've been apart, I've learned to listen to my heart, to follow it. I know it's a dramatic change. But I'm not lying: Since the last time I saw you not once did I ever forget you. Not once did your place in my heart change; not even the slightest."

"So when did you decide to send the picture? What happened?" I said. I was curious like that. I wanted to know the motivation in people.

"I listened to my heart talking to me," Greg answered. "But when it struck was early last week. I was talking with this woman who was dejected about pretty much everything in her life. I was trying to be positive with her, help her see things differently. One of the things she was upset about was money problems. And in the midst of talking to her, I told her that money and other material stuff did not assure happiness. And I continued to talk to her.

"When I hung up, I started replaying in my mind what I said to her. And the fact was, I was not following my own words to her. I realized then that the money I had meant so little if I had an empty heart. And that's what I had. So really that woman changed my life.

Or at least woke me up. Talking to her made me realize I really had an empty life.

"I cherished the money and not what we had. I know that now. I know it was a mistake. And I know it had to be bad for you to end things. I just hope that you'll let me show you just how much I've changed."

Those were the words I had hoped to hear but never thought Gregory was capable of uttering. Really, that was the entire point I wanted to make with him when I walked away. He just did not see it then; he had to learn it on his own. Or never learn it.

The time apart worked in another way, too. I realized how blessed I was when I had him, although his hangup on money was a big deal. The brothers I ran across after Greg were either disingenuous, rude, phony, arrogant, corny, weak, or all of the above. They were all definitely looking for some booty. It was, in short, a nightmare.

I found myself hanging with Alicia more and more, which was to say I was on the wrong end of blind dates Alicia arranged. One guy seemed nice enough. He had a decent conversation and a pleasant disposition. But as the night wore on, the drinks loosened his tongue, until he finally went for his.

He whispered into my ear: "I'm thinking about taking you home with me."

When I pulled back and said, "For what?" he responded: "So I can get up in your guts."

Needless to say, I was outta there. Another guy had no manners, no gentlemanly qualities. He was unfamiliar with chivalry. Another guy dressed like he was Big Willie, in one of those big-collar, fake-Versaci shirts, a white suit with gold buttons, and a gold rope thick enough to choke a cow. I sat through dinner cringing.

Although those bamas made Greg look even better by comparison, he stood out with me on his own merits. And with this seemingly changed Gregory, I was ecstatic. Ecstatic, not crazy. As good as I felt, it would not leave me that he had hurt me badly. And although I wanted him back, I was not so willing to jump right back into his arms.

If he really changed and really needed me as he said, he was going to have to show it. And if he did, then I'd know it was genuine because Gregory was not into impressing people.

"Gregory, I really want to believe that you've changed," I said. "I do. But after all this, I can't just say, 'OK, let's pick up where we left off.' I have to protect myself."

"I understand that," Greg said. "I do. And I'm not asking you to pick up where we left off. I'm asking you to let me show that I've changed, that I honor who you are to me. I want to win you back. I don't want you to come back to me until you FEEL it in your heart that I am what I should be as your man."

"You really want to do that, Gregory?" I said.

"I do," he said. "I think it'll be fun for both of us. It seems like I've spent almost every minute of every day recently thinking of ways to let you know that I refuse to let us go on without each other."

"That sounds so good."

"Can you hold on for a minute? I've got to do something real quick."

When he returned, he told me that he'd like to see me on Friday. "I want you to come over for dinner. I'm cooking," he said. Greg had not so much as boiled an egg in two years with me, so that was a date.

"This I've got to see," I said.

"Good. Now, I'm going to let you go. I'll call you tomorrow. But I want you to hear something first," he said.

"I want you to listen to something," he added. "Once this ends I'm going to hang up the phone so I'm saying goodnight now. But I want you to listen closely. I'll talk to you tomorrow."

Then he placed the phone in front of a speaker and hit "play" on the remote control of his CD player. He had set it up to play Anita Baker's "Love You To The Letter," a beautiful song that said, among other things, "I'm going to learn to love you better, to the letter."

It was the first song we slow-danced to. It hit me immediately that Greg had played our song, and I just blushed, outside and inside. I held tightly to the pillow and softly sang along with Anita.

THIRTY EIGHT:

South Ka-Ka-Laki

Julian

Thanksgiving was two days away and I had much to be thankful for. None of it, however, had to do with women. Mostly I was thankful that I had gotten through the ones I had recently met without having total disdain for ALL women. It was that bad.

So, I decided I'd take the drive to Orangeburg, S.C., during the holiday weekend to see my cousin James, but mostly to find—one Alexis Miller. I arranged for my graduate assistant to cover my Monday and Wednesday classes. Since I had no Tuesday class, I didn't have to return until Wednesday night or early Thursday morning. The best thing was that I had been on top of grading papers. Unlike many of my colleagues, I did not spend holidays with red pen in hand.

Certainly it was a long shot that I'd be able to find her, but ever since the L.A. trip, she'd pop into my mind from time-to-time. She had a presence about her that had me sprung. I was very attracted to a women with poise and personality. No doubt, I was all about a nice ass and breasts and all that physical stuff, too. But as striking as she was to look at, Alexis was more striking to listen to, to talk to.

And it bothered me that she expected my call while in L.A., and I was unable to make it. Chances are she would never see me again, but I wanted to at least try to find her, to let her know the good feeling we shared the night we met was real, that I was real.

But I was not going anywhere until after a hearty Thanksgiving meal of turkey, ham, chitlins, fried chicken, yams, collard greens, corn pudding, macaroni and cheese, stuffing, homemade rolls, and cranberry sauce. For dessert, it was pound cake, pineapple cake, sweet potato pie, red velvet cake, and peach cobbler.

My plan was to leave a few hours after eating, but I was hit with a common black-person affliction: on a full stomach, I went to sleep.

In the middle of the night, I woke up long enough to go to the bathroom, eat some more chitlins and macaroni and cheese, belch, and then go back to sleep.

I called my cousin James the next morning to let him know I'd be leaving then. "What happened?" he said. "You ate and fell asleep, didn't you?"

We laughed. He knew me well, having served more as my big brother while we grew up in the same house. I never understood why he was with us and not his parents, never even asked, but I was glad he was there. He taught me about toughness and sports, and he was the first man I knew who knew how to juggle a couple of honies at a time.

He was five years older than I was, and while I fought a drastic case of shyness as a pre-teen, he got his groove on. Finally, sadly, however, James moved to South Carolina. He just did not feel "comfortable" in D.C. anymore and wanted to go somewhere to start fresh. How he picked Orangeburg, I never knew.

In any case, I was excited about seeing him. It had been about 18 months—when he visited the family in D.C.—since we hung out. I figured I'd stay with him a few days and we'd go through the Yellow Pages to find pediatrician clinics I could visit to seek out Alexis. I mean, how many could there be in a small town like Orangeburg?

Before I left, I called my platonic friend, Nicole, to see if she had changed her mind about riding South with me. She first said she'd go, but then begged off, saying once I found Alexis, she'd just be in the way. I wondered if she was a little jealous.

But when I called her one last time, she told me she had met some guy and had a date with him over the weekend. Then I felt a little jealous. Or at least over-protective. "Julian, you don't need me in the way," she said. "You're trying to find a woman. How would it look when you find her that I'm there with you? I hope you find her, and I hope she's who you think she is when you do."

"What do you mean?" I asked "You think she portrayed herself to be something she wasn't?"

"I don't know," Nicole said. "But, listening to you, she sounds perfect. And we both know nobody's perfect."

"I know what you're saying, but this woman had something extra, something special. I guess I'll just see," I said.

With that, we ended the conversation, and I got my things together and got on the road. It was an eight-hour drive, but I was determined to make it in seven. I was going to push it, stopping only for gas.

To entertain myself on the road—and to keep myself awake—I

imagined that I found Alexis on her job and introduced myself to her. She was receptive in my daydream, telling me she never stopped thinking of me and that she prayed one day that we'd find each other.

I imagined dialogue between us. When I finally ran out of stuff to dream up, I wondered if I was so hyped about her because she was so great or the other women I had recently dealt with were so bad. Whatever the case, it was too late then. I was just three hours away.

When I took the exit for Orangeburg, I saw that the town was what I imagined. There was not much to it. The city was divided by railroad tracks. On one side, the somewhat affluent (meaning mostly white folks) lived on nicely paved streets, in brick houses with sidewalks. On the other side of the tracks lived mostly blacks. Many of the houses were old and run down. There were no sidewalks and few streetlights.

James lived on the black side of town because that was important to him. But he had a nice all-brick house with a well-manicured backyard. He did not have a sidewalk, however. He was sitting on the porch drinking corn liquor—they called it "white lightening"—out of a jar when I pulled up. My D.C. license plates attracted much attention. It was about five o'clock—meaning I made the drive in seven hours, twenty minutes.

"What's up, cuz?" I said. "Damn, you're drinking out of a jar, huh? You really have converted. Next thing I know you'll be blowing into a big jug to make music."

He laughed and showed me inside. "You look good, boy," James said. "So what's up? I know you came down here to find a lady."

When I tried to assert that I came to see HIM, he interrupted. "Come on now. Come on," he said. "I've been here five years and you haven't been until now. It's cool. I ain't tripping on it. But this girl must have some good pussy."

"I don't even know," I confessed.

"What?" James said. "Come on now. You're telling me you never got with her? So what are you doing here? I thought only some good booty could make a man drive eight hours."

"Not in this case," I said. "I told you how we met. I just thought it was a good time to see you AND see if I could track her down. And I needed to get away from D.C."

James got up and went into the kitchen. He came back with a harmless looking bottle filled with a clear liquid, a glass and a sheet of paper. That clear liquid turned out to be "white lightening," or corn liquor, and the glass was for me. He poured me a healthy drink, and when I smelled the "white lightening" my eyes got watery.

"Why do they call it 'white lightening?' " I said, wiping my eyes.

"Because it looks harmless, but is strikingly powerful," he explained.

As I took tiny, tiny sips from the most potent alcohol I'd ever had, James ran off a list of children clinics in Orangeburg from the sheet of paper. There were seven. "You said her name is Alexis Miller, right?" James said.

"Yeah."

"Well, on Monday and Tuesday, I called around to six of the clinics and none of them had an Alexis Miller working there. I told them that I was a cousin from California trying to track her down. None of those places had heard of her. I tried. I thought I'd surprise you and locate her job, and all you'd have to do when you got here was go see her. But I couldn't find her."

"What about the other place? What's up with that?" I said. I braced myself for his answer. No way I had driven all that way to find out in five minutes that the woman I was looking for was unfindable. I did not need to hear that so soon. Maybe after a few days, or even finding out over the phone myself. But not like that and right then.

"I called the place," James said. "It's open tomorrow, so we can go there in the morning. It's called, 'Child Care Professionals." They would not give me any information. The lady on the phone put me on hold for about five minutes and then came back and said, 'We can't give out that information, sir.' I wanted to smack her."

"She was just doing her job," I said. "Maybe that's the one she works at. It's got to be."

"Why?" James said.

"Because I need it to be. I'm not obsessed with her or anything, but wait till you meet her—she's righteous. Not just how she looks—and she is fine—but the kind of person she is," I said.

"I'm trying to figure out how I don't know her or haven't seen her," James said. "This town ain't but so big. I should have run into her at some point."

"That's a good point," I said. "But you haven't seen her—because if you had, you'd have remembered. No doubt."

We talked about life in South Carolina, the family, sports. It wasn't much happening there, so he offered to take me to a nightclub in Columbia, about a half-hour away. But the drive down had gotten to me. We had some other cousins there, so I did the right thing and visited them. I was tired and did not really want to go, but I was glad

I went after we left. They seemed genuinely happy to see me after so much time, and I actually felt the same way.

James and I returned to his house at about 10. We downed a smaller glass of "white lightening." It served as Sominex for me. "Cuz, I'm gonna hit the sheets, man. That drive and that drink got me sleepy. What's on the agenda tomorrow?"

"Let's hit that clinic to find your girl when you get up, and then I'll take you to get something to eat, and we'll play it by ear. Oh, there's a good basketball game we could go to: Norfolk State is playing South Carolina State. That'll be something to do."

I agreed with him on that, but my plan was to find Alexis and then find the nicest restaurant in town and have dinner with her. It was a grandiose plan, but I had to think that way after traveling so far and wanting to find her so badly.

The only dream I remembered that night was not a positive omen for me. In it, I found Alexis, but she was married and said she barely remembered me. Then, her husband and dog chased me down a long, dark tunnel. When I got through the tunnel, I followed a path that led me down a winding passageway. Finally, there was a dead end and nowhere to run.

I turned around and there was Alexis and her husband with axes, slowly approaching me while laughing menacingly. The dogs barked with slobber falling from their mouths. I closed my eyes and tried to push past them but was knocked down. As Alexis raised her axe over her head to pummel me with it, I opened my eyes.

"Damn," I said out loud as I sat up in bed. My heart was pounding. I was so relieved it was a dream, but I started wondering what the hell it meant. I had seen the movie, *Eve's Bayou* the previous week, but I was not about to have the dream interpreted. I did second-guess whether I should try to find her.

"Hey, Julian, you up?" James said, peeping through the door. "I heard you tossing and moaning in there. You either had a wet dream or a nightmare."

All I could do was laugh. "Let's go find your girl," my cousin added. "She's out there waiting to be found."

"She'd better be because I'm coming," I said.

THIRTY NINE

Where Ya At?

Julian

The Child Care Professional Clinic was on the black side of town, a small brick building at the end of a string of establishments. There was the furniture store, the flower shop, a real estate office, a boutique, a video store, and the clinic—all connected and all facing Route 29.

My heart pounded as we stepped into the lobby. I felt like I was taking the game-winning free throws in an NBA game, or a comedian in front of an Apollo Theater crowd. There were black women with their kids sitting in the waiting area. The receptionist sat at a low desk behind a closed glass partition. It might have been bulletproof.

I stood there a moment while she wrapped up a phone call. James took a seat and grabbed an Ebony magazine. The lady looked up at me and showed me a finger, as if to say, "One minute." That one-minute turned out to be about five, which surely tested my patience.

I definitely was in the South. All the ladies waiting to have their kids see the doctors said hello when we walked in. That was a surprise, because it sometimes was difficult to get women in the North to say hello when YOU spoke to them first. And the fact that the receptionist was slow in handling her business before getting to me was a Southern thing, too. We had stopped to buy a newspaper at a little corner store, and it took five minutes to do even though there were just three people in front of me.

But I was OK with waiting at the clinic. I looked back at James and gave him a look like, "What's up with this?" and he just smiled and shook his head.

Finally, the receptionist slid back the glass door in the partition and said, "Yes, may I help you?" All the women in the clinic lobby looked up to see what I wanted there; I did not have a child with me, and it was a pediatrics clinic.

I stuck my head through the little opening. "Hi, how are you?" I said. "My name is Julian. I'm here to see Dr. Alexis Miller. Is she in today?"

I did not want to seem like I was a bounty hunter or the police of a former boyfriend trying to track her down. I wanted to present it so it seemed like I KNEW she worked there and that it was no big deal.

The woman looked at me for a second, and as she was about to speak, the phone rang. "Just a minute," she said and answered the phone.

Of course, that "minute" took five minutes, with her leaving her seat and going into the back of the office. When she returned, she finished the called and looked up at me and said, "I'm sorry. What is it you wanted?"

"Dr. Miller," I said calmly.

"Oh," she said, "that's right. Dr. Miller is not in today. She's on vacation. Gone to see her 'suster' out 'der' in California. She won't be back for two weeks. Want to make an appointment?"

Damn, I thought. "No," I said. "I'm a friend of hers from out of town. Could you call her answering machine at home and leave a message for me?"

"I don't have her home number," she said. "I'm only part-time. But I can leave a message for her here—she'll call in sometime today."

So I wrote down James' number and my D.C. number and hoped that she'd recognize my name when she heard it. "Tell her it's Julian who was in L.A. when she was there last summer, OK? And tell her to leave her number on the answering machine if I'm not there. Please do that. I'm here visiting my cousin. Tell her that, too, because she'd wonder what I was doing here."

"I thought you said you were friends," the receptionist interjected.

"We are, but we haven't talked to each other in a while," I said.

"Oh," the nosy woman said. "Well, she said yesterday that she'd check in with me today at about 12. So, I'll make sure I give her the message."

"Let me ask you one thing," I whispered to her. "Is Dr. Miller married?"

The lady smiled. She shook her head. "No, she's not. Why?"

"Just wanted to know," I said and smiled back. "Thanks."

I gave James a pound when we stepped outside. "Good looking out," I said to him. "You saved a whole day of going from clinic to clinic. All right, let's get something to eat and get back to the crib."

Cuz said he had the ideal place to take me to eat. "But it's not a restaurant. It's a part of Orangeburg you have to see. I can't let you come here and not experience it."

"Cool," I said.

I sat in the passenger seat daydreaming about receiving a call from Alexis, when I looked up and noticed we were riding on a dirt road that had tall cornfields on either side of us. "Yo, where are we going?" I said.

"Don't worry. We're going to see Chippy. He lives back here in the woods, in a house by himself with a shotgun and all the best-tasting country meat you can get," James explained. "And he has 'white lightening' too."

"You've gone country for real," I said.

After a few minutes of kicking up dust on the dirt road, the cornfields finally ended and suddenly there was this old, teetering house. To the left, smoke came out of the ground, where Chippy had his barbecue pits. There were about four cars parked on the dirt and grass on the right of the house.

"That's Chippy right there," James said.

Chippy was a slender man with a big, barrel belly. He was dark and looked greasy, like he'd been tending to those grills for hours on end. He wore an apron that used to be white. "Hey, Jimmy, who ya got wit ya?" he said to James, who introduced us. We shook hands. Chippy's hands were big and rugged, like he'd been lifting boulders all his life. "You from up North, huh, boy?" he said to me.

I did not take kindly to being called "boy" by any man, but I did not think he had malicious intent, so I let it go. "Yeah, from D.C. What you got on the grills?"

"Oh, you're hungry, huh? OK, come on over," he said.

At two picnics tables sat six people with their heads so close to their plates I thought they were hunchbacks. The food was so good they did not bother to even raise their heads to say hello, which was different for the people in that friendly Southern town. Oh, yeah. Each of them had a glass of "white lightening" next to them, too.

Chippy walked me over to the pits in the ground. On one was one of the biggest pigs I'd ever seen. He was smoked. I'd heard of smoked pig, but I'd never seen it, never had it. Chippy had five chickens going in another pit and a huge side of beef and ribs in another.

"Let me sample it all," I said.

"My kind of man," Chippy responded.

We took our orders to go, and I bought a tall bottle of "white lightening" to take back with me to the District. Total: $20.

The food smelled so good in the car I had to open a bag and pull off a piece of beef. "What you think?" James said.

It was so good, so tender and tasty that I didn't know what to say. So I didn't say anything. I just reached back into the bag and got another piece, a bigger piece. Enough said.

"I hear you," James said. "I go see Chippy at least twice a week. But you've got to be careful, because it can be addictive. Plus, it's probably not the healthiest food you can eat, either."

"Yeah," I said, "but when it's that good, health issues don't come up until AFTER you finish eating."

And it did not take us long to finish our meal after getting to James's house. We stopped at Piggly Wiggly, the grocery store, on the way and picked up some macaroni and cheese, collard greens, and cornbread from the deli. We threw down.

James's phone rang a few times, but it was a couple of his women and my mom making sure I arrived safely because I forgot to call her when I got in the day I arrived.

Nothing from Alexis. It was getting late, nearly four, and I still heard nothing. If she checked her messages at noon like the receptionist said, I had hoped to hear from her by then.

"Julian," James said, "call the clinic and see if she called for her messages yet. Then at least you'll know if she got it and didn't call or if she just didn't get it yet."

I needed James's levelheadedness at that time because I could not think clearly. And usually I was pretty resourceful. "Good idea," I said to him.

The receptionist answered; I could tell her voice. I identified myself, and she put me on hold. For five minutes. "I don't believe this woman," I said to James, who laughed.

"I'm sorry, Mr. Morgan," the receptionist said, "but I have not heard from Dr. Miller. I think she's already in California, so she probably won't call in until Monday. We're about to close in two minutes."

"OK, thanks," I said. "But make sure she gets it on Monday."

"Can you believe this? I get down here, and she's gone back to where I met her. Shit. What am I going to do now?" I said.

"Nothing you can do," James jumped in. "You've done all you can do. You came down here, you found her, and you left your numbers. From what you tell me, you guys made some kind of connection. Just like you haven't, she probably hasn't forgotten it either."

"Yeah, I hope not," I said slowly.

We spent the next three hours sipping "white lightening" and visiting some of James's friends. I was amazed at how James had adapted a country lifestyle after spending the majority of his life in Southeast D.C. It was admirable, really. But I could tell at the core he was the same person. He still was caring and funny, with a love for fun, food, and sports.

"You want to go to the game?" he said after returning to his home at seven. "After that, we can take the ride up to Columbia and go to this little spot I know up there. They usually party pretty good."

"I'm down," I said. "Why not?"

So, we showered and changed clothes and headed over to South Carolina State. The gym was small and crowded with coeds. It was hard to tell how old those young girls were, but they were healthy and bouncy and tempting—especially with the buzz I had from sipping that "white lightening."

James and I split the first half watching the game and watching the girls. But I was there for one woman only. At halftime, I decided to get some chips and a hot dog. James kept his seat in the stands. I watched the girls walk by as I stood in line.

After getting a frank, I went to the condiment table up against the wall for some mustard and onions. A woman bent over to dress a hot dog for what looked to be her young son. Me being me, I noticed she had a nice ass.

When she finished with the spoon she used for onions, she turned around and handed it to me standing behind her. I looked into her eyes as she handed it me. Then I dropped the spoon on the floor.

Unless I was dreaming, that was Alexis Miller right there before me.

***

Alexis

I noticed that he dropped the spoon, but I just turned and walked away. Then I heard him say, "Excuse me, Miss."

I figured he was talking to me, so I stopped and turned toward him. The look on his face said that he recognized me. And he definitely seemed familiar to me, but I couldn't place from where at that second.

"Alexis?" he said.

Now wait a minute, I thought. How does this guy know who I

am. I was paranoid about men, especially in Orangeburg, who tried to step to you as if they were your friend.

"How do you know my name?" I said.

He just looked at me. Finally, he said, "I can't believe it's you."

I looked at him closely; he looked familiar. And it felt good to look at him, like from wherever I knew him was positive.

"What?" I said.

"Remember me? I'm Julian Morgan," he said. "We met in Los Angeles about five months ago, at the club in El Segundo."

I literally took a step back. It came to me so quickly that it jolted me. Every so often I thought of this guy I met in L.A. who made me feel so good and who then just disappeared. Never returned my call. After a while, I just chalked it up to "typical man." But I never felt that way during the time I was with him. If he were not this pleasant, bright guy that I met, he was one hell of an actor. Which, I guessed, men could be.

"Sure, I remember," I managed to get out. "But what are you doing here?"

An answer to that question, I really wanted to hear. Nobody just came through Orangeburg, S.C.

"You're not going to believe this," he said, "but I'm here because of you. I came here to find you."

I was really thrown for a loop then. I was right there in L.A. when he was there and he didn't call me, but now he comes to Orangeburg to find me? It didn't make any sense.

Before I could tell him that, I got interrupted. "Hey, you all right?" my younger brother said. He was tall, about 6-foot-5 and strong, home for the holiday wearing an Alpha Phi Alpha tee shirt, jeans, and an angry look. In recent years, he has become very protective of me.

I said, "Yes. Why don't you take Alex back inside, and I'll be there later, OK?"

My brother, Derek, gritted on Julian and took hold of Alex's hand, and they went back into the gym. I'm sure Julian thought Derek was my man. Far from it. In fact, I had such bad luck with men that I stopped even hoping.

I looked up at Julian, whose bright eyes captivated me the first time I saw them. His eyes reminded me of that one night we had together, how tension-free and fun it was.

"I don't believe this," I said. "I don't believe this. You came here to find me? Well, here I am. Now what?"

FORTY:

Pressed To Impress

Renee

The three days between Bible study and Sunday passed slowly for me. I could not believe how intrigued I was by Larry. We talked a few times on the phone for up to forty-five minutes, and the conversations made me even more excited about seeing him again.

I was at work on Saturday when I checked my messages. There was one from Larry. "Hi, Renee, this is Larry. I know the kind of hours you keep and how demanding work can be, so I wanted you to have a message from me when you got home. Just to let you know you've been thought about today. Also, I've been looking forward to tomorrow ever since I last saw you. So I'll see you at 10:30. Take care. Bye."

To say I was surprised would be an understatement. It didn't sound like he was expecting a return call, but I called him anyway. He deserved one.

"Thanks for the message, Larry," I said. "I was blushing the whole time. You're sweet. I'll call you when I get home."

And I did. We talked for a few minutes before I took a shower to begin relaxing. Before I went to sleep, I read the Bible as I lounged in bed. I had the TV on, but the volume down. This was peaceful time for me, time for me to reflect on the day and study the Word before saying my prayers and getting some Zzz's.

After I got off my knees, I slid under the covers and closed my eyes, leaving the TV on. I had worked a ten-hour day and expected to go right to sleep, but couldn't. I laid there thinking about Larry.

He had come into my life at a time when I needed male companionship. Not sexually; I was a born-again Christian and premarital sex was out. But I still enjoyed the comfort of a man and listening to a man's perspective on things. I had met three guys at various times who seemed nice in the two years since I had been "saved" and each of them turned out to be insensitive jerks who hurt my feelings and affected my thoughts about all men.

When I made it clear to them that sex was out, so were they. They stopped seeing me, stopped calling. It made me feel like a piece of meat, like since intercourse would not be a part of the relationship, they had no need for me. After the last guy stepped off, I made a vow to myself that the next guy who got close to me would have a difficult time, if any time at all.

However, two weeks after the last disappointment, Reverend Davis delivered a sermon that spoke directly to my heart. He titled the sermon: 5 Steps To Forgiveness. In it, the minister talked about the importance of forgiving those who mistreated you in some way.

Step 3 in Reverend Davis's plan was "The Enemy Has No Chance Against God." He addressed the congregation, but it seemed like he spoke directly to me. "You have to realize," the preacher said, "that nothing happens by accident. God puts people in your life for a reason, and you have to thank Him for the good and the bad."

Then he told a story about an old minister, a Reverend Gray, who spoke to his church for the final time after 40 years on the pulpit: "And the old man said, 'I want to thank all of you who supported me over all the years, who treated my family nicely, who treated me nicely, who were good in fellowship.' And before he sat down, he said, 'And I want to thank the other folks, too. I want to thank you all who talked behind my back, who did not support my vision for the church, who were mean to my family. Because if it wasn't for you, I would have gone home and chilled out and watched TV. But because I knew you were against me, backstabbing, I got down on my knees and prayed. So I don't know who to thank more—those who prayed with me, or those who MADE me pray.' "

The church rocked. The organist played, people stood, and cries of "Amen" rang through the air. I sat there with tears in my eyes. Reverend Davis spoke to me all right, and the pain that those men caused me vanished and did not come back. I simply prayed. I was no longer the victim.

So, when I thought of Larry, I thought of how comfortable I felt around him and not that he possessed the potential to disappear like the others did. I thought about how genuinely interested in me he seemed. He complimented me on my appearance, made me feel beautiful with his words, not bedroom eyes.

Then I clasped my hands together and offered one final prayer before going to sleep. "God, thank you for bringing a man into my life who seems to be a man I should know. I'm comforted in knowing that You will allow his true self, his true intentions to show. And I know that in any case, he will be a blessing in my life. In Jesus precious name I pray, Amen."

Praying always relaxed me. And in an instant, I was asleep.

***

Larry

I stood in front of my closet, trying to decide what to wear to church the next day. Usually, when I contemplated my attire, it was for a party or a date. But this was different. I wanted to look sharp, but not like I would go dancing after the service.

So I settled on conservative: a navy blue suit with a light blue shirt and pinstripe navy tie. I steam-ironed the slacks and pressed the shirt. Although I had not confirmed it with her, I planned to take Renee to a Sunday brunch I heard about in Santa Monica, near the pier.

That I was even home on a Saturday night was so unlike me. If I wasn't with a woman, I definitely was at a club trying to meet one. I liked to be in the mix. But being prepared for church, and prepared for Renee were my main concerns.

In the morning, I picked up the Bible off the kitchen table that Renee gave me and headed out the door. There was a coolness in the morning air, but it was refreshing. I looked up at the sky, and I believed it was going to be a good day.

The ride to church was uneventful. Renee apologized for not being ready on time. She wore a long beige dress that buttoned all the way down in the front. But I caught a glimpse of her legs as she crossed them. "Nice," I thought.

We arrived just after 11 and had to sit near the back. We stood as the congregation joined in on an upbeat hymn. I did not know the words, but I clapped my hands to the beat. All the while, however, I noticed the many attractive honies in the church. I thought: If a disco light fell from the roof and a deejay started spinning records, one hell of a party could take place.

But I was confused about the way many of the women dressed. It had been a long time, about eight years, since I had gone to church, but I did not recall seeing mini-skirts as I did that day. There was a woman with a leopard-print blouse, unbuttoned to show her cleavage and a skirt so tight she practically had to lean sideways to sit down. Another woman wore a sweater dress that gripped her juicy ass. And there were plenty others in gear inappropriate for church.

I leaned over and whispered into Renee's ear. "I know I haven't been to church in a long time, but when did the dress code change?"

Renee smiled. She, too, had a problem with her sisters' attire in the House of the Lord. "I don't know when," she said, "but they need to change it back."

After the announcements and a song from the choir, visitors were acknowledged. I didn't want to, but I stood as a member of the Welcoming Committee greeted us and asked each of us to say a few words. I started perspiring under my expensive suit when the other visitors before me seemed so comfortable addressing the church. "I'm Diane Thornton and I bring greetings from First Baptist Church of Rayville, Louisiana, and Reverend Charles Lawson. Isn't it a blessing to be in God's House? It's great to be here. God bless you, Pastor Davis and your congregation."

The people said, "Amen" when Diane Thornton finished. Then a very stately gentleman stood up and said with a thick southern accent, "Good morning brothers and sisters. My name is Kenneth Carmon." You could tell he wasn't finished. "Our Lord and Savior, Jesus Christ, has blessed us to be with one another on this glorious Sunday. And when I say 'glorious' I'm not talking about the weather. I'm not talking about this beautiful edifice." He then paused for effect before continuing. "And I'm not talking about the Dodgers' big game against my home team, the Atlanta Braves." Many in the congregation couldn't muffle their laughter. Carmon was on a roll. "It's a glorious day because we are here today with the singular purpose of doing the Lord's bidding and celebrating his unconditional love for us. And if He can love us unconditionally, it isn't asking much for us to reciprocate. We come together this morning to honor His devotedness to us and our devotedness to Him." I had to speak next, and he was raising the bar to uncomfortable heights.

Carmon could feel the crowd. "I didn't come here deliberately; I just 'happened' by. I could hear and feel Jesus as I passed your House of Worship this morning so I just 'happened' by. But nothing ever 'just happens.' This is the Lord's doing. And even though I'm here on business, I'm really here, he paused, "on His business. There's nothing like the 'business' of the Lord.

"I bring you blessings and greetings all the way from Atlanta by way of Poseidon Baptist Chuuurch, Reverend Dr. Ansel Marshall presiding, and I am honored that I could spend this Sunday as your guest. I can feel Jesus up in here. Thank you for bearing with me this morning. I know I was a little long-winded . . ." Someone in the crowded chimed in, "That's all right Brother," Carmon went on, "But you know how it is when you get the Feeling. I don't need to explain it. I just . . ." Some in the congregation gave praises, Amens, and a few "Hear him Lords." He sat down like any well-trained speaker or, for that matter, actor, would do with that "I'm really very shy" look. Never give the audience enough, first rule in showbiz.

What could I say? I had no church home, and I was uncomfortable invoking God's name for the sake of sounding sanctified. I looked down at Renee, who smiled at me. I didn't know if she was laughing at me or offering comfort.

But it was my turn, so I started talking. "Good morning," I said shakily like I never said the words "good morning" before. "My name is Larry Thompson. I live in Studio City. I don't have a church home, but I know it's a blessing to be here. I'm a guest of Renee Braxton, and I feel welcomed. Thank you."

The people shouted "Amen" and "Hallelujah."

When I sat down, I searched for a handkerchief, a napkin, anything, to wipe my brow. It was like I was asked to perform in front of a live audience with no material. I just said what came to me and hoped it was appropriate. Renee reached in her purse and gave me some tissue. I thanked her and dried my face and forehead. Renee patted me on the thigh.

"You were great," she said softly. "I know you were nervous and didn't expect that, but you were great."

Her words calmed me. "You could have warned me," I said.

"I know," Renee answered. "But I asked you last week if you liked surprises and you said you did. So . . ."

". . . So I owe you," I jumped in.

After another selection by the choir, Reverend Davis stepped to the microphone. He thanked the visitors for coming and made some more announcements and then began his sermon. It was "Learning How to Pray." Although I had not gone to church in several years, I thought I knew how to address God when I had to.

I prayed for forgiveness from time-to-time when I knew I needed to, which usually was after I dogged some woman. I prayed before auditioning for roles. I prayed for a safe trip on an airplane. But in each case, it was haphazard. It was not structured.

I learned from Reverend Davis to get on my knees, to confine himself to a "prayer closet" and to speak to God with an open heart. The minister talked about praying for thanks for all things and praying for others; not to just call on God when something was needed. He told the congregation to learn Bible verses by writing them down on index cards and studying them. "The understanding of God's words aids in your ability to address Him," he said.

Reverend Davis taught his listeners in his fiery, enthusiastic way that incited noise. And he cited Scriptures to illustrate his points throughout. And I realized I did not know how to pray, after all. But I did after the minister finished.

I was amazed by the reverend. He spoke with passion and without a hitch. He looked to have notes on the podium, but he seldom referred to them. I thought it was like an actor having learned his lines. But I knew this man was anointed, a man of God. I could tell. And it was especially comforting that the minister did not use theatrics to get his point across. He was matter-of-fact but still exciting.

When the doors of the church were opened and the invitation was presented to join the church for Baptism or a recommitment to Christ, I was tempted to walk down the aisle. The knowledge Reverend Davis gave up at Bible study and in his sermon made me thirsty for more. Learning was like a habit to me; I loved to be able to talk intelligently about everything. But it was surprising to me that my interest in God and the Bible had grown so much, so quickly. But I resisted his urge to join the church, mostly because I did not want Renee to think I was frontin'.

Afterward, as Renee and I stood outside on the steps of the church, I reached inside my jacket pocket and pulled out my sunglasses to offset the brilliant day. "It's a nice day to have a big, healthy brunch," I said. "Wouldn't you think?"

"I agree," Renee said. "We can go to . . ."

"No, no, no," I interrupted. "I've done some research. I've found a place in Santa Monica that has a great reputation."

"You've done some research?" she said.

"Yes. I wanted to make sure that we went somewhere where, first of all, the food is good with a variety of stuff; and also somewhere with a nice atmosphere," I said. "This place is near the pier and on the beach. A jazz brunch."

Renee was impressed. I could tell. It seemed like she liked me more and more. And I felt even better about her too. So good, in fact, that the women in the hoochie gear did not even draw my eye after church. I was focused on Renee. I raised my sunglasses so Renee could see my eyes. I stuck out my folded arm for her to clutch.

"May I?" I said.

She smiled and locked her arm under mine. "You certainly may," she said.

FORTY ONE:

Seeing The Light

Julian

There was so much going on in my life and Greg's and Larry's that we hardly talked to each other directly, so we left each other lengthy voice mail messages. I noticed the last two messages I received from Larry were different in tone from the hundreds he'd left over the previous years.

Usually, Larry was animated and sometimes boastful about his latest conquest. He said stuff like, "It ain't easy being me," or "I'm a king. Come on out here. I need help with all these honies. They're on my jock." And on and on.

He was nothing like that in his more recent messages. He was calm and almost formal, totally unlike him. "Ju, I hope all is well with you. We've been missing each other, but I want you to give me a call when you can. Things out here are good, real good and peaceful. I'm just trying to live right. Get with me. Peace."

I thought: "Just trying to live right?" Larry was hardly devilish, but I'd never heard him talk about living right. I wondered what had gone on out there. The last time we actually talked, he told me about meeting Renee again and that they were going on a date. That was the last I'd heard.

Two weeks had passed since then, and when Larry and I finally talked, he told me the deal. The things he said to me were things I'd never expected to come from him. I called Greg and got him caught up.

I told Greg that Larry spent his free time either with Renee or planning to get with her. He told a core of women who continued to call him that he was involved with someone and, basically, to get a life.

"He tried that before, but he couldn't," Greg said. "You know

193

Larry. He kept playmates."

"But not this time," I said to Greg. "He wasn't so happy with the women he was dealing with, and now when he compares them to Renee, well, he said it's no contest. He talked about having peace in his life because of Renee."

"Peace?" Greg said. "You know Larry always had some drama with women. I don't even know if he knows how to function with stability in his life."

"I know what you're saying, but this Renee person has a lot of influence over him," I told Greg. "From what he told me, all he does is work, play ball, and get with Renee. Every now and then he goes on an audition. But it seemed like she gets a lot of time."

"Well, that's good, really," Greg said. "If he's happy with it, I'm all for it. He left me a few messages, and you're right, he did sound a little different. Like he was real chill. He told me to call him on Sunday, because he knew he'd be home Sunday after church."

✳✳✳

Larry

Renee was true to her convictions, but not the overbearing type that tried to force her lifestyle or beliefs on others. She never, not once, FORCED the Bible or church or the virtues of God on me. When a time came that she wanted to interject her feelings, she did so in a way that kept me at ease, which made me receptive.

Many born-again people tried to force their faith down people's throats, to the point where it was difficult to even talk to them. I remembered a fellow student at ACT virtually stalking me about attending Bible study or reading some religious literature or citing verses or anything involving church to the point where I just tried to tune him out.

It was a shame, but every time I saw him, I felt like turning the other way. That was no way to be, but that dude never stopped.

Renee never started, and it made me more eager to learn. It was funny how that worked. I compared it to this: An attractive woman in an office setting got asked out regularly for dates by nearly every man in the building, single and married. She shot them all down, but the attention flattered her. Then she noticed that one guy in the office never made an advance toward her; he only respectfully greeted her and maybe engaged in some small talk. That was it.

Well, the attractive woman was moved to make advances toward the guy who did not ask her out. She became intrigued by him because he was different from the others, didn't try to force himself on her. And she ended up being interested in HIM.

That's how it worked with me and Renee when it came to religion. It got to the point where I actually asked her questions about religion. And I enjoyed listening to her talk about the Bible. She spoke with pride and passion, the way a man does about his family. It made me want to learn more.

Between that first Sunday at church and the Sunday before Christmas, Renee and I attended Bible study and church together each week. Despite her busy schedule, she found time for me. She enjoyed my company so much—and the fact that sex seemed not to matter to me. I still couldn't figure out how I looked at Renee for what she was—a beautiful woman—and not just a piece of meat, like I normally did.

When her best girlfriend, Kim, came from Oakland to visit for a weekend, she invited me to hang with them. I did, and by the time Kim left, she endorsed me with two thumbs up.

"Girl, he's fine," I heard Kim say to Renee in the kitchen. "And he's cool. He seems real calm. I like him. Shoot, does he have a twin?"

My stock, which was already high, rose even further with Kim's vouching. Women usually treated their partner's approval as the ultimate seal. I was in there.

Often, a man like me—who truly believed it was an honor for women to be in my presence—felt trapped in a relationship, limited, like he was being kept from servicing his public.

That summer, I had told my crew: "I'm beginning to think that there is not a woman out there who can hold me. Even when I meet one with the whole package—beauty, brains, ambition, sweet, whatever—eventually my interest fades. She can't hold my interest. It's a trip."

Well, Renee held me as if with a vice grip.

✳✳✳

Julian

When I finally talked to Larry and not his voice mail, nearly every other sentence was about something Renee said or did. I had never heard him so excited about a woman. And considering their relationship was limited—no sex—it was remarkable Larry was "gone" like he was.

"L," I said, "it sounds like you're whipped without getting the pussy."

"You're a trip," he said. "But you know what? You have a point."

Something else I noticed about Larry during that 40-minute talk. Not once did he mention another woman, and he did not once use profanity. And while I should have felt good about the way his life was—he was in a monogamous relationship, and he cleaned up his mouth—I felt weird about it. I did not know Renee, but this new Larry made me feel like she had taken away some of my boy.

So I asked him, "Ever since you met Renee, you've sounded different. I don't know. I can't really pinpoint it, but there's a difference. You all right?"

"Nah, he said, I'm great." "The difference is that I'm just chilling with one woman. I got tired of the way I was rolling—one honey this night, another honey the next. It got tiresome. And you know what? It was wrong. We've talked for years about finding somebody who could hold us. I thought it wasn't possible. But I know now that it is."

✳✳✳

Larry

It was 68 degrees and sunny on the Sunday before Christmas. Although I had been in L.A. long enough to not be surprised by the December weather, every year I still would laugh out loud about it. "How can it be this warm in December?" I'd say.

In what had become my usual Sunday routine, I picked up Renee for church, the sunroof open and the radio turned to an A.M. gospel station.

On this day, we took seats on the church's right side, on the aisle. I liked to be there so once the service was over, Renee and I could make a quick escape. On this day, Reverend Davis announced his sermon's title was "Finding God in Yourself."

"This morning, saints, I'm speaking not to all of you, but to you," he said. "Don't look over your shoulder or to your left or right. I'm talking to you. You know who you are. In fact, those of you who turned and looked at someone else, you are exactly the ones I'm really addressing. I'm talking to you. Not the man sitting next to the man, sitting next to the man."

The congregation laughed.

"I'm talking to YOU!" Reverend Davis bellowed.

My eyes and attention were transfixed on the pastor. It was like I was hypnotized. If he had anyone's undivided attention, it was mine.

"YOU," the minister continued, "you have the brightest of lights within you and you don't even know it. And you know why? Because you're too busy existing in darkness, stumbling through life, bumping into walls. Oh, you've got the fancy clothes and a nice car, and you know what to say to present yourself as this person with your stuff together.

"But inside, you're dark. You have no light. And we know that Jesus is the way, the truth, and the—what?—light! So to abandon the darkness, to reconcile with the Creator, to make yourself whole, you must—like with any other problem you might have—first REC-OGNIZE that there is a problem."

All of that was me. I'd never even allowed myself to think of the person I REALLY was. I didn't have anything, really, except my family and my strong friendship with Greg and Julian. Other than that, I had the presence of someone with his stuff together. Just the PRES-ENCE. Not the reality. Inside, I had no spiritual foundation. I had no morals. Reverend Davis called me out. I was dark.

"Sometimes you can lie to yourself," the pastor continued, "about something so much that you start believing your own lies. Some people say O.J. has told his story so often that he really believes he didn't kill those people. I don't know what happened, but God does, and so that's already taken care of. But with YOU, right now you probably believe that you're this person you've presented yourself to be all these years. You've got the women pursuing you or the men, and the job is going great, and you feel physically healthy, and you think: What more could I want out of life? Well, you can start by finding God within yourself.

"And, oohh, I'm talking about finding the one gift that can brighten your whole life, because you can have all the material things there are, but if you're dark inside, you'll never truly, truly be happy. Think about this: Any person you've ever been around who has dis-covered God and has a relationship with Him is the most peaceful person you come in contact with, isn't it? They are comforted in knowing that as they travel in this world, the path is lit by God. It's the ultimate security blanket."

I absorbed Reverend Davis' words. It was like no one else was at the church. He talked to ME. Everything the pastor said applied to me. I began to look at my life right there, in the sanctuary, and admit to myself that as far as I had come to get what I had, there was dark-ness within. There was no light.

One night, when Renee and I discussed the challenge of making a relationship work, she told me, "Where the struggle comes in is one party—usually the man—either does not know how to or refuses to open up his heart to the other person. If you truly love someone, opening your heart completely and letting that person in is what you should do. Why hold back? All you're doing is limiting yourself.

"Take it from a religious standpoint," she went on. "A Christian's heart is filled by God because he has opened his heart up to Him. He stripped himself naked, confessed his sins and weaknesses, and let down any guard he had up. That's what God wants and needs to come into your life."

I recalled that talk as Reverend Davis continued his sermon, which got more fiery as he went on. The organist heightened things by pounding the keys to emphasize a point. Most of the people stood, including Renee. I sat. I couldn't get up. My heart raced. A feeling of weakness came over me, as if I were drained. Then I could not see; a blinding light filled my eyes.

Suddenly, I could not hear Reverend Davis or the organist or the people shouting. I began sweating as if sitting in a steam room. I tried to move but I could not. Then, I began to cry profusely, uncontrollably, to the point where snot ran down toward my lips.

I had let down my guard, opened up my heart—and the Holy Spirit entered it. I knew immediately that my old life was over, and my new life was controlled by God. Renee looked down and saw me weeping. She sat next to me and put her arm around me. She knew what had happened, having experienced it herself.

"Larry, you've been blessed," she said.

The tears continued to flow, but I did not bother to wipe them. I nodded my head, and Renee began to cry with me. She got some tissue and wiped my face and nose.

I did not speak, couldn't speak. I just sat there and trembled at Macedonia Baptist Church, on December 20, 2000. That was the date that grew from a lust conquering women to a total, committed love for God—and for the woman who introduced me to that glorious way of life. The only way to a peaceful life.

I closed my eyes as Renee sat with an arm around me. And then I grabbed her hand and whispered a prayer: "Thank you, God. Thank you for saving my life. Thank you for forgiving me of my many sins, for allowing me to survive that hellish life I lived to get to this point. I am committed to You, to serving You, to living my life the way You intended for me to live. You are the Most Merciful. Thank You, oh Lord. Amen."

Never before had I spoken like that. But then, I was definitely a *new* person.

FORTY TWO:

Guess Who's Coming To Dinner

Greg

I called my mom in D.C. for cooking instructions. I had two days before the most important dinner of my life, and I definitely needed help. The idea of cooking for Brianna came to me in a flash: If that was supposed to be the quickest way to a MAN's heart, why couldn't it work in reverse?

And considering that Brianna knew of my total disinterest in lingering in the kitchen beyond getting something out of the fridge, I figured she'd view cooking for her as something extraordinarily special.

My mother told me how to prepare a roasted chicken, potatoes, and broccoli. It was a simple meal, but not for someone like me. I mean, I considered cooking hamburgers and french fries an exotic culinary achievement.

I had my mom speak slowly so I could take meticulous notes. I asked the guy at the liquor store what kind of wine went best with what I planned to cook. I bought new dishes for the occasion. I wanted everything to be just right.

When Friday came, I began cooking the meal about an hour before Brianna was due to arrive. It had been a long day already. I got a haircut that day, picked up clothes from the cleaners, and cleaned my crib as if a "white glove" test would be taken.

I peeled the potatoes, sliced them, and placed them in bowl. I cleaned the whole chicken, stuffed it with celery and onions, and seasoned it with herbs and rosemary. I cleaned the fresh broccoli and set it aside in another bowl. I greased a pan and placed dinner rolls in it. I placed the wine in the freezer.

All the while, I smiled to myself. So far, cooking was fun, although I had not actually COOKED anything yet. But I had done my part; the rest was up to the stove and oven.

I preheated the oven at 350 degrees and placed the cleaned and seasoned chicken into it at 6:15. To make sure it was cooked all the way through, I was told by my mother to keep it in the oven for about an hour. I poured a cup of water into a pot and shook seasoning into it. When it came to a boil, I slid the potatoes into it. I steamed the broccoli and baked the rolls.

At 7:10, the doorman phoned me from downstairs to let me know that Brianna was there. He allowed her to come up, and I stood at the door waiting for her to turn the corner toward my unit. I was pumped. I had not seen her since that day in July, four months earlier, when she ended our relationship.

But there she was, strutting toward me, a vision of class and poise. It seemed like she moved in slow motion. Her hands were in the pockets of her full-length coat, which was open and revealed a black, above-the-knee dress and a black jacket.

She wore black suede pumps that complemented her shapely legs. And she smiled the smile that used to make me weak to her.

When she got to me, I extended my arms, and she walked right into them. We embraced for nearly a full minute right there in the hallway. We both took deep breaths. I got lost in the moment—until I smelled smoke.

"Oh, no," I gasped. "Come in. I smell something."

Brianna came in, and I rushed to the kitchen. She took off her coat and smiled as I scurried about. I opened the oven door and smoke came billowing out. Thankfully, the chicken was fine. The dinner rolls, however, suffered a fiery death.

"Is everything OK?" Brianna yelled from the living room.

"Yeah," I said. "I've got everything under control."

"Doesn't smell like it," she said.

"Yeah, yeah, yeah," I said playfully. "Just have a seat. I'll be right out."

When I finally did emerge from the kitchen, I was sweating, but I held two glasses of wine. Brianna had taken a seat in the recliner, her legs crossed. I stopped in my tracks and admired the woman I, at one point, thought I'd lost.

"Thirsty?" I said.

"And hungry," Brianna answered.

I offered a toast. "To you—for finding it in your heart to be here tonight. Thanks."

"Thanks for asking me," she said. "You know, through the smoke I think I smell something that smells good."

"Yeah, you do. It's almost ready," I said. "Give me two minutes."

I then took Brianna's coat and hung it up. I came back and stoked the fire that burned in the fireplace. I put on a Norman Brown CD. Then I lit two long candles on the dining room table, which was decorated with the new plates I bought.

I was about to go into the kitchen, but then it hit me to go back over to Brianna. I asked her to stand up. She did, and I hugged her again. "The other hug was interrupted," I said. "Bri, you look great. You smell great. You feel great in my arms. I've missed you."

Brianna just smiled. "OK," I said, "have a seat at the table. I will serve you now."

Everything looked good, edible. I fixed Brianna's plate and placed it in front of her. I made a plate for myself and sat across from her. She grabbed my hand and blessed the food.

To my delight, the food was good. The chicken could have used a little more seasoning and the potatoes a little less salt, but for a first effort, I was proud of myself.

"All right, Gregory," Brianna said. "Who cooked this?"

"Don't even insult me like that," I said. "Girl, I put a lot of work into this. I burned the dinner rolls, but something had to go wrong. At least it wasn't the chicken."

"Well, I must admit, I'm highly impressed," she said. "This is really good. Remember the time I asked you to help me with dinner, and you didn't know where to begin? After that, I knew you'd never become a chef. Now this? What happened?"

"Well, I know that taking you out to dinner could be nice, but we've done that before," Greg said. "I want to do things we haven't done before. Not that what we did in the past was bad—shoot, it was great. But I've had a lot of time to think about things. Whenever we did something, you made all the plans, came up with all the ideas.

"I was comfortable with that because you always made good, fun plans. But, to be honest, maybe I got a little comfortable—a little *too* comfortable. I don't want us to go back to what we had. I want it to be better. I want to help make it better."

Brianna smiled, rubbed my hand, which was on the table, and got up and took her empty plate into the kitchen. I followed. We then participated in a post-dinner ritual: I washed and Brianna dried the dishes.

It was a minor thing, really, but it was something that I missed about not having Brianna around. We always had great conversations and big laughs washing and drying the dishes. With her out of my life, I simply tossed them into the dishwasher.

When we finished, we pounced on the couch. I brought Brianna her glass of wine and made myself an Absolute and cranberry. The fire was going strong and the music nice, and I could feel that Brianna was definitely on her way back into my life.

But I could sense that she was not totally comfortable, that she was cautious. So, I decided against a movie I had rented from Blockbuster and, instead went for something I thought would loosen her up and make her feel good. I pulled out a photo album that featured us over our two years together.

This was a psychological move. I thought that the photos would make her reminisce, make her get sentimental. And if things went absolutely great, they'd make her more eager to relive the past with me. And it seemed to work.

Each photo had a story and started conversation. For more than an hour, we laughed and talked and enjoyed each other's presence while recalling the past. This would help in our future, I believed.

"Remember this?" I said, pointing a picture of Brianna sprawled on the floor, hung over.

"I don't want to remember," she said. "I was so sick. Trying to celebrate the anniversary of the grand opening of your bookstore, drinking tequila like it was pop. Never again. It took me almost all of the next day to get over that. You know I haven't had tequila since then?"

"I hated to see you like that," I said. "But I really did like trying to nurse you back to health. And the best part was getting you in bed and laying there, holding you most of the day. It was nice to just watch you sleep."

"That was sweet," Brianna said. "You did take care of me."

"You know what?" I said. "I don't want you to be sick like that again, but I do want to hold you like that again."

"You want a lot for someone who didn't want me not that long ago," Brianna replied cooly.

I did not expect that response. Things had gone almost exactly how I planned it in my head—except for that remark. So, I hardly was prepared. But I just went with the truth.

"I know," I began. "And, really, I don't have an excuse, either. I can sit here and come up with theories and plots and all kind of stuff. But to me, the bottom line is that I did not know what I had in you until I did not have you."

Brianna seemed to study me as I spoke. Like most women, she believed her intuition was deadly accurate. It seemed as if she was satisfied that I did not try to bullshit her. Still, there was something else bothering her.

"Who is Michelle?" she said.

"Michelle who?" I answered. "I know a few Michelles." Again, she looked at me closely. My facial expression usually revealed something about how I felt, and she knew that. So, she searched for an inkling but found nothing because there was nothing to find.

"Michelle Lowery," she said.

My heart skipped then. Michelle Lowery was a honey I knew through one of my buddies in Chicago. She was a sharp sister who I had gone out with on a sneak-tip a few times in the months before Brianna and I broke up. Although I liked Michelle and was attracted to her, I did not sleep with her. Never tried to, in fact, although she more and more seemed open to the possibility.

Once, I ran into Michelle at a house party on the north side of Chicago. She insisted we dance and spend time talking during the night. My friends from work and the gym knew Michelle, too, and they did not know her to be so friendly with a man who was not important to her.

And although I was only her friend, I did not make that clear to my friends when they implied that I was sleeping with her. Instead, I just smiled as if I were keeping a secret. The pressure of being a man made me go out like a sucker. I was too anchored in machoism to say, "Nah, we're cool, but I have a honey, so I'm not trying to hit it. We're just friends." Instead, I let them believe the untruth so as to build on my rep. Immature.

"Yeah, I know Michelle Lowery. I met her through a friend of mine earlier this year. Why?" I said to Brianna.

"Well, I've been hearing some things about you and her."

"What things?"

"You know I'm not a he-say, she-say person, Gregory," Brianna said. "But some people who are your friends—or supposed to be your friends—all said you had something going on with this . . . this person."

"Friends? What friends?" I said. "Nobody I know would say something like that because it's not the truth. I know her, and I talk to her on occasion. I haven't actually seen her in awhile—but that is it. Who told you this?"

Brianna then reluctantly ran off a list of names that shook my world. "Kelvin, Hawk, and Maurice."

"Come on, Brianna. No way," I said. "You're telling me that they told you this? Those three guys?"

"Yes, they did," she said. "I saw Kelvin and Maurice at Water Tower. They were together. Maurice asked me about you, and I said I hadn't talked to you. This was about a month ago. He said, 'Well, I'm glad you're all right. I heard you guys broke up because of that stuck-up girl he was seeing.'"

"I said, 'What girl?' Kelvin said, 'Oh, you didn't know? Well, it doesn't matter now. Michelle Lowery.' Even though we weren't together, it still hurt me. They acted like all of our friends knew about it except me. I felt like a fool. I was upset, so I just told them it was good to see them and I left."

"I don't believe this," I said. "Listen, Brianna, I told you the extent of the relationship—if you want to call it that—with that girl. That was it. Period."

"How did you meet her?"

"Hawk introduced me to her. We were at his house watching a Bulls game, and he introduced her as a chick he went to school with. That was it."

"He said you asked him to introduce you to her because you wanted to get with her," Brianna said.

"He said what?" I said. "Hey, listen. That's bullshit."

"Gregory, calm down," she said. "I'm just telling you what he said. He called me—"

"He called you?" I jumped in. "What's he doing calling you?"

"That's what I thought, too," Brianna said. "I didn't even know he had my number, but he said he had it from that house-warming invitation. He said he was just checking to see how I was doing because he knew we broke up. Then, after a few minutes, he said he saw your 'new girlfriend' that day."

"I can't believe this," I said.

"It's strange three of your friends are telling me the same story," she said.

"What are you saying, you believe them? Look, it's obvious they're not my friends. I don't know what's going on with them. Even if it were true, why would they tell you? But it's not true. I'm telling you right now, when we were together, I never cheated on you. Never."

"To be honest, Gregory," she said, "I never felt like you did. I really didn't. But I know that you're a man, which means you're capable of cheating. The other thing, though, is I never really felt good about Hawk, Maurice, and Kelvin to begin with. I asked myself: 'Why would they tell me that?' It's just weird, Gregory. But it was always something about them that rubbed me wrong. You couldn't see it because you're too nice to people. But they just wanted to use you, to use the connections you've made in the city to get them into an event or Bulls tickets or parties. You just couldn't see it.

"They weren't like you are with Julian and Larry," she added. "All you all want from each other is friendship. I know what you have with them. As for those three guys, they're just users."

I listened to Brianna, but my mind was on my so-called friends who turned out to be straight punks. The fury within me made me want step to each of them. A wrong word from either, and I was going to punch someone right in the face.

The evening I prepared for like crazy blew up like a volcano. My emotions were split. On one hand, I wanted to tear one of those sucker's heads off. On the other, I wanted to assure Brianna they were lying.

It did not get any better for me when she got up and said, "Well, I'd better go now."

"What? Don't go, Brianna. You haven't even touched your wine all night," I said. "Have a drink with me. Let's finish talking this out."

"There's nothing left to talk out, really." she said. "You said they're lying. What else can you say? Their word doesn't mean anything to me. But at the same time, I can't help but wonder why they'd all lie. It's so weird. But I'm glad I got to see you. I was going to tell you this over the phone, but it's better that I got to see your reaction in person. I believe you."

"If you believe me, stay for a little while," I said. "I don't want you to leave with this nonsense being the last thing we talked about."

"I'm a little tired, to be honest," she said. "I've been dragging lately, so I just want to get a hot bath and some rest. But I'll call you tomorrow, OK?"

"I guess it has to be," I said. As she left, I wondered if she was playing me off, you know, just telling me anything to get out the door. That wasn't her style; she was straight up, usually.

I walked her to her car. We hugged, and her embrace was firm. That made me feel a little better. I kissed her on the side of the face.

"Call me to let me know you made it home," I said. I expected a better ending to the date, but maybe I expected too much.

FORTY THREE:

Ships Ahoy

Greg

When I woke up the next day, I almost literally sat by the telephone. I didn't even call the store to see how things were going. I wanted to hear from Brianna. I NEEDED to hear from her. I was very happy with our first time together in four months—despite the revelation that a few of my "friends" turned out to be far from that—but I was a little uncertain if she had really believed me about Michelle Lowery.

I told myself that if she did believe me, she'd call, as she said she would. But it was unlikely that she'd call as early as I got up. Although I had been out of the Army for a few years, I was still into starting the day with the birds. This was also a good rule of thumb to apply in business.

I knew that Brianna liked to start her days early, too, so I hoped that she'd call first thing. To kill time, I called Larry. It was 9 o'clock in Chicago, 7 in L.A.

"I know you're not still sleeping," I said when Larry answered the phone.

"What's your problem?" Larry said with a frog in his throat. "You need to start taking sleeping pills. It's too early to be up on a Saturday morning."

I continued as if Larry told me he was wide-awake and waiting for my call.

"Man, I got with Brianna last night," I started. "Cooked dinner, too. We—"

"Wait a minute," Larry said. "You cooked dinner? You really do want her back, huh?"

"I told you, Larry. I'm on a mission," I said. "Everything went great last night, but she did hit me with some heavy stuff. You know

206

those dudes you met the last time you were out here—Maurice, Kelvin, and Hawk? Well, they told Brianna that I was *fucking* with this honey out here, Michelle." It felt strange cursing in front of Larry, even over the phone.

"Come on," Larry said. "I thought you were cool with them."

"Yeah, me too," I said. "I want to go and punch them right in the face. Right now, though, I'm just trying to figure out why they'd go out on me like that. I'm tripping."

"Greg," Larry jumped in, "don't trip on those fools. To hell with them. Your focus is on Brianna. You know you didn't do anything with that woman. I remember you telling us about her. Just make sure Brianna knows the real deal. As for those guys, this is what you do: You pray for them. You pray for them because they need it. You pray for them, and it takes the burden off of you. When people do something against you, you feel like the victim. Praying for them lifts that off you."

"Since when did you start praying for people?" I said.

"Since now," Larry said. "Try it. I promise you'll feel better. Meanwhile, I'm going back to sleep. I'll get with you later. Peace."

"Peace," I said. Then I dialed Brianna's number but hung up before it rang. I realized I was getting beside myself. "She'll call," I said aloud. "I need to stop tripping."

I went to the corner store and bought the Chicago Sun-Times and the Chicago Tribune. When I returned home, I noticed the date. It was November 28th, Brianna's birthday. I hurried to my date book to make sure I was right. I was. How could I have let that slip up on me?

Immediately, my mind began to race. I wasn't big on celebrating my birthday, but Brianna was definitely big on enjoying hers.

She would expect me to send flowers—I always did—so instead I sent balloons that read "Happy Birthday" on one side and "From Gip" on the other. "Gip" was a pet name she had for me that I wasn't crazy about. But I knew it would draw a smile from her.

Later, I arranged dinner on the Spirit of Chicago, a ship that offered dinner and dancing as it cruised along Lake Michigan. It was a romantic, seductive ride that Brianna had mentioned to me more than a year before. Of course, I basically ignored her request back then. So, I knew she'd be surprised and excited about that gift.

I felt so good about myself that I decided to be risky. I called the Palmer House and asked about rates for a suite. When told $350, I swallowed hard—and then booked the room for the night.

Finally, I went shopping on Michigan Avenue. I stopped at

Victoria's Secret and, after 30 minutes of searching, purchased a gold teddy with spaghetti straps. I smiled as the woman at the register wrapped it; I thought of how sexy Brianna would look in it. Then I went across the street to Marshall Fields and bought her a dress for the night. It was black silk, above the knee, and came with a sheer top that tied at the waist. Sexy.

After all that, all I had to do was get Brianna to spend the evening with me. Turned out that was not so easy.

I called her on my cellular as I walked back with all the bags. "Hi, Bri, how are you? Happy Birthday," I said.

"Thank you, Gregory. Where are you? Sounds like you're outside."

"Walking on Michigan Avenue from shopping. What are you up to?"

"I'm about to go visit my parents and see what they have planned for me for the evening. Why?"

"They don't have anything planned for you."

"How do you know that?"

"Because I have something planned for you."

"Oh, you do, huh?" Brianna said somewhat agitated. "Well, Gregory, I wish you would have asked me first. You could have done that last night, but then you'd have to remember it was my birthday to ask me about it, wouldn't you?"

"You've got me there," I said. "I can't lie. I didn't think about it then. I was just excited about having you there. But I am thinking about it now."

"Well, I have to be fair to my parents," she said. "I can't just break the plans they've made. I told them I would spend the evening with them because I had no plans. They were excited about that because I never spend time with them on my birthday. So, I really have to see what they have put together."

"Bri, can you ask them to take a *rain check*? I have a big evening planned for us," I said.

"Doing what?" she said.

"It's all a surprise. I can't tell you. But I KNOW you'll enjoy it."

"Well, if you want them to take a rain check, YOU call them and ask. That's the best I can think of. Otherwise," she said, "I've got to do something with them because I told them I would."

That was a scenario I did not anticipate. I had a cool relationship with Brianna's folks—BEFORE we broke up. I was not sure how they looked at me since then because I knew Brianna was very close to them and that she told them about most everything in her life. So, I had no doubt that they knew she ended the relationship with me because I was trippin'.

But I had to call the Banks. When I got home, I took a deep breath and dialed the number. I hoped they were not home so I could leave a message. But on the first ring, Brianna's mother answered.

"Hi, Mrs. Banks, this is Greg Gibson." I held my breath in anticipation of her response. If she was short, like, Yes, what can I do for you? I knew I would be in trouble. But if she was cordial, I had a shot.

"Well, hello Greg. Haven't talked to you in a while," Mrs. Banks said.

That response was in between, but I took it as favorable.

"I know. How've you been?" I said.

"Just fine. What can I do for you?" she said, getting straight to the point.

"I'm sure you know that Brianna and I stopped seeing each other for awhile. It was my fault, no doubt about it," I began. "But we've been talking lately, and we had dinner last night; I cooked. Anyway, it did not hit me until this morning that today is her birthday. So I immediately got on the phone and made a bunch of plans for us for tonight. But when I spoke to her, she said you and your husband might have big plans for her, too."

"So, what are you getting at, Greg?" Mrs. Banks said.

"Well, I've been trying to show your daughter that I want us back together," I said. "Mrs. Banks, I love Brianna. I really do. I always felt I had, but I know now that I REALLY do. And on her birthday I'd like to really show her that."

Mrs. Banks did not speak, so I continued. "Now, if you all have something special planned that can't be changed, I respect that. I understand. But I had to ask because I want to do some special things for her today."

Mrs. Banks asked me to hold on. I could hear her telling her husband about what I said. After a moment, Mr. Banks took the phone. "Hi Greg, how you doing?" he said in his distinctive, hoarse voice. "My wife told me that you want to see Brianna tonight. You know how I feel about my baby, I'm sure. We planned something small here at the house with her aunts and cousins. Family. But . . . we can do that tomorrow; they all live nearby. That's if it's OK with HER. If it is, you just make sure she has a good time. But not too good of a time. You understand?"

"Yes sir," I said. "Mr. Banks, thank you and Mrs. Banks. I really appreciate it. And I'll make sure she has a nice time. I promise that."

That out of the way, I called Brianna back with the news that she was mine for the night. "Can I come see you at about six? We can go from there."

"What should I wear? I'm not sure how to dress," Brianna said. She was sincerely concerned about her attire for the evening, but her biggest goal was to get me to tell her what was up. She loved surprises AND hated them. They were good when she had no idea they were coming. But to know a surprise was in the offing was like torture to her to not know. This was a woman who would snoop, days before Christmas, to find out what was in presents marked with her name.

"Nice try," I said. "We don't have to leave until seven, so I can tell you what would be appropriate when I get there."

"Whatever," she said, irritated that I would not give in.

I got my wardrobe together for the night: a black three-button Hugo Boss suit with crisp white shirt and tasteful black and gold tie. I shaved my head so that it would glisten under the moonlight. I brushed my suede split-toe shoes. I was ready.

When I arrived at Brianna's house, it was the first time I'd been there since she ended our relationship, other than dropping off the candle. It was not lost on me, either. I just wondered if I should bring it up or ignore it. I felt so good about everything, I went on and brought it up when she opened the front door.

"Hi, birthday girl," I said with a wide smile. I put down the shopping bag of goodies for Brianna. She stepped outside, and I gave her a prolonged hug.

"You look sharp," she said. "And you smell good, too."

"Thanks," I said. "You know, Bri, I know it's your birthday, and we're definitely celebrating that. But it's a celebration for me just to be right here again, on your front porch. I didn't think I'd ever be here again."

"Well, I'm glad you're here," she said. "But now that you are, let's go inside because it's a little chilly."

"What's in the bag?" Brianna said as she locked the door. "Anything for me?"

"A few things," I said. "Check it out."

And so, she did. First, I gave her a birthday card. I had gone to Hallmark and personalized it. There was a big heart on the front with "Happy Birthday, Bri" and inside, I wrote: "Dates of birth are to be honored once a year. I honor you always, Brianna. And in all ways."

On the left inside portion of the card, it was signed and sealed by a notary public. Under that, I wrote, "Now, my commitment to you is in this legal document. There's no denying it."

"Gregory, you actually went to a notary? I can't believe you," Brianna said.

"Yep," I said, trying to downplay it. "The guy thought I was crazy. He said, 'This woman must be special. I've never had anyone bring in a birthday card.' "

She leaned over and kissed me softly on the lips. That was very encouraging. Then she was back to gift receiving. "What's next?" she said anxiously.

"There's more, but you can't receive them until later tonight," I said as I handed her the box with the dress in it.

Brianna acknowledged the nice wrapping paper before ripping it up. She pulled out the dress and held it up against her body. "Gregory, this is beautiful. And it's my size. How did you know my size? You never bought me any clothes before."

"You told me you wear an 8 in most things about a year ago," I said. "It may not seem like it, but I remember everything you say to me. And I'm glad you like the dress because that's your outfit for tonight."

"Oh, yeah? Where are we going?" she said mischievously.

"To dinner. Don't worry about where."

Brianna left to get dressed and emerged from her bedroom about 45 minutes later, looking tight in the dress I picked out for her. I was proud. She was happy.

And she was hungry, so we headed for the pier. When we got close, Brianna got curious. "Where are we going down here?"

I didn't answer. I just kept driving. Then, when I pulled into the parking lot for the Spirit of Chicago, Brianna knew. And she was excited. "No!" she said. "We're going on the boat? You know I've been wanting to do this for a long time."

"I know," I said. "I was just waiting for the right occasion. Your birthday is it."

Brianna just looked at me for the next several seconds. I could see her with my peripheral vision. I already had made her birthday seem like a birthday.

Larry, Julian, and I had talked about how it really did not take much to please a woman. Just a little creativity and a lot of attention. The real chore was being motivated to actually do it.

And that part of it was easy for me then. I was hyped about pleasing Brianna. I had more emotional energy than ever before, probably because the first time around I hardly used any. Really, I didn't even know I had a romantic side. I took advantage of romantic situations.

But I didn't CREATE any.

But this really was a new me. Money did not matter. Time did not matter. It only mattered that I showed Brianna Banks that she meant more to me than anything. And I learned that it could be so much fun pleasing the one I loved. And the night had just really begun.

FORTY FOUR:

Fancy Meeting You Here

Julian

All the words I practiced on the eight-hour drive to South Carolina evaded me. I had found Alexis, but I was caught totally off guard. Usually, I prided myself on my ability to wing it on a moment's notice. But I struggled for a clear thought with her standing in front of me.

"This is so wild," I said finally. "I came here to find you. I believed that I would. But at the same time, I can't believe that I have. But I came here because ever since we met in California, you've been on my mind."

"But why didn't you call me in L.A.? I called you. I was waiting to hear from you," she said.

I absorbed her every word. There had been times in my life when I met a woman who looked good on first appearance and less than what I recalled or wanted the second time. Too many times. Alexis Miller—clad in white cotton blouse and blue jeans—only enhanced my image of her. Like the night we met, her makeup was neat and her hair on point, although it was long and flowing and not pinned up like at the club in Los Angeles.

From a few feet away, I could smell the fragrance she wore. It was the same as the night we met. And her eyes were just as delicate and vulnerable, yet inviting. Although she was surprised to see me, she remained poised.

"I would have called you if I could," I said. "You're not going to believe this, but about three minutes after I walked you to your car, my friends and I were in an accident. A serious accident, on Sepulveda."

Alexis placed her right hand over her heart. Her shoulders dropped and her face showed an expression I had not seen.

"Oh, my God. Julian, I saw that accident," she said. "Well, I didn't see it when it happened, but we rode past it not long after it happened. It was horrible. It was so bad that I covered my eyes. It was two jeeps, wasn't it?"

"Yeah, it was bad," I said. "We're all better now. We spent a few days in the hospital. I was unconscious for a while and ended up with a serious concussion and a broken arm and other little stuff. My boys got banged up, too, but we're fine now. Anyway, when I got to my clothes at the hospital, your number was gone. I tried 411 here, but you're not listed. So, finally, I just came down here."

"I can't believe this," she said. She blushed. She was flattered and not at all bothered that I was there. That gave me hope. "But how were you going to find me?"

"Well, I have a cousin, James, who lives here," I said. "I knew what you did, so I went that route. Child Care Professionals, right? I found your job. I went there this afternoon. The receptionist told me you were in L.A. So I left a message there and had her leave one for you at home. All that and I find you at a basketball game."

"I can't believe this," she said.

"You keep saying that," I said.

"I know, but it's unbelievable. When you didn't call me back when we were in L.A., I just thought that you were a typical guy, just shooting a lot of game."

"Game?" I said. "You were there. There was no game involved. We just talked. It was the best conversation I've ever had with a woman. Because of that conversation, I'm here."

"I'm sorry, you're right. The conversation was great. That's why I was looking forward to seeing you the next day," Alexis said. "When you didn't call me, I really didn't know what to think. In cases like that, you tend to think the worst."

As we stood there talking, the basketball game resumed. I had been gone so long that James got concerned and came looking for me. He found me with hot dog in hand, talking to Alexis.

"Hey, this is my cousin, James," I said. "James, this is the very elusive Alexis Miller."

"Who?" James said. "Nah, you can't be serious."

We all laughed. James went over and hugged Alexis. "All that detective work I did and he finds you here?" he said. "Oh, well. Whatever works. I know this is a happy young man right here."

"Well, I'm happy, too," she said. "No one's ever done anything like this for me."

James excused himself and returned to his seat. I wanted to continue the conversation, but she did appear to be with someone.

"Who are you here with, may I ask?" I said timidly.

"That little guy was my son, Alex," she said.

We talked for a long time in L.A. and never did she mention she had a son. That news surprised me. But I knew I really was interested in her because I was unfazed. And this was new for me, because I had a few things I would not tolerate: no women with children, no women from out of town.

I did not want an "instant family" that came with a woman with children. And what if I wanted to go away for a spontaneous trip? If she didn't have a babysitter, she was stuck at home. I had vowed to not partake in that kind of situation. I wanted a woman with the latitude to roll whenever.

As for the distance, when I was horny, I certainly wanted my woman in driving distance, not long distance. On a nice summer night, I'd want to do a movie and dinner with my honey. If she were 500 miles away, how could I? Trying to maintain an in-town relationship was hardly easy, so trying to be in one when I was in one place and the woman was in another, well, it was not something I would get down with.

But I learned something about myself as I stood in front of Alexis Miller, mother and South Carolinian: I had some fucked up hang-ups—I mean a whole lotta *baggage*. But it was not until then, at that very moment, that I realized that.

I looked into her eyes after she told me about little Alex, who was three. I could tell my response was important to her, based on how she zoomed in on me. And those eyes also told me that she wanted it to be all right with me. It took me a nanosecond to process all that, AND my feeling of wanting the woman, no matter the circumstances.

"Is that right?" I said, trying to sound surprised, but not fazed. "I get it: you called him Alex. Alex and Alexis. That makes sense. Was that his father with him?"

"Please, don't bring up his so-called father," Alexis said. "That was his uncle, my brother, Zack."

"Yeah, well, he gritted on me like I did something to him," I said.

"He's just very protective of me, that's all," she said.

"You seem like a big girl who can handle herself."

"I thought I was too, until . . . well, let's talk about that later, OK? So, what are you doing later?"

"We were going to go to Columbia to hang out," I said. "But that was before I saw you. But I thought you were going to L.A."

"We were, but my sister is coming here next week, so we—Alex and I—decided we'll just hang out here. But he's staying with my mother tonight and—I still can't believe you're here—we can get together and have a drink or something."

"Yeah, I like 'white lightening.' " I said.

"What do you know about 'white lightening'?" she said in astonishment. "That's an Orangeburg thing."

"My cousin had some. Then I bought a bottle this afternoon. So, I'm down with it." I said.

She laughed and shook her head. Then we made plans to talk after the game and then hang out. Before rejoining her son and brother at the game, Alexis took a long look at me.

"You look good," she said, "like I remember. But there's something different about you."

I knew what it was, but I didn't volunteer anything. I just continued to write my cousin's number on a napkin, and, for good measure, I added my cell number, home number, pager number, and even my work number. I remembered how we lost contact before, and I was determined not to let that happen again. When I finished, I looked up at her. I enjoyed looking into her eyes. After a few more seconds, it came to her.

"The goatee. That's different," she said. "You didn't have that in California. But I like it. It's neat and distinguishing. It gives you a real professorial look."

"Really? Well, thanks," I said somewhat embarrassed but definitely flattered. "If you like it then, hey, cool. Until you said something, I hadn't really thought about it. But that's about the only real change with me. But you certainly look the same, which is great."

"Thanks," she said. "I'm just glad to be on vacation."

We hugged and went back to our seats inside the gym. I watched the game with James, but every so often I zoomed in on Alexis across the court. I observed how she interacted with Alex. She hugged him. She disciplined him. She even popped him when he tried to wander off.

I took her willingness to spank him as a real strength. It always annoyed me when I heard women talk of disciplining their children by "putting them in timeout" or using harsh words while wagging a finger. Inevitably, kids who got that treatment and not a belt—or whatever was handy—across their butts were bad asses I did not want to be around. That contributed to me not wanting to deal with a woman with children.

But Alexis had been raised like me: with love, which at times was illustrated by the impact of a belt. I did not like the beatings as a child, but I later knew that I'd definitely be a physical disciplinarian as a parent. It worked. Of course, it was action to punish but also to teach. These days, kids needed the belt in the worst way.

I was so hyped about finding Alexis—and her response to me—that I needed a drink. So, when the game was over and we returned to James', I made a beeline to the "white lightening." James had a glass, too, and we sipped and laughed until the phone rang.

"If that's Alexis, I'm in business," I said. She said she'd call, and I believed she would, but I could not be too certain.

James answered and handed the phone to me. Alexis said she had dropped off her son, and after some small talk, she gave me directions to her house.

"You said you had some 'white lightening,' didn't you? You should bring it," she said.

And so, I did. When I arrived at her brick ranch-style house, she greeted me at the door before I even knocked. She showed me inside. Her place was tastefully decorated, and the smell of scented candles filled the air.

***

Alexis

I asked Julian to sit in the dining room adjacent to the kitchen as I poured boiled peanuts from a pot off the stove and into a plastic bowl. I brought the bowl and two glasses to the table. I lit the candles on the table and turned down the lights.

We sat there eating peanuts and sipping bootleg liquor. And we talked and talked about everything. Julian told me more details about the L.A. accident. And he even told about Joanne, and the drama of her being pregnant by someone other than him.

It was nearly three in the morning when he said, "Now, tell me more about Alex. I watched you two at the game. I could see right away you guys have a tight bond."

"We do," I said. I was so happy that he asked me about Alex. Without exception, we were a package deal. If I a man could not deal with both of us, if I sensed at all that that was a problem, then I couldn't possibly deal with him.

"Alex is my little man," I told Julian. "He's three years old, but acts a lot older. We do everything together. He's the one great joy in my life."

"Do you have room for more joy?" he said.

That man sure knew how to say things to make me feel good. But I would not assume anything. "What do you have in mind?" I said coyly.

"Me," he said assertively, looking directly into my eyes. Then the words just started coming from Julian.

"Alexis, it seems to me that my life is at sort of a crossroads. The things that were very important to me are hardly that anymore. It took a lot for me to get to this point. The person I've been with you is not the person I've been all my adult life. I'm not proud to say that I've made lots of mistakes in relationships, mistakes that I could have controlled, but I didn't because I didn't want to, I guess. I've been dishonest with women and . . . cheated in relationships. I don't know how I got to that point, but that was me."

I didn't say a word. I just looked into his eyes. Julian's eyes did not dart around the room. They were locked on mine, and vice versa.

"I don't often believe in the cliche that things happen for a reason," Julian continued. "One of my friends, Larry, is big on that stuff. 'It's all in divine order,' he says. But in the case of meeting you, I do believe that. I do because although I lost your number in L.A. and had no way of reaching you, I somehow always felt that our paths would cross again.

"I was bothered that we lost touch, but it was all in divine order, I guess. In a way, I believe I was in that car accident so that we would not communicate right then because I was not ready for you. I met you at the right time, but it was not the right time. I was involved with someone and thought she was pregnant with my child. To maintain both of you would have required me to lie and be deceitful, which I had been good at doing.

"Instead, I lost the number, and later found out that Joanne was not the woman I thought and the baby was not mine. Over the next months, I met women who just did not move me, but certainly did frustrate me. All of that led me back to you—with no woman, no *baggage*, just an open heart and a changed outlook."

He finally stopped long enough for me to interject. I was impressed that he admitted how badly he treated women in the past. And I was spooked that he felt it was the wrong time for us to meet when we were in L.A. I felt exactly the same way, but for different reasons.

"It's so funny, Julian," I said, "because I've wondered about you. And what's so scary about the things you just said is that I thought the same thing about divine order. I was so happy to meet someone like you, who I could talk to, feel good about, and be comfortable with. There was just no pressure. But I had things going on in my life that would have been complicated to deal with AND you, at the same time. But like you, I've gotten beyond that stuff. So, you don't know how good it is to see you here, although I still can't really believe it."

He got up from his chair and walked around the table to my side. I stood up, and we hugged. He kissed me on the top of my head, which was nice, but the lips would have been better. I couldn't tell him that, but that's what I wanted. Then he kissed me on the side of my face.

Finally, I couldn't take it anymore. I raised my head and pointed my lips in his direction.

Our mouths met as if drawn together by magnets. We looked into each other's eyes as our lips touched. His lips were soft and moist. Then I closed my eyes and creased my mouth. He did the same, and we stood over the candle-lit dining room table and enjoyed a long passionate kiss.

FORTY FIVE:

You Sexy M.F.

Julian

For the first time since knowing Alexis, I thought about sex with her. That one kiss took me there. I was embarrassed that a bulge developed instantly in my pants. I tried to pull away so that she would not notice, but it didn't work. But it was quite comforting that she pulled me closer to her. She wanted to feel it.

"I like you close to me like this," I said to her. "You feel like you belong here."

"I like you this close, too," she said while looking up at me. "I haven't been with a man in a long time. About a year. But I've got to tell you—and it's a little embarrassing, but we've been honest and open with each other—that I find you very sexy. It's not just one thing. It's everything together—your eyes, the way you smile. Your tall, lean physique, your dark complexion, the way you carry yourself, the way you dress. All of that together makes you so sexy."

"I don't want to sound like I'm trying to top you or give you a compliment because you've given me one, but I do want to say something," I said. "And it's a little complicated, so stay with me. Until now, I never thought about sex with you, and that's probably more sexy than anything. When we met in L.A. and all of tonight, I've soaked up the feeling of being around you. It's feels good. It feels right.

"You're great. But the thing that is most attractive and sexy is that I don't think about sex with you. Or I hadn't. I think about how good I feel with you, how natural the conversations are, how REAL you make me feel. I've never, ever felt like I had to be honest with someone until you. You make me feel differently about myself, better about myself. And it's something very sexy about that."

She hugged me tighter. I hugged back. I rubbed her back gently and kissed the sides of her face. Alexis stepped back.

"I want you, Julian. You don't know how badly," she said. "But this is too soon. Too soon. And we probably should talk some more."

"Alexis, I was not trying to get you in bed. I agree that it's too early."

"OK, I'm sorry. I guess what the real problem is, is I need to talk to you about my life and why I wasn't ready for you four months ago when we met. It's so late, though, that we probably should get into it tomorrow."

"That's fine with me," I said. "I guess I should go back to my cousin's and let you get some rest. I need some, too."

"No," Alexis said. "I know I said it's late, but I don't want you to go. Let's sit on the couch and rest. If I could just sleep in your arms on the couch tonight, that would be good."

"Good for me, too," I said.

So, I used her bathroom and joined her on the couch. She had slipped out of the jeans and into some sweats and a tee shirt. She reached down and slipped off my shoes and leaned back on the pillows she had taken off her bed. She covered us with a spread and rested her head on my chest. It was nearly 4 a.m.

We lay there quietly for a few moments. I thought she was asleep when suddenly she said, softly, "Julian, are you asleep?"

"No," I said.

"Well, then. Can you tell me a story?" she said. "I love stories."

I had no story in mind, had never told a woman a story, not the way she talked about. But my aim was definitely to please her, so I said, "Sure. What do you want it to be about? Should it be a funny story or a dirty story or what?"

"Whatever you like," she said seemingly agreeable to anything.

"Well, I don't have any stories in my head, but I'll think of one as I go along," I said. "OK. There was this guy who met this woman. He was the kind of guy who loved women, who had a lust for women, that was very strong. He noticed her beauty, but he was more captivated by the person she was. He couldn't believe how genuine and charming she was without trying. It was just her.

"Well, they exchanged numbers and planned to get together the next day. But they both lost the other's number and never talked. He hoped she'd call. She hoped he'd call. But neither did. Finally, after months and months, the guy got tired of dealing with women he did not want to be with, so he set out to find that woman who captured his imagination.

"Finally, he found her. He couldn't believe it. He was relieved that she was as glad to see him as he was to see her. They talked and talked, just like before and vowed to always keep in touch."

"What finally happened with them?" Alexis said.

That was a loaded question, a fastball right down the pike. I could have answered that in any way I wished to make her feel good. Instead, I went with what I truly believed.

"They grew as friends and lovers. He felt like he needed her in his life, something he never felt with a woman. He could depend on her for anything. She needed him in her life. He comforted her, made her feel secure. He was honest with her, and she appreciated that. And he became really good friends with her son."

For a moment, Alexis did not say anything. Finally, she said, "Julian, do you believe that's what will happen with us, or were you just filling out the story?"

"I think with us it can be just like that, or better," I said. "That was a story from the heart."

She did not respond. I was on my left side, with her on her left side up against me on the couch. Alexis let out a sigh and softly lowered her head back on my shoulder. I kissed the top of her head.

"Julian," she said. I waited for her to say something, but she paused a few seconds. "Thanks for finding me."

"You have to know it was my pleasure. Truly my pleasure."

We did not talk again until we awoke about five hours later. The entire left side of my body seemed numb. I had awakened a few times during the time we lay there and I wanted to move, but I would not, for fear of breaking her sleep. Because I was so tired, from the long day and the alcohol, I just went back to sleep.

Finally, we struggled off the couch. Alexis insisted that I stay for breakfast, and who was I to argue? I wanted every minute I could have with her.

She gave me a face cloth and a toothbrush—the tools I needed to be refreshed for a new day—and after she took a shower, I went to work on myself. I was greeted, after leaving the bathroom, to a table of bacon, eggs, grits, sausage, toast, and orange juice. How she whipped that together so quickly surprised me.

"So you're a Renaissance woman, huh?" I said.

"I try," she said.

We ate and talked and laughed, just as we had before. It was difficult to impress me, but Alexis could do so without trying. She teased her hair, but did not put any heat on it. She had on lipstick—a goldish color—but no makeup. She wore a button-up blue blouse and a pair of loose fitting prewashed jeans. Remarkably, she was elegant.

I had to go to great lengths to not stare at her. Her skin was radiant. Her complexion was a little darker than caramel, yet it seemed to light up the room.

"Are you staring at me?" she said.

"I can't help it," I said. "I feel good when I look at you."

✳✳✳

Alexis

I smiled, but I did not respond. I got a little emotional, so began clearing the table—anything to keep busy. Julian offered to help me, but I refused. "You're company. Relax. I got it," I said.

Julian was observant, and he noticed that I was not myself. "What's wrong?" he said.

I did not want to reveal the *baggage* I carried for fear of running him away. But I wanted to be fair to him and to let him know what I had dealt with. So, I took a deep breath, and got it out.

"Well," I said, "I, uh, I was just thinking about my past. You make me feel good by the things you say, the way you look at me, just being here . . . I never thought I'd feel this good about a man."

"Thank you," he said. "I'm glad to hear that."

I sat back down at the table, across from Julian. I struggled with the words I needed to share.

"I told you I wanted to talk to you last night," I said. "I actually at one time thought I'd never deal with a man again. I really did, because my son's father took me through so much shit—excuse my language. But that's what it was."

It pained me to get into my past. Julian could tell, and he reached across the table and rubbed my hands, which were clasped together.

"Alexis," he said, "we don't have to talk about this."

"Yes, we do," I said sternly. "Julian, I like you. I really like you. And you need to know exactly who I am if you're going to be in my life. My past is part of my life because it helped make me who I am."

He could not argue with that.

"I was engaged to Alex's father," I went on. "His name is Butch. I thought I was in love with him, but it was really the idea of being in love that I was drawn to. Anyway, after we'd been dating for about a year and were engaged, he became incredibly jealous. I couldn't talk to another man, no matter how casual. Every man was staring at me, according to him—and I *wanted* them to stare at me, he said. It was so crazy.

"Finally, the baby came and he calmed down, for a while. After about a year, it started again. It was driving me crazy, so I finally said, 'Butch, would you please get off my case? Just leave me alone.' I had never really talked back to him. That drove him over the edge.

"Alex was in his play pen, playing. Butch came up to me with a crazed look in his eyes. He said, 'Don't you ever talk back to me. Ever.' I started to say something, and the next thing I knew I was on the floor. He had punched me right in the jaw.

"My lip was bleeding. I was dizzy. I didn't know what happened. He picked me up and grabbed me by my hair with both hands. I could barely see his face, even though he was about an inch away. He said, 'Didn't I tell you not to talk back to me? Didn't I? Let me tell you something else. If I ever see you talking with another man, you're going to be sorry. You hear me?'

"I was so scared. I nodded my head yes. He pushed me down on the bed."

I stopped then to compose myself. Tears streamed down my face. I got myself together and continued. "Then," I said, "right there in front of my baby, he . . . he raped me. I was screaming for him to get off, trying to fight him. But I was really weak and still groggy from that punch. I was crying. Alex was crying. When he finished, he said, 'Don't act like you didn't want it. I know you did.' Then he got up and left.

"I thought I was going to die right there. I knew I had to get away from that man. But he wouldn't let me."

Tears rolled down my face. I trembled. Julian handed me a napkin. I could tell he wanted to say something. "Are you all right?" he said softly.

I nodded my head yes, but I was not so sure. I blew my nose into the napkin and continued.

"I called the police on him I don't know how many times. He stalked me everywhere I went. Out of nowhere he'd just pop up. He put his hands on me at least three different times. One night, I was in bed sleeping. I'm a light sleeper, but I didn't hear anything. All of a sudden . . ."

The memory of that horror got to me, and I cried some more. Then I began to open my blouse, which I was sure confused Julian. I pulled my blouse back to reveal my left shoulder. Then I pulled it back farther to show the burn marks on the upper back of the shoulder.

"I was sleeping, and Butch broke in the apartment I was living in and burned my shoulder with an iron. Those are iron marks," I said. "I woke up and almost had a nervous breakdown. I was so scared I didn't even feel the burn. He said he was going to burn my face. I jumped on the other side of the bed, screaming.

"Butch didn't know my brother was staying with me because I didn't want to be alone. Before he could get to me, my brother came in and jumped on him. Butch somehow got away from Zack and ran."

"What?" Julian said. "I have heard of brothers lunching out and stalking women, but it was always somebody else's friend, not someone I knew. This is unbelievable. What happened to this guy?"

"Well," I said, "he was so crazy that he didn't even hide from the police. They went to his house, and they said he was sitting there, eating an apple and watching TV. He's been in jail for assault for two years. He's got about three more to do."

"Damn. I'm sorry to hear you had to go through something like that," Julian said. "That's crazy. So how long did it take for you to get over all that."

"Well, I'm not sure that I am over it," I admitted. "When I met you in L.A., that was only the third time that I had been out since he went to jail. It's been tough. I was literally afraid to deal with men for a long time. I finally got to the point where I could go out again. But these guys come up to you with all these games. It takes about five seconds to realize they are not real or that they have one thing in mind: sex.

"It gets so tiresome. I resigned myself to believe I'd be by myself for a long time. But then you approached me. I noticed you coming toward me probably before you noticed me. I liked your approach. You were, I don't know, just comfortable, confident. It was like you knew me before saying a word to me—or at least that's what I wanted to believe so I wanted to get to know you. I remember saying to myself, 'Hhmm. I wonder what's up with this guy? I need to find out.'"

Julian could not help but blush. "Yeah," he said, "well we were thinking the same thing. Now, we can really find out."

FORTY SIX:

Turning A New Leaf

Julian

"I have given my life to Christ," Larry told Greg and me on a conference call. "I know it's probably hard to believe, but I have. My first priority is to live the way God intended for me to live. And that's as a Christian."

It was such a shock that neither Greg nor I said anything. I had heard of such dramatic change in people, but I never even dreamed it could occur with Larry. He seemed so unlikely because it was so natural for him to live an unstructured, haphazard lifestyle devoid of Godly influence.

But I could tell in the prideful way that he spoke that it was real. God had taken over.

"L," I said, "congratulations. You have received the greatest gift there is. I'm happy for you."

"Yeah, me, too," G said. "It's the best thing that can happen to you. The best thing that can happen to anybody."

"That's exactly right," Larry said. "But one thing about me could never change. You are my boys. You're the first people I've told because that's how we are, how tight we are. That's not going to change. And don't change the way you deal with me or talk to me. I'm still the same person, in the sense that our relationship means a lot to me. We can't let that change because I'm living different from before."

"Cool," I said. "Just one thing. Don't join the choir because you can't sing worth a damn."

We all laughed, like always. In a way, I was jealous of Larry. He really had received the ultimate gift. At the same time, I wasn't envious because when I was young, my parents sent me to a holiness church where every five seconds it seemed someone got the Holy Ghost. And that scared me. People gyrating uncontrollably, falling

226

all over the place, screaming, speaking in tongues; it all frightened me to the point where I did not want any part of it.

I later learned it was wrong to be scared, but I was. And even though as an adult I knew more about God and how He entered and brightened lives, I still carried a part of that childhood fear with me when Larry was touched.

Since the three of us could talk about anything, I shared that with Larry and Greg. "I know the feeling," Larry said. "I had similar fears. But in this case, fear comes with ignorance. If you don't know, then you can hardly be comfortable. I didn't know, either. But I had been going to Bible study, which helped me understand."

"So what is it about you that's different?" Greg asked.

"First of all, I feel so at peace with myself," Larry explained. "I feel like no matter what, I know that I am protected by God. He loves His children and provides for them. All that's required of us is to worship Him, to uplift His name. I do that now, and I can't even describe how much more joyful and peaceful I feel inside.

"And as a Christian, I don't drink anymore; I can't poison my body. I don't use profanity. I get joy out of reading the Bible and praying. It's a real miracle. It's a blessing. I spend my days focusing on God and praising Him because He has saved my life."

"So what about women and sex?" Greg said. "What about Renee? When you met her, you talked about how sexy she was."

"Renee is born-again also, so we both understand that premarital sex is not a possibility," Larry said. "I can sense you guys' eyes bugging out. But it's true. Christians do not have sex before marriage. We're all weak to the flesh. I know that. While I've changed my ways and made a commitment to God, I have not lost my senses. Renee is very sexy. But there are ways to be intimate with her without being INTIMATE. That's what we'll explore.

"But you know what: I love her. I love her for the woman she is and, most definitely, for pointing me to Christ. I'll always owe her for that. She changed my life. So, as I grow closer to God and His Son, I'll grow closer to Renee. I feel like everything that happened that led me to her—which really means that accident out here—was arranged by God."

***

Renee

Larry said the accident was God's will. I sat in his apartment, gushing, because I felt, in a small way, that I helped save Larry's life. That wasn't my intent. Not really. But I was so happy for him, so proud that he opened his heart.

I already had fallen for him because he made me feel like a woman. But in the back of my mind, I wondered if he'd be able to deal with my no-sex terms. I wasn't blind. He had a way with women, and I was sure he was active sexually before he met me. Very active. But after he got "saved," I did not have any more of those concerns.

"You do not know how happy I am for you," I said to Larry. "I mean, I know how you feel right now—like a different person. It's a great feeling."

"You know what else is a great feeling?" Larry said. "Having you in my life, knowing that we're spiritually linked. I feel close to you. Thank you for taking me to that first Bible study class. That's where it all began. If you were an average woman, we would have gone to the movies or poisoned our bodies with liquor or something else we probably should not have been doing.

"Instead, you stayed true to yourself. You did God's work, bringing someone who needed spiritual uplifting to church. That's how it all began for me."

"Well, really, Larry, it would not have begun if you were not so persistent at the grocery store," I said. "You have a certain charm about you that I really like. And something just told me that you'd enjoy the Bible study. I'd never done that before. But it was something about the way you think that made me bring you."

In the many weeks after we met, Larry was as gentlemanly a man as I'd ever been around. He did not make any advances toward me. We'd usually greet and depart with a hug, but that was it.

So, I'm sure he found it curious that I slid up under him on the couch. "Larry," I said, "Can I kiss you?" It was quite forward for me, but it got to the point where I wasn't sure if he would ever touch me.

"If you promise to keep doing it, every day." he said.

I loved that answer. "I promise."

And so, we kissed. Next thing I knew we were caressing each other's bodies. It got hot and heavy, with no cool-down in sight. Finally, I pulled out the fire hose. I had not been that excited by a man in who knows how long.

"I think it's time for me to go," I said, wiping my face.

"Yeah, you're right," Larry said. "But I want to ask you something. Will you take a trip with me?"

"Where?"

"Does it matter?" Larry said.

"No, not really," I said, and it didn't. "I was just asking out of curiosity. I mean, I would like to know where I'd be going."

"That's reasonable," Larry said. "I don't know. Santa Barbara. San Diego. San Francisco. Napa Valley. I don't know. I'd just like to go somewhere with you outside L.A."

"I have some time off coming up," I said. "All of those places sound great to me. I'll let you pick one."

It really didn't matter to me. I hadn't been out of California my whole life. Not even to Las Vegas. I told Larry that, and he ended up picking Miami for our trip. I was so excited I didn't know what to do.

Larry had a friend who moved there and worked at an exclusive hotel in Coconut Grove. So, he got a "hookup" on a lavish room. He would not give me the details of the room. He wanted it to be a surprise. But he did say that his buddy came through with a reasonable rate that we could afford.

I was thrilled with the idea of flying cross-country. It was a long flight, but I didn't mind one bit. Larry slept a lot, but I was too excited to sleep. I looked out the window, read some magazines, and even walked a little on the plane.

When we got to the hotel room, I was relieved to see that Larry had arranged for two beds. That showed respect.

The room was just beautiful. There was a baby grand piano off to the left side. I had never SEEN a baby grand piano in person. "Look at that," I said. "I can't believe it."

"Check out the bathroom and the patio with the jacuzzi," Larry said. "This is serious."

It was nearly 7 p.m., so we decided to find a place for dinner. "Let's go to South Beach," I said. "I've read and heard a lot about it."

And so, we got directions from the concierge, dropped the top on the Sebring we rented and drove to South Beach. It was a warm evening, in the mid-60s, perfect for eating in a sidewalk cafe.

We ate a great meal at A Fish Called Avalon, watched the people go by, and soaked up the feeling of true affection for one another. It was a relief for both of us to be on vacation, to not have to worry about what time to wake up or the phone ringing or ANYTHING.

"See," Larry said, extending his arms at the table, "this is why I need to be rich—materially, in addition to being rich spiritually. I enjoy just doing nothing so much."

***

Larry

When we finished eating, we walked along the strip and then crossed over to the beach. We took off our shoes and walked in the sand. All the while, I held Renee's hand, something I'd never willingly done before. There were times when women grabbed my hand, but I always felt uncomfortable. In this case, I WANTED to hold Renee's hand.

After about fifteen minutes, we plopped down on the beach and watched the moonlight glisten off the Atlantic Ocean. It was storybook.

"Larry," Renee said, "this is so nice. We're so blessed."

"I know," I said. "I can't think of another time when I've felt so good, mentally, physically, and definitely spiritually. I look back on my life, and I know God had a plan for me that I was not even aware of. There were times before I moved to L.A. where I was just surviving. Then I got to L.A. and was caught up in that whole party scene."

I shook my head. "I guess I had to go through all that to get where I am," I said.

"Well, where were you before? I mean, you weren't unhappy, were you?" Renee said.

"I didn't know enough to know if I was happy or not," I said. "I couldn't see anything then, really. So, in a short time, I've come a long way. Listen Renee, we held hands walking along the beach. I never, ever thought I'd do that. It just was not me.

"The idea of actually caring and being really affectionate with a woman was something I did not do. Let me tell you, I loved to be around women, but I resented them, too. I never allowed myself to get close to one. I tried to, I think, but it just didn't happen. And I'm thinking that my mother had something to do with that."

I had only told Greg and Julian about my mother, but Renee had graduated to that status. I had to unload my *baggage*.

"When I was young," I explained, "about four, my mother just up and left the family and moved to New York, to go to nursing school or something. She had these career plans, and she went for it.

"It was crazy. I loved her, was attached to her. Even at that age I felt connected to her. I mean, I can still remember the feeling of when I realized she was gone and wasn't coming back anytime soon. It wasn't until 12 years later that she came back. My father raised me and my brothers. I love my mother, don't get me wrong. But I think that experience affected me in the way I dealt with women. It was like I believed they would leave one day, too. I didn't trust women."

Renee grabbed my hand and spoke as passionately as she ever had to me. "Listen, honey," she said. "I would NEVER leave you. As you've put your faith in God, you can put in me, too. You give me credit for changing your life, but guess what: You've changed mine, too. You've changed my whole outlook on men—even before you were born-again. I don't know if you've ever felt secure, like no one could harm you. That's how you make me feel. I feel like you're my protector. I feel like you're my friend, my very, very special friend who I hold close to my heart. I feel like you're the only person in this world who I can talk to about anything. All of these feelings are new to me, but I love feeling this way. So, I'm not going anywhere. However you felt about other women, leave that where it is—in the past. I'm here, God willing, always."

All I could do after those words was hug her.

FORTY SEVEN:

Miami Nice

Larry

When we returned to the hotel, I found that the concierge did as I'd asked: A beautiful floral arrangement was left on the coffee table with a note attached.

"Where did those come from?" Renee asked

"I don't know," I said, holding back a smile. "But it looks like there's a card."

Renee picked up the card and then sniffed the flowers. There were daffodils and lilacs, violets and carnations—her favorites. That made her figure they had to be there by my doing more so than compliments of the hotel.

"You sure you don't know anything about this?" she said, sounding suspicious.

"I'm going to take a quick shower," I said, this time unable to suppress a smile. "I'll be back shortly."

Renee sat in the single chair near the sliding glass door and opened the card. I grabbed a bag and went into the bathroom as she began to read it. It read:

"I see why these are your favorite flowers. They brighten a room—just like you do. Truly, Larry."

***

Renee

I sat back and took a deep breath. I smiled to myself and recited a short prayer. "Thank you, Lord, for Larry. I know that all things come through You. I understand that relationships are challenging, but I'm committed to making sure our relationship with You gets stronger, which I know will make us stronger as a couple. In the precious name of Jesus, I pray. Amen."

I opened my eyes and consumed the room. I was awestruck by it. The room was beautiful, with the baby grand piano set off to the left. There was an entertainment center with a CD player, television, and VCR. On the far wall was a bar with a mirrored background. To the right of the entranceway sat a cherry dining room table with an elaborate chandelier hanging over it.

I thought to myself: "This is so nice, I can't believe it."

I heard Larry turn the water off in the shower, so I went to my suitcase and contemplated what to wear to bed. It was the first night we would spend together, and I felt more awkward than nervous.

I brought along some Victoria's Secret items, but I was kind of afraid of actually putting on something slinky. Then I said aloud: "What the heck?" I grabbed a long white gown that was elegant and not too revealing.

A few moments later, Larry came out of the bathroom, wearing a black silk robe and slippers. I couldn't help it; I wondered if he had on anything under it.

"How do you like the flowers?" Larry asked.

"They're beautiful. Thank you," I said. "And the card was very nice, too. You're something else."

We embraced and Larry kissed me on my face. I kissed him on his lips. We stood there in the middle of the room looking into each other's eyes, without blinking, as if we were having a contest.

After about fifteen seconds, we kissed again.

∗∗∗

Larry

Then I let out the words I never expected I'd be moved to say to a woman. "I love you, Renee."

I had told Julian and Greg how I felt about Renee, but I'm not sure they took me seriously. I didn't mean to even tell Renee at that moment, but my emotions took over.

That new me wanted everything to be just right when I did anything concerning her, even the little things. Like, when I decided to give her a key to my apartment, instead of just handing it to her, I put it in a small white box with a note inside that read: "You hold the key to my heart. You should have this one, too."

So, on something like my first time ever telling a woman I loved her, I wanted it to be in the ideal setting. I'd actually planned to tell her a little later, while we took in the night air on the patio. But she was there in my arms, and I just got weak. I could not hold back.

"Oh, Larry," Renee said. "I know you've never told a woman that, so you don't know how much that means to me. I love you, too, Larry."

Tears welled in her eyes. "I've loved you for what feels like a long time, even though we've only known each other briefly," she added. "But I couldn't tell you because I didn't really know for sure how you felt. You made me feel like you loved me, but I was scared because it would have killed me to tell you that I love you and for you to not feel the same way. So I just went on, hoping that one day it'd happen. And it did."

I used my fingers to brush away the tears that streamed down Renee's face. "I do love you," I said. "It feels good to say it. And you know what: It hit me as suddenly as God hit me on that Sunday. We were at your place, playing Scrabble. It was your turn to go, and you were moving the letters around to find a word. I sat there, and I stared at you. And it seemed my heart just opened up. Then it seemed like you could sense I was looking at you because you looked up at me and gave me a look like, 'Chill out.' You thought I was trying to pressure you to hurry up so I could get my turn, but it wasn't that. I was just taken by you. It was then that I felt for the first time ever that I loved a woman. I was in love with you from that moment on."

"Do you remember what word I put down when I finally did go?" Renee said.

"Yep. It was l-o-v-e," I said. "And when I looked down and saw that, it was just confirmation for me."

We embraced. "I'm going to take a quick shower, now," Renee said. "Don't go anywhere."

I watched her as she walked to the bathroom. Then I folded my arms and waited. Suddenly, I heard what I expected. "Oh, my goodness," Renee yelled.

After taking my shower, I set up a relaxing bath for Renee. I cleaned the tub and then ran it full of hot water and bubbles. I pulled two scented candles from my gym bag and lit them, placing one on each end of the tub. I placed a small tape recorder on the vanity with a sticker on it that said, "Play me."

Renee stood in the doorway of the bathroom, shocked. I came up and hugged her from behind. "I hope you don't mind me arranging this," I said. "But it's our first night together, and I want you to be totally relaxed. It's a special night. You're a special woman. So go ahead, enjoy it. Soak as long as you want. I'll be right out here."

She turned around to look into my eyes. "You make me feel so special. Thank you." Then she hugged me again, tightly. "We can't have sex, but I'd still like to romance you," I said.

"By all means," Renee said. "Romance me."

She played the tape—the Clark Sisters gospel recordings, a Renee favorite. As she bathed, I went into my suitcase and pulled out a bottle of sparkling apple cider. I raced to the vending area and filled a bucket with ice and chilled the beverage. I pulled out a pair of wineglasses and two more candles.

When I heard Renee letting out the water in the tub after about thirty minutes, I placed the candles on either side of the piano, lit them, and turned off all the lights. Then I positioned myself at the piano, waiting for Renee to enter the room.

She spoiled my plan somewhat by making a grand entrance from the bathroom in a smooth, sexy gown. I was thrown because I could see her hardened nipples. I did not expect that. But Renee was surprised, too, at the ambiance I created. Still, she slowly, seductively walked over to me, her hands running up and down either side of her body.

I got up from the piano and allowed Renee to waltz all the way into my arms. She whispered into my ear as I embraced her: "That bath was wonderful. I feel so good, so relaxed. Thank you."

She then reached down and pulled the string on my robe, revealing my bare chest and a pair of silk boxers. "You look nice," she said.

"Not as nice as you," I quickly responded. "Sit right here. Why don't you pour us some cider. I have one more surprise for you."

I sat down next to her on the piano bench. I then took a deep breath and began playing the piano. Renee had no idea that my father forced me to take piano lessons for seven years starting at age ten. I could not play ball on Saturday's until I finished my early-morning piano lesson. Since I had to take the lessons, I begged that they be in the morning so that I could prevent my friends from learning about them. I looked at playing the piano as stuff for girls then. But when I started putting the trip together and learned we'd have a piano in the room, I decided I'd sharpen my skills and play for Renee.

As I played, I could sense Renee's amazement. I hadn't told her about my ability with the ivory keys. I played a few classical songs that I remembered, although I could not remember the names. Then I played Stevie Wonder's "Ribbon In The Sky."

When I got to the part in the song that said, "We can't lose, with

God on our side . . ." Renee put her arm around my shoulders and sang the words.

"That was beautiful," she said when I finished. "You didn't tell me you could play the piano. I've never had anyone play anything for me."

"I've never WANTED to play for anyone," I said. "I really didn't want to learn how to play at all. My father made me—and my brothers. But I'm grateful that he did now. I practiced a little at church in the last week or so, just so I wouldn't embarrass myself trying to play for you. But I'm still rusty. I hadn't played in years."

"It was great," she said. "That was so nice. I just don't know what I'm going to do with you. What were the names of the first two songs you played?"

"You know, I don't know," Larry answered. "I just remembered them from my lessons. One of them is by a guy named Richard Strauss. They're classical songs. I remember being excited about learning them because they were very deliberate, very slow, and romantic. I played them so much that I memorized them."

"Now I'll never forget them," Renee said.

I played around on the piano for several more minutes. Finally, we decided it was time for the wonderful, but long day to end.

So, we got on our knees and prayed. When we were done, I invited Renee to my bed. Not for what the old Larry would want, but rather so I could read to Renee from the Bible.

"What are you going to read?" she said.

"Songs of Solomon," I said. "It's a love story."

I began at chapter one, verse one: "Let him kiss me with the kisses of his lips, for his love is better than wine."

Renee stopped me right there and kissed me. "I'm going to let you finish, but I just want to say one thing," she said. "I really do not know if I've ever had a better day in my life. My first time out of California, a beautiful room in Miami, dinner at a sidewalk cafe, a walk on the beach, flowers, the man I love telling me he loves me, a soothing bubble bath, songs played for me on the piano. And now this. This has been unbelievable.

"But I've got a question for you. Do you mind if I sleep in your bed tonight—with you? I want to be close to you. We know our limitations. It would kill me to sleep over there knowing I could lay on your chest."

I smiled, but did not answer. I just put my arm around Renee and gently pushed her head down on my chest. Then I continued to read.

FORTY EIGHT:

Boat Load of Fun

Greg

The passengers on the Spirit of Chicago came from many walks of life. There were African-Americans, Italians, Croatians, Germans, Irish, Koreans, Chinese, Nigerians, Ghanaians, Brazilians, Indians, Antiguans, Trinidadians, Jamaicans, you name it. There were young and old, and in-between. It was the kind of crowd that Brianna enjoyed. She loved black people, made sure she bought a home in an all-black neighborhood and frequented black-owned businesses. But she often talked about the importance of being diverse and knowing and meshing with other cultures.

I was less into such mingling; I didn't think it was NECESSARY. I thought it was good if it occurred, but I wasn't pressed about it. But even I could admit that the atmosphere on the ship was refreshing. It was good to see the many races enjoying the same space with no obvious hostility in the air. And for Chicago, that was rare, divided as that city is.

At the table next to me and Brianna was an Italian couple celebrating their fifth wedding anniversary. John and Mary Joe Raffini introduced themselves when Brianna caught Mary Joe staring at her.

Finally, Brianna just smiled at Mary Joe, who awkwardly apologized and then explained herself. "I'm sorry, but I was just admiring your dress. It's beautiful."

"Oh, thank you," Brianna said, blushing. "Actually, my friend, Gregory, picked it out for me for my birthday."

Then the four of us shook hands and exchanged pleasantries.

"That's great," Mary Joe said. "I've been married five years and this guy hasn't bought me a piece of clothing."

"Oh, so you don't count lingerie, huh?" John chimed in.

"No, I don't," she said. "That's more for you than for me."

And we all laughed.

"Gregory—it's Gregory, right?" Mary Joe said to me. "I'm very impressed. You have good taste. But did Brianna say 'friend?' I noticed she is not wearing a ring, and you guys look like more than just 'friends.' Isn't marriage in the offing?"

"No," Brianna said. "And we're not going to go there, are we, Gregory?"

"No need to," I said.

"I asked because I tried to get John to take me on this ship since before we were married. So it's taken me about six years to finally get here," Mary Joe said. "Girl, if you can get a man to buy you a dress AND take you here and not be married, you're good."

"Why can't it be that he's good?" John said. "Spare me your pro-woman stance on at least one issue."

"Thanks, John," I jumped in. "I agree."

"Yeah, you would," Brianna said. "Mary Joe, I don't know, to be honest. I'll give him credit because he has been very sweet—recently, anyway. But it's hard to say if it's me or him."

"I can answer that," I said. "It's you." Then I looked at the Raffinis and said, "It's her. She's inspired me."

"When are you going to be that sweet?" Mary Joe said playfully to John.

"Wait till we get home," he shot back with a grin that conveyed his intent.

Brianna and I considered that our cue to let them get into their own little nasty world. But white folks being white folks, John and Mary Joe continued to share their world with us, telling us all kinds of personal information that black folks would not dare share with perfect strangers.

By the time we finished eating dinner, we knew how many times John and Mary Joe slept together in a week, Mary Joe's breast size, John's favorite sex position, and that they did it on an airplane and in her mother's bed. And this couple did not have alcohol to fall back on as an inducement to such running of the mouth; they did not indulge.

Brianna and I nudged each other under the table as the personal information continued to flow. When they finally paused, I seized the moment. "Hey, excuse us for a while," I said. "I'm going to take the birthday girl to the dance floor."

And so, Brianna and I got up and slow-danced to Prince's—oh yeah, I mean the Artist's—1980s classic "Adore."

I felt great. That close to me was where she belonged.

"Promise me something," I said into Brianna's ear.

"What?"

"Promise me five years from now we won't be telling our business to strangers," I said.

"Aww, they were all right. They were a nice couple," she said. "They were just having a good time."

"Yeah, I guess so," I said. "Let's forget about them and get back to us . . . It's good to have you back in my arms. It's good to have you back in my life, period."

"Who said I was back?" Brianna said casually but with an undertone of bite.

I hoped she was kidding, but it didn't sound like it. Throughout the night it seemed that Brianna was fighting against herself. Her mind versus her heart.

"What?" I said. "What?"

"Well, I think I have a say if I'm back in your life, you know?" Brianna said.

I stopped dancing. "Are you serious?" I said.

"Yes I am, Gregory," she responded. "These last few days have been good, very good, but it's hard for me to just let go of what happened and throw myself right back into the same old stuff."

"The same old stuff?" I said. I stared at Brianna shaking my head. I felt desperate, like I was losing her. I grabbed her hand and led her to the ship's deck.

I took off my jacket and placed it around her shoulders. There was the breathtaking view of the lit-up Chicago skyline from Lake Michigan. It was a mild winter night for Chicago, about 35 degrees. There were a few other couples outside taking advantage of the crisp air and romantic scene. "I know it's a little cold out here, but I wanted to talk to you some place where it wasn't so loud," I said.

"I want you to understand something," I went on. "Maybe I spoke too soon in there. Maybe I'm just rushing things a little bit. But it's only because I love you. I've been without you for the last four months, and I learned a lot about myself during that time because I spent more time by myself than I probably ever have.

"And one of the things I learned is that I'm not a needy person. I don't need to be out at the club and I don't need to have someone push me to do my job, and beyond Julian and Larry, I don't need so-called friends to call me all the time or to get with all the time. I'm independent, almost to a fault.

"But I do need YOU. I know you're hesitant to trust me, to believe in me. And that's cool. I'm not even sweating that. Whatever hoops you want me to jump through or hurdles to clear, I will because it's important for me that you feel comfortable with me and trust and believe in me. I need that."

Brianna started to say something, but I stopped her.

"Just a second," I blurted. "I said all that and I mean it, but if you don't have an open mind about me earning my way back to where I SHOULD be, then I can't do it. If you've already decided that you'll never feel the same as you did before, then there's no need for me to go on, really."

"No, Gregory, I do have an open mind," Brianna said. "If I didn't, do you think I'd be here? It's just that no matter what you say, I don't understand why we had to get to that point for you to get to this point. I talked to my mother about it, and she said that some people don't realize the obvious. It takes something to happen for them to see what's right—and what's right there in front of them. And sometimes they don't ever see it.

"But whatever caution or hesitancy I have, it's just me," she went on. "It's not you; you've been so nice, made me feel like you really love me. I knew it before, but I didn't always feel that way. Still, all the time we were apart, I never stopped loving you. I have to admit that. I couldn't if I wanted to. I was angry with you and disappointed, but my heart always was open to you. When you sent me that picture, I felt like I willed it to happen. I really did."

My heart started pounding faster and faster. I hugged Brianna. I noticed her nose was cold and I rubbed mine on hers.

"This is nice and pretty out here, but I think we should go back inside," she said. "It's cold."

So we went inside, to the bar, where I ordered a vodka martini for me and a rum runner for Brianna. When the drinks were made, I paid for them and offered a toast. "To a wonderful night. Happy birthday."

We sipped on the drinks and watched the flow of people. One of my favorite pastimes was "joning" on someone, anyone. So, every so often I'd whisper something funny into Brianna's ear about something someone wore or did.

"You're bad," she said. "Stop talking about people."

I excused myself and went to the bathroom. "Don't move," I said to Brianna.

In the bathroom, I ran into John as we both washed our hands.

"I noticed your wife had a beautiful ring," I said to him. "I plan to go ring shopping in the near future."

"When you do, I've got the place for you to go," John said. "My father has a jewelry store in the Diamond District. Great stuff. Here, here's a card. I run the place for him when he takes off every three months to gamble in Vegas or Atlantic City. He usually loses about $10,000, but I think he just goes for the excitement or to break up the monotony. But when you're ready to shop, definitely come see us. We'll take care of you."

John left me standing in front of the mirror, staring at the business card. I thought to myself: White folks always have something right there for them. His father has a business for him whenever he wants it. He blows ten grand to break up the monotony of work, and he probably writes it off anyway.

I occasionally would mention leaving behind a legacy for my future kids, a business they could assume. That was a driving force for my opening a bookstore. Many people would get motivated by driving through a palatial neighborhood or checking out expensive cars or dreaming about exotic trips. Not me.

What motivated me was talking to people who already had the loot. Once, we went to a Lakers game in L.A. and worked our way into the Forum Club at halftime. I somehow got into a conversation with Jerry Buss, the Lakers' owner. It was only about two minutes, but when Buss excused himself, I was geeked. I wanted to be in his position, not necessarily owning a professional sports franchise—but hey, you never know. John Raffini was nothing in the league of the owner of the Lakers, but he still had a similar effect on me.

When I returned from the bathroom, I paused to get a look at Brianna from a distance. She was lovely. I decided then that I'd initiate a game we played from time to time. We called it "Strangers." In this game, one of us would initiate a conversation as if we were meeting each other for the first time.

It usually began with one of us pursuing the other, who played hard to get.

"How are you, miss?" I said to Brianna to get things started. "Mind if I join you?"

She immediately picked up on where I was going. "It's a free country. You can stand where you want," she said dryly.

"I've been checking you out and I noticed that you're here alone," I said. "I am, too. Why don't we spend the rest of the evening together?"

"What, do I look like I need to be picked up?" she mocked.

"It's not like that at all," I said. "It's just that I'm interested in getting to know you. What's your name?"

"Do we have to go there? I mean, what's the point?" she said, suppressing laughter.

"Oh, I see. You're out here alone because you're pissed off with some man," I said. "It's easy to see the animosity. What did he do? Stand you up? Lie to you about something? Whatever he did, you can't let that spoil your evening."

"What's your deal? There are a lot of women here alone. Why me?" Brianna said.

"Forgive me for being blunt, but I like the way your dress is clinging to your breasts," I said, smiling. "That's a great dress, by the way. Looks very expensive, classy. You paid a lot of money for that. But you have good taste. You did buy it, didn't you?"

"No I didn't, as a matter of fact. This sucker I once knew bought it for me," she said. "But what's this about my breasts? Why are you looking at them? I'm offended."

"Oh, don't be," I said. "I'd rather jump into Lake Michigan than offend you. It was truly meant as a compliment. Listen, I have a suite at the Palmer House. How about when we dock you let me lick those fat nipples of yours?"

"You're crass. And you probably don't even know where the Palmer House is," Brianna said.

"If I do, will you come with me?" I countered.

"We'll see," Brianna said.

"I think you want to kiss me," I said. "Go ahead, you can do it."

Brianna could not hold back her laughter. "You're so crazy," she said. "You'll try to get a kiss any way you can."

"Can't blame me for that," I said. "Maybe I won't have to plot or ask for one later tonight. Maybe you'll just smother me in them."

"Why? What's happening later?" she said raising her eyebrows suspiciously.

"A lot," I answered. "A lot."

FORTY NINE:

Sex Machine

Greg

After the boat docked, we made our way to the Palmer House. "You were serious about the hotel?" Brianna said.

I just smiled.

"So, you were confident that it would be all right with me, huh?" she said. "Confidence can be very attractive at times—and embarrassing at others."

I did not answer. I WAS confident, almost cocky. I simply released her seat belt as the valet opened her door. "Be careful getting out," I said. "We're on the 19th floor. It has a nice view. You'll like it."

When we got to room 1906, I had trouble getting the door open with the card key. "Hurry up, Gregory. I've got to go to the bathroom," Brianna said.

I finally got the door open, and Brianna practically sprinted to the bathroom which was to the left of the entranceway. While she did her business, I called room service and ordered another martini for me and a rum runner for her.

Then I laid out the gold teddy I bought for her on the bed. When Brianna came out of the bathroom, she surveyed the room. The living area was adorned with antique-like furniture, a 19-inch television in an armoire, and large pictures depicting country-side roads and rolling hills.

To the left, behind tall french doors, was the bedroom with another bathroom off to the right. I pulled back the curtains to display a majestic view of the city. Brianna noticed it all, but locked in on the teddy on the bed. "Is that for me?" she asked rhetorically.

"It's not for me," I answered.

Brianna picked up the teddy and held it against her body. "Oh, this is beautiful, Gregory. Thank you," she said. "You sure this isn't for you? Remember: John said he buys lingerie more for himself than Mary Joe."

"No," I said. "Mary Joe said that, not John. There's a big difference. In my case, it's for both of us. It'll feel good up against your body, and I'll get a great pleasure out of seeing you in it."

"You must want me to wear this tonight since I don't have any clothes with me," she said. I slowly nodded my head as I gave her a suggestive look.

"Well, I'm going to take a quick shower," she said.

"I'm going to do the same in the other bathroom," I said.

I hurried in and out of the shower before her because I had a few other things to set up for the rest of Brianna's night. I called it her night, but it was my night, too. Really, it was both of our night. And I had to make everything right.

After the shower, I slipped into a pair of silk boxers and a silk robe just as the doorbell rang. It was the drinks—right on time.

I found the "Quiet Storm" on the radio and climbed into bed with the drinks. I turned off all but one light near the bed. A few minutes later, Brianna emerged from the bathroom. She posed at the door, her hands on her hips in that gorgeous lingerie.

"You like?" she said seductively.

"I love," I answered.

She got onto the bed with me, and I passed her a drink. "Where did these come from?" she said.

"Magic," I answered. "One more toast. To my ace on her 31st birthday. I plan to spend all your other birthdays with you."

Brianna blushed, and we tapped glasses. We enjoyed the drinks and talked about old times and times to come. I contemplated for a second telling Brianna about Theresa. Then I came to my senses. What purpose would it have served for her to know I slept with someone when we were apart? None.

Sometimes the truth did no one any good. Sometimes the truth was better off as a lie, or at least untold. I had Brianna going, and an honest moment like that could have spoiled it all. Ultimately, I decided that she did not even want to know. Plus, what I did with Theresa did not matter at all.

And when Brianna said, "Gregory, I went out on a few dates when we weren't together," I didn't want to hear it.

"Don't tell me. Don't even want to know," I said.

"I've never seen you jealous," she said. "It's kind of cute. But you never did get jealous, did you? Why's that?"

"Because I was confident that you were a faithful woman," I answered. "And you never gave me reason to be jealous. Trust me, if there's a reason to be, I would be. The things that matter to me I'm very protective of."

"I matter?" Brianna said. Clearly she sought compliments, because that question was so academic. How could a man trying to win back a woman tell her she did not matter?

"Come on, now," I said. "That's rhetorical, right? I know I don't need to answer that. Right?"

"I guess not," she said.

"Good," I said. Then I downed my drink in one gulp, took it to the head.

"Aaah!" I said. "OK. I've got one more present for you."

I reached over Brianna to turn out the light, making sure that my lips brushed up against hers in the process. Then I turned to the other side of the bed and flicked the switch on the lamp.

The room turned a pale red. I had switched bulbs while Brianna showered.

"All right now," Brianna said.

"I'll be right back," I said. Then I disappeared into the darkness of the living room, closing the french doors behind me. I turned down the radio so Brianna could not hear it and searched for a hip-hop station.

When I found a station playing a series of Jay Z remixes, I turned up the volume and announced from the other side of the door: "Miss Brianna Banks, the Palmer House proudly presents for your exotic pleasure, Go-Go Greg!"

I then pushed open the French doors and came in dancing in my robe. Brianna blushed and put her hands over her face. "I don't believe you," she said. She had asked me many times to be an exotic dancer for her, but I always quickly refused.

"Believe it," I said as I worked my hands over my body, approaching the bed.

Suddenly, I hopped onto it. Brianna sat there with a huge grin on her face. "Take it off," she yelled. "Take it off."

And so, I ripped off my robe, revealing my bare chest, covered in baby oil, and silk boxers. Brianna screamed. I stood over her, gyrating to the music. Then I slowly slipped my boxers down. Brianna never blinked. I got them down to my ankles, revealing the pair of black bikini drawers Brianna bought for me the previous Valentine's

Day. I'd never worn them and told her that I never would.

She saw the bikinis and screamed some more as I waved the boxers over my head with one hand. Still dancing on the bed, I tossed the boxers aside and straddled Brianna, who was sitting up with her back against the headboard. I slowly danced toward her.

She reached out and started rubbing my legs which I also had smothered in baby oil. She could hardly believe what was happening. She took the last of her drink to the head and tried to set the glass on the night table, but missed. It landed on the floor.

I then jumped and turned around in midair. Now I faced the other way, my ass in Brianna's direct view. She screamed again. Then she reached up and rubbed my thighs and worked her way up to my ass. "Oh, Gregory, you know I love your butt," she said.

I bent over and gave it all to her. And she rubbed and rubbed, and then got up on her knees and reached around and caressed my dick. Almost as soon as she touched it, it grew in her hands. I missed her touch.

"Aww, you know I've missed Max," Brianna said, using her pet name for my dick. I asked her why she called it "Max" and she said because it gave her "maximum pleasure."

"And I can tell Max misses me, too," she said.

She then turned me around to face her and pulled down the bikinis. "Max" popped out like a jack-in-the-box. Brianna began stroking "him" as I put my palms on the ceiling for balance. The dancing was over. I didn't think either of us heard the music anymore. We made our own rhythm.

Brianna reclined on the bed and gently pulled me toward her by my throbbing wood. I held onto the headboard as she slowly licked the base of my Johnson, up and down and around. Then she worked her way up to the head, teasing it with her tongue for a moment before slowly covering much of it with her mouth.

She sucked and licked my manhood as if it were a Popsicle. She did it passionately, lovingly. Brianna enjoyed fellatio, took pride in pleasing me. I used to ask her why she did that so well, and she said, "Well, I want to please you and also my pride is such that I strive for the best in whatever I do." I loved that answer.

It had been so long since I had been so sexually pleased that I almost forgot how wonderful she was. I clutched the headboard tighter the more Brianna waxed "Max." When she finally stopped, after about five minutes ('cause I couldn't take no more, and she could sense Mt. Max getting ready to erupt) she whispered to me: "I hope you have a condom."

"I'd shoot myself if I didn't," I said.

I retrieved one from the bathroom and turned off the radio. "Baby, you don't know how good you made me feel," I said when I returned to the bed. "I love you."

"I love you," Brianna said.

I then began kissing her on her shoulders, over to her neck, and down to her breasts. I caressed her titties gently and licked and sucked each of them for several minutes. The sound of Brianna panting excited me. As much pleasure as she took in pleasing me, I took in pleasing her.

Still with a breast in my mouth, I reached under a pillow and pulled out a squeeze-bottle of honey. I raised up from Brianna and held the bottle high over her body. "You're just pulling out all the stops," Brianna said. "Where did that come from?"

"You deserve everything," I said.

Then I helped Brianna pull the teddy over her head. I was happy to see that she did not have on panties. "I miss looking at your body," I said. "I appreciate your body."

"Thank you," she said softly.

I let the honey drop onto Brianna, first on the right nipple and then across to the left and down her stomach to her naval and right down to the lips of her pussy. She moaned throughout the process.

The moaning grew as I slowly cleaned the honey off her body with my tongue. The honey was sweeter than normal coming off Brianna's soft, caramel skin. I started with the breasts and worked my way down her stomach and over her navel.

I made sure that I worked my tongue inside Brianna's navel, a point of pleasure for her. All that was left was the honey that rested on the lips of her plump vagina. I savored that most of all. I licked my lips and took a deep breath before going downtown.

I tantalized Brianna by showing her my pointed tongue, and then began kissing the inside of her thighs. Then I slowly, skillfully took on the honey. Brianna opened her legs wide, and I immediately slid my tongue deep into her hot, juicy tunnel. I worked it in and out and around her insides, and she swiveled her hips to my rhythm.

I placed my hands under her thighs and pushed her legs up in the air, allowing me to penetrate deeper with my tongue. Brianna enjoyed it all with her eyes closed. Every now and then she glanced down at the top of my head. Mostly she moaned in darkness, especially when I licked and softly sucked her clit. I know how to use my tongue as a feather which was as teasing as it was pleasing.

"Oh, Gregory, oh," Brianna managed to get out. "Baby, oh, baby."

Then she stopped talking and started gyrating. Her breathing got heavy. She sat up and grabbed my head. Finally, Brianna let out gasps and then screamed. She began to come and tried to push away from my tongue so she wouldn't. "Oh, stop, baby. OK, OK," she begged.

True, she eased up on me, but turnabout is not fair play. Her pleas made me go in for the kill. No way I was stopping then. I worked my tongue even harder. I was going to make her come so hard that she'd go from solid to liquid to gas. Having a woman melt as a result of giving her some "*good oral*" is the highest level most brothers could attain. I had taken her to the stratosphere.

I extended my tongue to its limits. I was sticking it out so far my forehead creased. She was mine, all mine now.

Can you imagine that you got brothers who don't believe in giving a woman head?

She pulled me up into her arms. She was shaking and breathing heavily—and unevenly. It got me kind of scared. "Baby, oh God. You're going to drive me crazy," she said totally exasperated in a voice that was totally unrecognizable. If the color didn't come back to her face soon, I would have dialed 911—for real.

I watched her closely, but I did not respond. Instead, I searched the bed with my right hand for the condom. Once I found it, I quickly opened it and got that jimmie on. The next feeling Brianna had was the hardness of "Max" inside her.

So, her panting and screaming started all over again. I talked over it. No doubt, a hard dick was a source of power to a man over a woman. It often led to out-and-out arrogance.

"Have you missed this dick?" I said as I stroked my girl.

"Oh, yes, Gregory, yes," Brianna said. "Give it to me, baby. Don't stop."

"Stop? Who's thinking about stopping?" I answered.

Brianna raised her legs high, and I maneuvered my arms inside them so that they were parallel to my body. I grabbed her by the ankles and spread her legs, all the while still inside her. Then I stroked her in rapid-fire succession—I jet-rocked her—a technique I knew Brianna liked.

She rocked her head from side to side as I thrust inside her. I got so into it that my dick slid out. Instead of putting it back in, though, I reached for Brianna's hand and pulled her up and off the bed and led her to the window.

I hugged her and kissed her on the neck and then turned her around. She leaned over and rested her hands on the windowsill as I inserted my rock-hard instrument from behind. I told Brianna, "Enjoy the view," and then began stroking her.

It was our favorite position. She bowed her head and pushed her body toward my thrusts. She wanted to feel my hardness as deep as she could take it. She was a soldier like that. I massaged her ass and occasionally smacked it as I went in and out of her.

I tried to enjoy the view, but it was difficult for me to take my eyes off my dick sliding in and out of my woman. After about ten minutes, I took "Max" out and sat down in a single chair near the window.

Brianna immediately mounted me and began to vigorously ride my dick. Later, I rose from the chair with her in my lap. She wrapped her legs around me, and I began to walk around the hotel room with my dick still inside her. I put her back up against a wall in the living room and delivered purposeful thrusts. Brianna put her nails into my back—an act of approval.

I carried her near a window and stroked her some more. The same thing up against the armoire and by the bathroom. Finally, our walk ended at the bed, where I slowly placed Brianna down on her back.

But I never came out of her. To come out would have only punished myself, she felt so good. Rather, I stayed in and made love to her in the missionary position. After five minutes on the bed, Brianna announced, "Oh, Gregory, I'm coming."

The very words excited me, and I stroked her harder. It also gave me the green light to come also. Excitedly, I told her, "Me, too!"

And so, we did, together. She gripped my neck tightly, and I pushed deeper and harder. When her juices flowed, Brianna repeated, "Oh baby, oh baby." All I could get out was, "Yeah baby, yeah baby."

We came, and collapsed in each other's arms. Our bodies were soaked in sweat. We were completely drained. And our hearts were full.

FIFTY:

It's In The Cards

Julian

I spent much of the afternoon telling Alexis about my life, my family, my job, my friends, my fears, my goals, my dreams. It all just came out. Something about her made my tongue loose.

She offered me her life story, and I listened as eagerly as humanly possible. I wanted to know everything about that woman, and, the more I learned, the more I liked. We grew up in totally different lifestyles—me in apartments in the city life of southeast Washington, D.C., her in rural South Carolina, on a farm.

This was a woman who milked cows as a child, who plucked headless chickens, who planted crops. The closest I came to any of that was catching tadpoles with a jar at a nearby creek. I would have run from a headless chicken.

Yet, while we were certainly different, we were very much alike in one fundamental way: Deep down, we needed someone special in our lives, but we were willing to be alone if it meant dealing with a bunch of drama.

"I know that's right," she said.

It was not until 4:30 that afternoon that I returned to James' house. And I really did not want to go then. Nothing against my cousin; he was my people. But he could not compete with Alexis.

"Damn boy, I thought you got kidnapped or something," he said when I showed up at his door. "You all right?"

"Hey, I'm great," I said. "I meant to call you, but it just didn't seem like a chance came up for me to do so. But I'm a tell you right now: This woman is the one. I can feel it. I've never felt it before with a woman. Now I know what people mean when they say you 'just know.' Like, you know how when you prepare a dish and you know before even tasting it that it's wonderful? That's how it is with

Alexis. I KNOW she's right for me."

I showered, called home to my mom's, and ate with James. We talked about the family and basketball and other stuff, but my mind was not really on anything but Alexis. We had planned to get together later that evening; she had committed to a friend's card party. She did not want to back out, couldn't back out, so she asked me to come along.

I would have accompanied her to a cotton-picking contest. She invited James, too, but he had a little honey from Charleston he had to go visit, so he passed. I was due to pick up Alexis at eight, and I wanted to take a short nap before heading her way.

But I pulled out a piece of paper first and wrote Alexis a letter. "Alexis," it began, *I'm writing this at 5:50 p.m., because I'm trying to sleep, and you're keeping my eyes open. And since you're with Alex, I decided I'd put pen to paper.*

By the time you read this, we would have returned from the card party. We would have spent time together around your friends, and more opinions of me would have been formulated by you. And that's a good thing. I believe we've met because of fate, that we were supposed to meet. So, here's what I think you went through during the party and how you feel now:

At some point during the evening, you looked at me and wondered where had I been all your life. You felt proud to attend the party with someone rather than go alone. You feel closer to me as you read this. When we were not together during the party, you could feel me looking at you, you could sense that I wanted to be near you. But you wondered if it was just you wanting to be near me.

The only uncomfortable moment came when you thought, if only for a second, that I'd be out of your life as quickly as I came into it this weekend. Then you realized that was not a possibility; you can feel how much I want to be with you.

In writing this, I'm not trying to come off as a psychic. I just want you to understand that I'm connected to you, and you are to me. I don't know how it happened so fast. But I know it's there, and I feel very good about it.

And one more thing: You can't believe how good I am at Spades.

It was weird, but I felt I could go to sleep after writing her. I felt at peace.

When I woke up, I felt refreshed. James left me a key and a note; he already had left for Charleston. I got myself together and picked up Alexis. Again, her presence was so elegant, so strong. She could be that way without even really trying. In this case, an above-the-knee blue silk skirt with a silk white blouse and navy suede pumps achieved the desired effect on me.

"As always, you look great," I said. "Being from here, I'd expect you to have on a pair of overalls and big plaid cotton shirt."

"Very funny," she said.

I wore a pair of taupe slacks, a cream shirt, and a taupe and cream blazer. I wasn't sure if I would be overdressed or not, but it was better than being underdressed. Plus, I knew I could just take off my jacket to be quite casual. On top of all that, I was in South Carolina. How could I go wrong?

"You look nice," Alexis said.

"Not as nice as you," I said. It was hard for me to not compliment Alexis Miller. Sometimes women needed to hear compliments. With her, I felt like I needed to GIVE her compliments. So weird.

When we got to the home of Paul and Lana Spence, three other couples were already there: Ralph and Karen, Kwame and Elizabeth, Randy and Flecia. All of them had gone to high school with Alexis. Later, a couple of guys came alone, and it was clear they already had been drinking.

Everyone knew everyone—except me. Alexis was good about checking on me throughout the evening, but she did not need to. I thrived on making myself comfortable in every situation, so I made my way around the room and chatted with most everyone.

I could see Alexis in the distance checking me out, watching how I maneuvered around her friends. I did the same with her. And when she offered me a drink, I insisted on "white lightening."

"You know about 'white lightening?' " Paul said.

"Oh, yeah," I said. "Got any?"

Before Paul could answer, Kwame pulled out a small bottle from his inside jacket pocket. "Get that man a cup," he said to Alexis. She obliged.

I called out to her as she walked away. I asked her to come close so I could whisper into her ear. "Young lady, you look great," I said. Then I produced the letter I had written and gave it to her. "Put this up. You can't read it now; I want you to read it later when we get to your house, all right?"

"What is it?" she said.

"It's something I wrote for you, but it won't make sense until later," I said.

"OK. I won't open it until later," she said. "But is it good? It's not a Dear John letter, is it?"

"You're not serious, are you? Of course, it's not. You'll enjoy it," I said.

She sighed heavily and placed her hand on my knee. Her touch was soft but firm. It made my heart skip.

"I think we're up next at the 'Spades' table," I said. "I hope you know how to play."

"I hope YOU know how to play," she said.

Sure enough, we spanked Ralph and Karen and then the two guys, all the while giving each other high-fives and knowing glances. We played off each other like we had been card partners for years. To me, it was another example of how in sync we were. We even both talked trash in similar fashion. It was great.

By the time we won the second game, I had downed two glasses of "white lightening," so I felt pretty good, had a nice buzz. It was almost midnight, and the two guys who came alone hung around with me and Alexis and Paul and Lana. It took me just a few moments to figure out that one of them anticipated Alexis would be there alone, and he'd try to push up.

Turned out that Lana had tried to hook up Alexis, not knowing that I'd popped up. She knew Alexis was a good woman and even felt sorry for her that she was alone. This guy, Kevin, peeped that I was with Alexis, but still wanted to try to get with her. He figured that since I lived in D.C., I'd be gone soon, and he'd have his shot.

I was aware of all that, but I made sure to give Alexis some space so Kevin could shoot his shot. I was not threatened by him, and I really wanted to see how Alexis would handle the situation.

So I leaned on the kitchen doorway and joked with Paul and Kevin's friend, as Alexis chatted with Lana in the living room. Kevin took it as his moment to seize, and so he pounced.

"Haven't seen you in a long time, Alexis," he began. "You look good. How are you?"

Lana got up and left them alone by the fireplace. "I'm fine," she said.

"You shouldn't be such a stranger," Kevin said. "You should let me take you out to dinner next week. I'd like to hang out with you."

Alexis smiled to herself. "Thanks Kevin, but I'm seeing someone—that gentleman right there," she said, pointing at me.

"Ah, come on. He lives in Washington," Kevin said. "You're not going to sit here waiting on him while he's up there doing whatever he wants."

Alexis was a sweet, polite woman, but I could see in her demeanor with her son that she'd blow up when pushed. Kevin pushed her.

"Whatever I do is my business, not yours, so don't tell me what I should do," she said, raising her voice a little. "You don't know him, and you don't know me well enough to say something like that. I think you should not worry about me."

Kevin wanted to respond, but before he could get a word out, Alexis was on her way toward me. I acted as if I did not hear the exchanged. She hugged me. "I'm glad you're here," she said.

"What's wrong?" I said.

"That guy was bothering me," Alexis answered. "But it's nothing."

Before I could respond, Kevin, eager to exact some sort of revenge on Alexis, came storming over. "What's your problem?" he said loudly to her.

I took over from there. "She doesn't have a problem; you do," I said. "And since you do, you deal with me, not her."

"You come down here from D.C.—big time professor and all that. So what, you think you're so big and bad?" he said.

"Nope, but neither are you," I said, glaring straight into his eyes. I was hardly a fighter, but I would not back down from anyone.

"So what you saying?" Kevin said.

"I'm saying you don't have any business over here. And if you feel you do, you have it with me. So, since it's with me, we can settle it right now, however you want to settle it."

I could see in his eyes that he was punked. He stood there a few seconds without saying anything. Finally his friend came to his rescue. "Come on, Kevin, it's not worth it, man. Let's just go," he said, pulling him away.

"I'll see you again—Professor," Kevin said to me on his way out the door.

"Yeah, I hope so," I said.

"Julian," Alexis said, clasping my arm, "I'm sorry."

Those were the first words she spoke to me during the confrontation. And that was the way it should have been. When I stepped into it, it was my deal then, not hers. It would have bothered me if she had jumped in saying something like, "No, Julian, it's all right. Let's not start something."

It was like the story Richard Pryor told on his album, "Bicentennial Nigger" from 1976. He said he took a woman to dinner at a Chinese restaurant in New York, and she complained that hair was in her food. So, he called over the waiter to complain. Then the woman jumped in, saying, "Oh, it's all right." Pryor responded:

"Shut up, bitch! If it's all right, why didn't you eat the shit?"

His point was: Once the man got involved, let him handle it. Alexis, however, let me handle the situation. Again, she impressed me without even trying.

"Sorry about that," Paul said. "Kevin's all right, he's probably a little drunk."

"No big deal," I said, and it wasn't. "As long as Alexis is fine, so am I."

I helped Paul take some trash out, which allowed Lana and Alexis time to talk. I returned in time to overhear something interesting.

"Girl, he's something else," Lana said. "I didn't know to the last minute that he was coming with you. Otherwise, I would have told Kevin you'd have a date."

"I know," Alexis said. "Lana, I really like him. I mean REALLY like him. And it's scary."

"Why?" she said.

"Because," Alexis said, "it's almost too good to be real."

FIFTY ONE:

So, Now What?

Julian

In the car after the party, Alexis said she wanted me to stay the night with her again; Alex was with his grandmother.

"Now how could I say no to that?" I said. "But we have to go to my cousin's house so I can pick up my toothbrush and something to sleep in and clothes for tomorrow."

While at James's house, Alexis found a photo album that featured pictures from what looked like my most recent family reunion, which was in Bristol, Virginia, and some flicks from our younger days.

When I came from the back with a bag of clothes, she was so deep into the photos that she did not notice I was even there. "What do you have there?" I said.

"Oh, just some pictures of you and I guess your family," she told me. "Come here. Tell me who all these people are."

I sat down beside her, and we went through the book, page by page. She wanted the identities of everyone in every picture. It was like she learned something about me through the pictures of others.

And the ones with me in them Alexis studied harder than the rest. "Look at that," she said. "You have nice legs, Julian."

When she got to the pictures of me as a child, she smiled. I was a skinny little guy with closely cut hair and an innocent look. And my eyes seemed too big for my head. The photos of me back then always made me feel a little awkward, but Alexis loved them.

"Ah, these are so cute," she said. "They look just like I would imagine you looking at seven years old. You know, you look like your mother. The same smile. And look at those eyes. Tell me this: Why is it that you smiled on your pictures when you were young and not so much when you got older?"

"I just don't like to smile too much on pictures," I said matter-offactly. "Why? I just don't like to see myself cheesing."

"I don't know why not. You have a nice smile."

"Anyway, you ready? Let's boogie."

When we got to Alexis' house, we sat down at the dining room table. The couch would have been more comfortable, but the table was where we seemed to do a lot of talking. I thought she had forgotten about the letter I'd written her because she did not mention it, but she had not. Not hardly.

"I'm going to open this now," she said. "But I'm scared."

"Why?"

"Good things never come in letters," Alexis said. "If you wanted to tell me something that I wanted to hear, you'd just tell me. People use letters to hide behind something or just for bad news. What are you hiding?"

"Maybe you should just open it," I said.

She did. I watched her eyes as she read. Alexis was cool, but I learned while in South Carolina that her eyes told a lot about how she felt. She began reading the letter with a strained look around her eyes, but that quickly changed to a softening and then a sort of relief and finally joy.

When she finished, she started reading it again immediately, her eyes expressing joy throughout. Finally, she spoke.

"You know what?" she said, "I feel like I could have written you this exact letter before going over there, too. I really do. I was glad to take you with me because I wanted you to be with me, but I also felt confident that I would learn some good things about you. And you're right: I did feel closer to you as I read this. And I did think that maybe you'd go back home and not come back. And I do feel so connected to you. This is just confirmation."

"And you know what the best part was?" I said. "When you told me in the car that you didn't know I could play Spades so well."

Alexis threw her head back in laughter, which made me laugh. Her laugh made me feel good.

"You are a trip," she said.

Without asking me, Alexis went into the kitchen and poured me a drink of "white lightening." "I'm going to take a quick shower," she said. "Be right back."

Before going to the bathroom, she put a couple of logs in the fireplace and got it going. I moved to the den and sipped on my drink and watched the fire. I then dozed off. When I awoke, Alexis was standing over me in a black long silk robe. It was open, revealing a slinky black top with thin straps and matching flute shorts.

It was the kind of vision a man would never get tired of awaking to. "Ah, suky, suky now," I said. That was the first thing that came to mind, so I just let it out.

Alexis blushed. "You look so nice," I said regaining my composure.

"Thank you," she said. "I'm going to make a drink. Want another?"

"Maybe when I come back," I said. "I'm going to take a shower, too."

In rushing to pack at my cousin's, I neglected to put in a t-shirt. All I had was a pair of cotton shorts and a pair of slippers. So, I entered the room bare-chested, which prompted Alexis to say, "Go 'head, boy."

I was sort of embarrassed, so I ignored her comment. Alexis sat on a comforter she had spread on the floor in front of the fireplace. There were pillows there, too. The room was warm from the fire, toasty.

I sat down next to her and immediately put my arm around her. She placed her hand around my waist. I kissed her face. I could smell the perfume she wore. It was the same fragrance from the first time I met her.

She ran her hand up my stomach and chest, which literally gave me chills despite the warmth of the room. I didn't think about anything. I just went with the flow. Alexis whispered to me: "Julian, I'm so glad you're here."

"Me, too," I said.

I kissed her lips. They were soft and inviting. I kissed them again. Then I slid my tongue into her mouth. We kissed and caressed each other until Alexis lay her head back on a pillow and I followed her down, never allowing my lips to part hers in the process.

No longer did I have chills. I was hot, in more ways than one. I whispered to Alexis: "Baby, you make me feel so good." Before she could say anything, I kissed her deeply again. I could feel her hands running up and down my back and then onto my ass.

When I finally allowed her to breathe, she said, "Julian, please don't take this wrong, but . . . I want you. Waiting probably would be the so-called right thing to do, but I don't feel that way with you. I feel like we need to seize every moment we get. It's like a miracle that we're even together. It's not like me to ordinarily be forward like this. Not at all. But this is no ordinary situation with us. I KNOW it's not."

I wanted her, and told her so. "All I can say is that it makes me feel good to make you feel special," I said. "And that'll never change."

Then, I got up. "Where are you going?" she said.

"I'll be right back in a few minutes," I said. "Trust me."

I went into the bathroom and grabbed the baby oil that rested on the vanity. I went through the family room on my way to the kitchen. "What are you doing?" Alexis said.

"Do you trust me?" I said. She answered affirmatively, and I said, "OK. Now, just give me two minutes, and I'll be right back."

In the kitchen, I found a container, poured oil into it, and placed it in the microwave. Alexis called out from the den: "What are you cooking?"

"I'll bring it in to you in a second," I said.

The oil nice and hot, I returned to Alexis's side. "This is for you," I said. "But to get it, you're going to have to do one thing—take off your clothes."

"Really?" she said, smiling. "OK."

I tried to not stare as she slowly, seductively stripped, but it was impossible not to. Her body was so smooth, so perfect. There was no indication that she'd had a baby, other than the bikini-cut from the Caesarian section. "You're beautiful," I said to her. "Now, just rest on your stomach, close your eyes, and enjoy."

I straddled her and leaned over and kissed her back and shoulders, even the burn mark, down to the small of her back. I tested the oil to make sure it was not too hot. Then I slowly allowed the oil to drip from the container onto her shoulders.

"Ahhh," she said softly. "Oh, that feels so good."

I slowly rubbed the oil over her shoulders and back. I could feel that she was tense, so I massaged those areas until they were loose. I poured more oil on her back and then over her plump, perfect ass. I rubbed the oil in. I couldn't help spending a little extra time on those cheeks.

Later, I moved on to her shapely, smooth legs and down to her feet. I was not much of a foot person, but all my hang-ups and inhibitions were dismissed when it came to Alexis Miller. So I massaged her feet with a passion.

On cue, she rolled over on her back, and I poured oil on the middle of her chest. I softly spread it over her firm titties, which caused her to moan. Before I covered her nipples with oil, I gently kissed and then sucked them. I appreciated the fullness of her breasts to the point where I almost forgot I was giving her a massage.

When I got back to rubbing her down, I covered the whole front of her body, enjoying every inch along the way. Alexis called my name and asked me to take off my shorts, which I did without hesitation.

She wanted to rub me down, but that would have to come another day. I was so horny that I would not have been able to stand feeling her hands all over my body without being inside her. So, I instead produced a condom.

I was going to put it on, but Alexis stopped me. "Let me do it," she said. And so, I did.

And we made love on the comforter in front of the fireplace like something out of a movie. It was all passion. She felt so good to me, but it was no surprise. Everything up to then with me and Alexis was in sync, and I expected that making love to her would simply follow suit.

And it did. My lips against her body felt so right. I made sure to caress every inch of her body with my hands. There were no uncomfortable, awkward moments. Every touch of hers felt perfect against my body. If a woman made me feel better than she did, I could not remember. I know that part of the reason she felt so wonderful was because I cared so much about her. My heart was into it. It was passion. In the past, it was more sex or the conquest than making love.

It actually was the first time that I desired a woman out of passion and not lust. Even with Joanne, my first thoughts were how I could get her into bed.

"Julian, thank you for being so delicate with me," Alexis said. "I needed that. Now you've got trouble because I'm going to want to be with you all the time now."

"Well," I said, "that goes both ways because I definitely will be yearning for you."

We kissed and kissed for the next several minutes. I got up and stoked the fire and added two more logs. When I laid back down, Alexis rested her head on my chest, and we took turns asking each other questions all night.

The warmth of the fire heated my body. The sincerity and openness of the conversation warmed me inside.

FIFTY TWO:

Love & Money

Larry

In the several weeks after we returned from the Miami trip, Renee and I were virtually inseparable. I had taken her on a Star Trek mission: places she'd never been before. In the process, I made it difficult for either of us to get along for a significant time apart.

If we did not eat together, we worshipped together or shopped together or even danced together. Not down at Roxbury's or Shark, but at home, in front of the window at my apartment overlooking the pool.

The fact that I could spend so much time with a woman and not get tired of her was a major revelation. I mean, I used to get my sex groove on and then be ready for the honey to leave almost immediately. The new me recalled my old ways, but I did not crave them. They were so empty.

Christian influence was at the heart of everything I did. And it was a blessing that Renee lived the same way. Our ambitions coincided, which meant that we did not pull in different directions. It was not an effort for me to try to please her, but I still was motivated to be more creative in letting her know that I cared.

The issue of sex was truly a non-issue. As long as we were not married—which was something neither of us was willing to discuss after just a few months together—we would have to experience each other without intercourse.

It was something neither Greg nor Julian could have handled. The old me couldn't have handled it either. Greg and Julian told me about how tough it would be for them to be with a woman and not BE with her. And I tried to break it down for them on one of our conference calls.

"It's really not that hard," I said. "When the commitment is

261

made to Christ—a REAL commitment—then it's not hard at all. It's a blessing. It's . . . it's like hitting that game-winning shot you made against Anacostia when we were in high school, Julian. Or that tackle you made, Greg, at the goal line to win the Homecoming game against Spingarn. Remember how good you felt because you helped the team get the victory? Well, it's the same with me now. I have the victory, the victory of LIFE.

"It's a victory to know God has taken over my life and given me a second chance to live the way I should. And being with Renee without sex is a part of living right. I know coming from me, considering how I used to live, makes this almost, like, incredible to hear and hard to believe. But she's lived this way far longer than I. And we've been able to show each other affection without going over the line. I told you about the Miami trip. It was the best time I've EVER had with a woman. It was the best because we shared real, true emotions and affection and love for each other. I know it might sound corny or whatever. But it's the truth. And I've never had that before. And we did not have sex."

I told them of how the most simple things could be ways of expressing love and affection without sex. For instance, I told them about taking Renee roller-skating. First of all, they didn't even know I was interested in roller-skating because I wasn't. Recreational activities—bowling, video games, cards—I usually didn't play. Well, at least the old Larry didn't.

But where Renee was concerned, I had no limitations. An evening of roller-skating with her was romantic.

"I know it seems like just something to do, something simple," I said, "but we held hands as we skated around the rink. We trusted each other to not let the other fall. We laughed and talked and watched the people, the kids. We sat on the bench and fed each other hot dogs. We shared cotton candy. We drank from the same cup with two straws at the same time. When you enjoy being around someone like we do each other, a night like that is like a great, romantic evening."

Neither Greg nor Julian could stop me from going on.

"When we drove home," I continued. "I put my hand on her leg. It wasn't like I was trying to get a sneak feel on, it was just that I needed to touch her, almost like to make sure she was still there as I kept my eye on the road. It was a great night. And then that night we went back to my crib, read the Bible, and called it a night. That was a great evening. We were totally fulfilled."

When I was the skirt-chasing, God's-gift-to-women Larry, nothing short of sex was good enough. I didn't even ever recall using the word "fulfilled" as it related to a woman. And even though I tried to make it clear to my boys that I was committed to my new life, it took a while for them to get used to me being so different. And I definitely was different in a lot of ways.

Even with money. I enjoyed a good time, and even though there were times when I did not have much money, I spent freely. Some of it was irresponsible, most of it just a strong desire to enjoy the moment. If that meant spending on drinks or too much on some gear I thought appropriate for an occasion, I'd do it.

But when I got a call from my attorney notifying me that the drivers of the truck that hit us in that L.A. accident had settled out of court, I was hardly careless with the $25,000, I received in the deal.

Rather, I paid off all my bills—credit cards and a loan for my training at Actors Conservatory Theater—leaving me with only my new car payment. For the first time in my adult life, I was free of financial worry. And I still had more than $15,000 left.

I did not tell Renee about the money until the next night at her apartment. She had whipped up some fried chicken, potatoes and spinach. We ate at the table and then sat in front of the TV in the living room. I took that as the right time to spring the news.

"You trust me, Renee?" I said.

"Of course, I do," she said. "Why?"

"OK. Now, I want you to do something for me, something you might have a problem with, but if you trust me you'll just do it," I said.

"What are you talking about?" Renee said.

"I recall you saying something about wanting to knock out your credit card bills and the last few months on your car loan so you could be done with bills and then you can look for a townhouse or condo," I said. "What I want to know is, how much would it take to do that? Don't ask me why. Just tell me."

"Well," Renee said, looking at me curiously, "I don't know."

"Guess," I said.

"Probably about . . . let me see, maybe $3,000," she said. "Why?"

"Thank you," I said. Then I got up and went to my jacket, which was on a hanger in the closet. I pulled out my checkbook from the inside pocket.

"What are you doing?" Renee said.

"Hold on a second," I said. I made out a check to Renee for

$3,000. I walked back to the couch and sat down, not yet revealing the gift.

"Renee," I began, "I was blessed with a check for more than $25,000, yesterday as a settlement from the accident Greg, Julian, and I had this past summer. I paid off all my bills, and I can't even tell you how relieved I feel inside to be bill-free—well, other than my car payment. I mean, it's a great feeling.

"I still have some money left, and there are a couple of things I want to do with it. One, is this." I pulled out the check made out to Renee and handed it to her.

"You're an angel," I said. "You've changed my life. I'd do anything for you. So, take this money and take care of your debt. If I could do more, I would."

"Larry, why would you do this for me?" Renee said, tears in her eyes.

"Because I should. Because I love you. Because I can," I said.

"But I can't accept this. This is too much. It's your money. You went through the pain and rehab. What about paying the rehab bill?" she said.

"It's taken care of as part of the settlement," I said.

Renee tried to talk, but I jumped in. "Renee, there is no reason for you to not accept this. This is a gift," I said. "God gave me—and my boys—a gift by not letting us die in that accident. I'm giving you a gift for leading me to God, for being my special friend. You have to take it."

"I don't know what to say," Renee said. "I mean, this is so sweet, so kind. I just don't know what to say . . . Thank you."

She hugged me tightly and would not let go. "OK, OK," I said. "You deserve it. But let me tell you what else I'm going to do.

"I still have more than $12,000 left," I said. "What I'm going to do on Sunday is give the church $5,000 for the new building fund in both of our names. What do you think?"

"Oh, Larry, that's so nice," Renee said. "You know I love Macedonia, but are you sure you want to give so much? And you'll only have $7,000 left."

"It's God's will," I said. "And I don't look at it as only $7,000. It's $7,000 more than I had. My bills are paid. The church needs the money. For all I get out of that church, it'd be wrong for me to not make that kind of donation when I have the money."

"But why in both our names?" she said. "It's your money."

"Because you brought me to the church," I said. "You brought me to God. And you're my girl. So it's coming from US."

Renee just sat there embracing me. She didn't say anything, and neither did I. I closed my eyes and prayed.

After several minutes, I said, "It feels good to have a little money. But you know what feels better? It feels better to be out of debt and to help someone else. I never thought about helping anybody before. I mean, not anybody other than my family and Greg and Julian. Other than that, everyone was on his own.

"I definitely never thought about giving a woman a dime. But you're no ordinary woman; I hope you know that. And as for a church, I didn't even have one. But I love Macedonia and Reverend Davis, and to be able to give a big donation feels good. And it's a different kind of good feeling than I've had in the past.

"Before, the things that made me happy, well, I don't even want to get into that with you. The point is, I'm feeling as good right now as I've ever felt."

FIFTY THREE:

Long Distance Love

Julian

I spent another day with Alexis before heading back to D.C. I was glad that I made arrangements with my graduate assistant to cover my classes. I even got to meet her son, Alex, which was a trip. I did not have much experience in dealing with kids, other than my sister's son, John.

But the little guy and I actually got along amazingly well. He definitely was apprehensive about me at first. When Alexis introduced us, I shook his hand and tried to initiate conversation. He was not very interested.

I certainly did not want to pressure him, so I basically ignored him and talked to Alexis. I could tell she felt bad that he didn't want to talk with me at the start, but I assured her it was all right.

After about ten minutes of not saying anything to him, I picked up a Nerf football and began throwing it up into the air to myself. I noticed him watching me from across the room. Suddenly, I looked at him and said, "Can you play football?"

He nodded his head "Yes."

I threw him the ball and he caught it. I asked him to throw it to me, and he did.

"Hey, Alex," I said after he threw the ball to me, "your mom probably does not want us to throw the ball in the house. So let's go outside and play catch, OK?"

Alex quickly got up and led me through a side door, down the driveway and to the backyard. We played catch for the next twenty minutes. Then I showed him how to kick the ball and how to hold it when running.

Alexis watched with a smile in her heart from the kitchen window. A parent hopes for the best in his child's life, and Alexis was

266

happy to see her son take to a man's influence.

When we came back inside, Alexis's cousin, Tammy, was there catching Alexis up on the Orangeburg gossip. By then, according to Tammy, most everyone knew in town knew I was there and had heard about my confrontation with Kevin.

I was unfazed by it. I let the women do their thing and took Alex with me to get some ice cream. Even though it was maybe an hour before lunch, Alexis allowed him to have some because she just could not believe that he'd actually leave her there to go with me. I was just as surprised at myself.

Kids and I just did not go together. I did not have the patience or desire to deal with them. But I found through Alex that I had limited myself. He was a joy to play with. And I could tell that he had a great interest in sports, but no man ever took up much time teaching him.

I must admit that at first I decided to pay the kid some attention because I knew it was what Alexis wanted. But it became a challenge when he would not take to me and then a joy when he did. I genuinely liked little Alex, and he could sense that I did. And the biggest motivation for me was that he was a part of Alexis. She was so wonderful that I knew he had to be too.

When we went to get ice cream, he actually initiated dialogue. I told him some jokes and he laughed and we sat on a bench outside Diary Queen, enjoying ice cream and each other.

Then, out of nowhere, he hit me with a tough question that kids sometimes do. He asked: "Do you know why my daddy is in jail?"

To myself, I said, "Oh, shit." I could have told him "no" to get out of it, but I didn't want to lie. He said his mother hadn't told him why, which I understood. How could she tell him the truth at his age? "Well, Alex," I said, "I think your mom should talk to you about that. But I do know that he loves you. And he loves your mom, too. Sometimes things happen and people make mistakes. We all do."

That was about the only thing I could think of. I wasn't sure if he sought some answers about his father or whether he sought some sort of comfort. I chose the comfort route. He was too young to begin thinking he was unloved by anybody, especially a parent. And it would not have served any positive purpose to tell him his dad beat up his mom.

He seemed satisfied enough with my response; or he just refused to pursue it. So, we finished off the cones and headed back home. By the time we arrived, Tammy was at the door on her way out, having filled Alexis' ears with the town's news of the week.

When we approached the door, Alexis quickly came out to greet Alex on the porch. "Hi, baby, how you doing?" she said.

"Fine," Alex responded.

I looked on smiling. "Did you have a good time with Mr. Julian?" she said.

"Yes," Alex said.

Alexis looked at me and smiled. "Hey, Alex. Do you want to spend the night with Miss Tammy and Buck?" Alexis said, referring to Tammy's four-year-old son.

Alex got excited.

"Good," Tammy said. "I'll be back in about two hours, and pick you up."

As Tammy talked to Alex, Alexis gave me a look I had not seen. It was seductive, which took me off guard. I received that to mean my last night in town would be shared with her.

I nodded my head knowingly. Tammy left, and Alexis took Alex inside to have lunch. He ate maybe half of his chicken fingers and fries, the ice cream effectively having spoiled his appetite. Alexis was stunned when he said "yes" when she asked him if he'd like to take a nap.

She eagerly took him to his room. On the way, however, he turned around and waved to me. "See you later, big boy," I said.

I had planned to go back to my cousin's and allow Alexis to do whatever she needed to do before Tammy returned, but she had other ideas.

"Do you have to go? Because if you don't, I'd like you to stay. You're going to be gone tomorrow, and there's no telling when I'll see you again," she said.

That was reason enough for me to stay. And it also signaled to me that it was time to plan our next meeting.

"You know I don't want to go," I said. "I know what we should do. Do you have a calendar?"

She went inside her Coach bag and pulled out her checkbook, which had a calendar in it. I invited her to D.C. after Christmas, leading into the new year. "We're going to spend New Year's Eve together?" she said. "I've never done anything on New Year's eve except go to church or watch the festivities on TV. There was this big party last year everybody went to in Columbia at a hotel. It was, like, $20 to get in. And I just couldn't rationalize paying $20 to hang out with people I see every day. I wasn't really into going out at that time anyway. But if I was, I was not going to pay $20 to drive to

Columbia to party with my everyday friends. I love them, but . . ."

We had to plan ahead. With her responsibilities as a parent and a doctor, and mine as a professor, we were both very busy. I was not tenured yet, and it is "publish" or "perish" in academia. Part of securing tenure was based on doing research, and publishing books and articles that were deemed scholarly. I had some articles published, but I knew that I needed to get started on a book project—and fast.

We picked out a date in February—Valentine's weekend and a date in March. "I really can't believe I'm charting dates to see you months in advance," I said. "That tells how excited I am about you. Also, I'm hoping that in between those set dates, we could maybe meet halfway between here and D.C. for a few days. Or one day, I don't care. I just want to see you. And you should bring Alex, too— if you're comfortable with that."

She just smiled at me. "Anytime you want to see me, you can," Alexis said, "because I'll definitely want to see you, too. And it seems Alex has a new friend."

That last night together was another wonderful time. She took me around Orangeburg. We went to Chippy's and got some food. She showed me where thirty years earlier three black youths were killed when they demonstrated to integrate the town's only bowling alley. She showed me where two boys, 14 and 15, were arrested in 1968 and put on a chain gang because they wanted a Coke at Kress's Five and Ten Store.

"So much went on in the South in the '60s," she said. "It's gotten better. Well, at least we can bowl wherever we want and buy a soda."

"And we can travel the world, take advantage of what life has to offer," I added. "Being with you makes me think about the possibilities."

"The possibilities," she said. "I like that."

Then we went back to her house and made love to the sound of her groans, my moans, and crickets. We put each other to sleep.

The next morning, Alexis showered after I did, and it hit me then that this woman that I had fallen so deeply for so fast would be out of my vision for a while. I knew she understood how I felt about her, at least I hoped she did. But I wanted to embed it into her mind and heart. Then, in a flash, it came to me a clever way to appease myself and to reiterate my feelings.

So, I got a sheet of paper and tore it into seven little pieces. And on each piece, I wrote a short note to Alexis: "I miss you," "I want you," "I need you," "You're beautiful," "Can't wait to see you," "I adore you," "We're good together."

Then I folded the notes and placed them in places around her house where she'd eventually find them. I put one in her purse, another in a drawer, in a kitchen cabinet, under her pillow, in her work bag, in her favorite coffee cup, and inside the shoes she liked to wear.

It took her several days to find them all, but she said her heart skipped each time she did. "You know, I've been searching my things trying to find them," she said over the phone. "But I never do. Then, one just pops up. I love it."

We did New Year's in D.C., which was great. We met in Raleigh, N.C.—a midway point. We went to Myrtle Beach for Valentine's Day. In March during spring break, I flew to Orangeburg and we drove to Atlanta for a long weekend. One Friday, I flew into town just for the night and returned home for work.

The next month, she visited me, and we went to Baltimore's harbor for a relaxing evening and fine seafood. It was then when she first met my mother, who was relieved to find Alexis to be as pleasant as I made her out to be.

When Alexis was not looking, my mother gave me the "thumbs up." That was important to me.

"Alexis, you can visit anytime, even without Julian," my mom said.

"Why would she want to do that?" I cracked.

"Boy, be quiet," Mom said. "I want to take her shopping. It'll be girl's night out."

"That sounds like fun," Alexis said.

She was a special woman, someone I didn't know existed. And she made me become someone I didn't know existed within me. She made me know that there were untapped qualities within all of us.

I wrote her frequently about the impact she had on my life. The only personal letter I had written to anyone before Alexis was to Santa Claus. That was it. My thinking was: Why write a letter when I could just call? Saved a lot of time.

But I was motivated to put my feelings down on paper to her. And when it was obvious that she enjoyed receiving mail from me, I flooded her with material each week. It was difficult to keep up the pace I started—three letters a week. But I did manage a mid-sized one weekly and maybe a card or postcard. I let her know that thoughts of her consumed me.

And I learned that a letter was an expression of something more. It put a true emphasis on my feelings. She told me she read them repeatedly. "I have them all," Alexis said. "They're special. You don't find a man who will take the time to actually sit down and write a woman. And I can tell it takes you a while because you're not just saying any old thing. You write me very specific and intimate stuff. I can tell that your heart is into it."

"You know what, Alexis?" I said. "They actually don't take me long to write. I start with a blank sheet of paper not really know what I want to say. And then I concentrate on you and the words just flow from my heart to my mind and to my hand. Next thing I know, there are two or three pages filled."

It even got to the point where I sent her a letter about my sexual fantasies with her. I wrote her a tale about me and her making love in a limo on the way to a red-eye flight to L.A., where we'd then go to Hawaii. On the plane, when everyone was asleep, I wrote that she'd meet me in the rear bathroom, and we'd somehow turn that cramped space into our little love nest. And the fantasy ended in Maui, on the beach, the moon the only provider of light. I'd lie on my back, Alexis riding me, as the coolness of the ocean covered our bodies.

She was so excited. "I really wish we could make that come true," she said.

I reminded her of her words when Larry called to say I'd be receiving a check for $30,000 as the settlement money in our L.A. accident. I didn't expect that much, but I guess I received the largest settlement because I was semi-comatose. It had been so long that I forgot that the case was pending.

My first plans after knocking out bills was to arrange that fantasy trip. "That will be my birthday present to you," I said to her. My next priority was to give Greg something for when he helped me. I know that he's looking to open up another store so this would be a good time for me to step up.

I also bought her a ticket to Chicago for June. It was time to see Greg, and Larry and Renee planned to come, too.

"I'll go anywhere with you, Julian," Alexis said. "Just say when."

FIFTY FOUR:

Ring For A Day

Greg

It was a warm, muggy, mid-June Chicago night. El Niño apparently still had things screwy, so sudden rain was always a possibility. And sure enough, it began to come down, at first lightly and then so heavily that I had to pull over because I could hardly see a few feet in front of me. Thunder rang through the air and lightening through the sky. That was the signal for me to turn off the radio.

As the rain pounded on the top of my car, I reclined my seat and closed my eyes. It had been a whirlwind week—and whirlwind several months, really. I had won back the woman I loved, solidified her faith in me, and received a check for $20,000 to boot.

I was happy. Almost strangely, however, the settlement money from the car accident did not mean as much to me as having Brianna. My first reaction would have been to open another store or invest the money—you know, let the money work for you instead of you work for the money. I smiled to myself when I realized that my filled pockets did nothing toward filling my heart. No amount of money could do that. Only Brianna could. And that was more comfort to me than money ever provided.

I said similar things earlier that Saturday morning to John Raffini, the Italian guy Brianna and I had met months back on the dinner cruise. Between that night and then, we grew to levels at which we had not been. And I knew that it happened because I changed. Brianna was the same woman she always had been. But, in a nutshell, I grew up.

I showed Brianna that my knack for romance was not fly-by-night. I sent her flowers when she got promoted to director on her job and for no reason other than she deserved some. I met her for lunch and took her on quick outings, blanket on the ground and all. I used to call those times "picnics," but I learned through reading

272

that "picnic" was a term white folks used back-in-the-day that meant they would pick and "nick," which was their synonym to "nigger," and hang him. So I never used "picnic" again.

Anyway, I made Brianna feel special, let her know that my mind was occupied by thoughts of her, that it was important to me that she feel special.

One day, when Brianna went out of town for a seminar for three days, I left her heart-felt, intimate messages on her voice mail—at home and work. And when she returned, she found a package at her front door. In it was a cassette tape with love songs I carefully selected.

"I chose each of these songs because in some way it reminds me of you or us," I wrote in the note. "I'd like you to play this tape at home and in your car, and listen to the words and how they apply to us. And then one night we'll listen to them together."

***

Brianna

I just did not know what to think. "Momma, Greg is so different from before," I said to my mother.

"He seems the same to me," Momma said. "He's still loud and funny—and very nice."

"No, I mean with me," I explained. "He's so caring. I never really wanted him to be something that he's not. I loved him the way he was. But it's like he got hit over the head and all the things any woman would want in a man went into him."

"Baby," her mother said, "your father is a unique man. I don't think I've ever told you this, but we broke up before we got married—just like you and Greg did. But we were miserable without each other. It only lasted a week. But when we got back together, we never had another major problem. Sometimes I've wanted to knock him upside his head, but for the most part he's been the sweet husband and father—and a strong provider.

"He's unique because he was mature at a young age. His parents died when he was a teenager, and he started working at 15. Maybe that made him mature faster than most men. I don't know. But he's always been very responsible, very solid. That's unique in a man. Not too often do they change. It takes something drastic to happen, and maybe not even then will they grow up. I think Greg just grew up. They say people can't change, but you can tell people now that you know they can.

"I've seen how much happier you've been. There's a pep in your step that no one else can put there but him. But also understand this:

He changed because of you. You brought out all that in Greg. So you're both reaping the benefits."

***

Greg

I truly felt like I reaped the benefits of change. I had Brianna. And I wanted more, so I visited John Raffini that morning. There was no need to delay the inevitable. I wanted Brianna to be my wife. I had no reservations about it at all. On the phone, I told Julian and Larry: "It's time. I mean, I don't have any interest in anyone else. Not at all. It's time for us to start putting our lives together, as one."

So, I wanted a hookup on an engagement ring, and John delivered. While sitting in the car during the downpour, I opened the case that contained a two-and-a-half carat princess cut diamond ring I'd purchased that morning from Raffini's. It was of high color and clarity. I was very careful with all my purchases, so I visited a jeweler who told me how to determine a quality rock.

Before purchasing the ring from John, I took it to an independent appraiser, a gemologist, who rated it $1,200 more than the $6,100 John asked for it. To be sure, I took it to another appraiser, who rated it of similar value.

Not many things made people happier than getting a deal, especially someone money-conscious like me. So, I was geeked. I just wanted the pouring rain to stop so I could get to Brianna and ask her to marry me. I told her to be dressed to go out because one of my employee's had a surprise party for his wife, and as the boss, I felt compelled to at least make a cameo.

The rain finally slowed enough for me to continue to Brianna's. When I got there, I placed the ring inside my raincoat pocket, and ran up to the covered porch. I rang the doorbell.

When Brianna answered, I asked her to come outside. "Why?" she said.

I didn't expect that response. I thought she'd just say, "OK."

"I'm all wet," I said. "And I need to talk to you about something—now. Come on, it's raining, but it's covered here and it's warm."

She came out. I sat on the bench, and Brianna sat next to me. "What's wrong?" she said. "You look nervous."

"I am, a little," I began. "I wanted to talk to you right here because the last serious talk we had was here. I'm sure you remember that. It's sort of symbolic to be in the same place now. It's like we've come full circle."

I licked my lips. Tears welled in my eyes. Brianna got concerned.

"Gregory, what's wrong?" she said.

"Everything's all right," I said. "It's just that I never thought I'd get to a point in my life where I believe I can't live without someone. But that's how you make me feel. I love you, Bri. I've loved you so long I don't remember when I didn't love you. I'm not perfect, but I do want to be the perfect man for you. Trying to be that is not an effort; it's fun. And I want you to allow me to continue having that fun forever."

"Of course," she said. "Gregory . . ."

Brianna seemed so transfixed on the tears that flowed down my face that she did not notice me reaching into my coat pocket. "Gregory," she said. "Why are you crying?"

"Because I got the best deal I've ever gotten in my life today," I said. "Whatever I paid for this is nothing compared to the value of what it means. Will you marry me, Brianna?"

I raised the ring in front of Brianna. "Oh, my God," she said. Before she opened the box, she answered me. "Yes, Gregory, yes. You know I will marry you."

Then we kissed and hugged. "Thank you," I said.

I leaned back and wiped the tears from my face. At first, I didn't know why I cried. But I was overwhelmed at where I was in my life. It was the first time I'd ever expressed tears of joy.

"You want to open that now?" I said to Brianna.

"OK," she said. "I'm so nervous.

"Oh, my God. Gregory, this is so beautiful. And it's big. Look at that. Look at that!"

Then she began to cry, which made me cry some more. We kissed and tasted the salt of each other's tears. "I can't believe this," she said. "I knew it would happen one day, I believed that it would. But . . ."

"It looks great on your finger," I said. "I agonized over which diamond to get for a long time. But John—remember John from the Spirit of Chicago?—he helped me out."

We got up and went inside.

"Do we have to go to that party tonight?" she said. "We've got some celebrating to do. I want to show my fiancée how much I love him."

"Oh, you do, huh?" I said. I knew what that meant—serious love-making.

"Well, let's just make an appearance," I said. "I promised the guy I was coming, and I could tell he was looking forward to us being there. We'll stay for an hour and then bounce. All right?"

"OK, husband," Brianna said. "But I've got to call my mother and father first."

As she dialed the numbers, I watched her glow. Seeing her happy made me happy and proud. When I looked back at the first two years of our relationship, I realized that I'd fallen short of being the kind of mate I should have been with her. And that made that moment more special because I saw growth in myself.

That was the difference in me. I grew up. There's no way to teach a man to truly become a man. Some men look like men and talk like men but are not the kind of men they should be in relationships. I never thought about that until I stopped looking for something else and looked at what I had in Brianna. That simple step changed my life.

My friends were surprised to learn that I could be so committed to one woman. I never did mess around on Brianna, but I put myself in positions to do so because I thought it was part of being a man. That was so much *bullshit*. I grew to learn that being a man in a relationship was to be committed and faithful to it.

I thank God I grew before it was too late.

"I can't believe this," Brianna said. "The biggest moment of my life and no one's at home. I spoke to them earlier, and they said they weren't going anywhere. Now they're not home."

"It's OK."

"I know, but I just want to tell somebody."

"Well, when we come back from the party, I'll watch TV, and you call up all your friends."

"I'll call them tomorrow. When we come back, I want to seduce my fiancée."

"Cool," I said grinning.

FIFTY FIVE:

Surprise, Surprise

Julian

The party was at the top level of the Shark Bar, a black-owned restaurant with locations in New York, L.A., and Atlanta, as well as this one in Chicago. It was one of Brianna's favorite places to eat.

Greg and Brianna pulled up right at 9 o'clock. One of his employees stood in the doorway awaiting their arrival. He went upstairs and told the guests that they had arrived.

When they entered the party area, the group of about forty of us screamed, "Surprise!"

I stood back and watched the surprise unfold. Brianna was confused. Everyone looked at her. She looked behind herself to see if the honoree was there, but there was no one. She saw a bunch of faces but could not make them out.

Finally, her mother stepped up to her. "Congratulations baby," she said and hugged her.

Brianna stepped back. "What? What are you . . ."

She could not finish her sentence as it dawned on her that the people were there to celebrate her and Greg's engagement. "Gregory . . . but how? You did this?" she said.

He just nodded his head. Her father put his arms around her. "Listen, sweetheart," he said, "that ring doesn't mean you're not my baby girl anymore. You'll always be my baby girl."

"Thank you, Daddy," she said crying.

After the sustained hug, a line formed to greet and congratulate her and Greg. "I don't believe you," she said to G. "What if I had said, 'no'?"

"It would have been your pre-funeral celebration," he said, hugging her.

Brianna was thrown by the people who came out. Her old college roommate, who lived in Detroit, was there. So was a group of co-workers. And when she saw me and Larry, she just screamed.

"Oh, my God!" she said. "I can't believe this." She hugged Larry and then me. "This is really a party now."

"Hey, " I said, "you know how the song goes: 'A party ain't a party till I run through it.' "

I introduced Brianna to Alexis. "Through Gregory, I've heard a lot about you," Brianna said. "Thanks for being here."

Alexis smiled. "I'm glad Julian brought me," she said.

In the past, bringing a woman to a gathering was tantamount to bringing sand to the beach. As a single man, it was important to ALWAYS make myself available to meet other honies.

But Alexis made that seem old and stale. As I drove back from South Carolina that weekend after finding Alexis, I reviewed my life and was really embarrassed by it. I'd lied and cheated on women, good women, so many times I couldn't even remember. I never gave myself a chance to be in a thriving relationship because I undermined it almost before it started.

Some of it was the fear of being happy. It might sound strange, but that was the deal. Dogging women didn't bring happiness. It brought a feeling of conquest, which is totally different. Unnecessary drama.

The more I dealt with Alexis, the more she helped me realize that I had so much more to offer someone, to offer MYSELF. All the creativity I used in deceiving women I could use in helping a relationship flourish. As bad as men can be, there is good inside. It just has to be touched. And when it's touched, the man has to feel it and react to it.

I did, and I lived a life with so much less confusion and drama. The change in me seemed drastic—dealing HONESTLY with a woman. But, really, the capability to do so was there all along.

That's what Larry told me, and I agreed with him. I thought about that as he introduced Brianna to Renee. "Let me hug you," she said to Renee. "Any woman who can have a great impact on Larry, I have to hug."

"There you go," Larry said. "But, taking nothing away from Renee because she's my angel. But God is the one who had the impact on me."

Brianna smiled. "He's about the only one who could, I guess," she said, laughing.

She continued greeting people, while Larry and I posted up at the corner of the bar. We had not seen Greg since we arrived the night before. He was busy arranging the evening and getting together the last of Brianna's gifts.

After we all ate, Greg suggested Brianna open her presents. There were only a few, two from Greg and one from me and Larry. The first was lingerie. The card on the box said, "Just a little sumpin', sumpin' for the honeymoon, you know?" Greg felt a little awkward because Brianna's father glanced at him as she read the card.

The next gift was a nameplate for her desk at work. Larry and I got that. It read: "Brianna Gibson."

"What if she wanted to keep her last name?" her friend from Detroit said.

"Then she wanted to marry someone else," Greg answered. Everyone laughed.

The last gift was a videotape. The restaurant hooked up a VCR to a TV. "Can I show this now?" she whispered to Greg, recalling a few tapings they had made of each other making love.

"It's OK," he said.

"What could be on this tape?" she wondered aloud.

As it turned out, it was almost her life story. When Greg decided he was ready to propose to Brianna, he took his camcorder around to her parents, who furnished him with photos of Brianna from an infant to an adult.

He selected several and put them on camera. Then he interviewed her parents about her and how far she'd come to being the woman she was then. They both told touching and funny stories that she might not otherwise have told.

Greg then went to her friends and taped them congratulating her. They also told short, funny stories. He asked Larry and I to get on tape our well-wishes to them. We did and sent them to him.

He took all that footage, including his words to Brianna, to a video technician. Greg picked out music he wanted to play in the background, and the technician gave it a professional touch.

The package was nicely put together, with Greg making an opening statement, leading in to photos of Brianna as a baby on up to a woman, pictures with her family and friends, and many with Greg. Then her parents talked lovingly about her to the point where Brianna shed some tears. Next was her friends sending love and encouragement and congratulations. Then came Greg's mom and brother. Finally, Greg said on the video: "If you didn't know it before, you should know now that you're not just special to me. But, thankfully, I get to have you."

Then there was another series of photos of a smiling Brianna, ending with the one of her and Greg on the steps of the library where they met.

Brianna threw herself into Greg's arms when it was done. She was overwhelmed. "You're so sweet," she said. "How did you do that?"

Greg didn't answer; he just hugged her.

"Greg, that was incredible," his mother said. "That was so nice."

Greg was embarrassed by all the attention, but he was happy that it went over so well. "I need a drink," he said to me.

I led him away from the crowd and to the empty bar. I got Larry's attention and waved him over.

It was the first time since the L.A. trip nearly a year earlier that we had some quiet time together. I ordered shots of Hennessey for me and Greg, and a shot glass of Pepsi for Larry.

Larry proposed a toast that sounded more like a prayer. "Thank God for guiding you back to Brianna. And may God guide you and her together to a married life of great joy and happiness, one that you both hold to the sanctity of God's words."

Before we tapped glasses, I jumped in. "Hold up," I said. "Here's my toast: To my boy, who's giving up the good life for . . . the great wife. You've got a good woman. I'm happy for you."

We tapped glasses and drank up. Greg then went into his pocket. He pulled out two $20 bills and handed one to me and Larry without saying a word.

I looked at Larry, and he looked at me. "What's this for?" I said to Greg.

"You don't remember?" he said. "You either, Larry? Shoot, I could have kept my $40. Think back to '91, when we ran honies so much that we vowed to never get married. And then we made a bet that whoever got married first would give the others $20. Remember? Well, I'm paying up."

"I had forgotten about that," Larry said. "I knew it wouldn't be me. I kind of always thought it would be Julian to go first."

"Me?" I jumped in. "No way! I always thought Greg would be the one, if anybody. But to be honest, it didn't seem like any of us would get married."

"That was then," Larry said, looking at Greg, "We won the bet, but you got the prize."

"You're right," Greg said. "Brianna's my ace. And you know, this night is kind of like a dream, a good dream. But it wouldn't be right without you two here. Thanks for coming."

Just then, Brianna came over and into Greg's arms. "How you guys doing?" she said. "Is this one of your infamous male-bonding sessions? Don't let me interrupt."

"No, you're not," Larry said. "We actually were talking about how blessed you both are to have each other."

"I know," she said. "But I think you three are blessed, too. First, to have each other, because you guys are the best friends I know of. Greg talks about both of you EVERY day. But I've talked to both of your girlfriends. They are both very nice, very sweet. They aren't like the women I've seen you guys with in the past. They seem really happy."

We laughed and joked for a few more minutes before Brianna, Greg and Larry left to join the others. I stood the bar. Alexis came over and hugged me. She knew something was on my mind. "You want to talk about it?" she said.

I said, "Have you ever experienced déjà vu?"

"Sure," Alexis said.

"Me, too," I said. "I have those little episodes less often now than I used to. I wonder how that happens. You think it's possible to make it happen?"

"No, baby," she said. "That's something I'm sure we can't control. Why?"

"Because every so often, I'd like to experience the feeling I have right now," I said. "My two best friends are happier than they've ever been. I know these guys as well as I know myself, and I can feel how happy they are. And I know that I've never been so happy."

Alexis did not say anything. She knew how to let the moment take care of itself. I put my arm around her and watched everyone mingle. Through the crowd I spotted Greg whispering to Brianna. Our eyes met and he winked. Then I found Larry on the other side of the room with Renee. He pointed at me, and I pointed back.

All those years, and we still had that connection, that oneness that only came with the tightest of friends. A oneness that was both healthy and unhealthy. At its best, the oneness allowed us to bare our souls and fend for one another against anybody or anything. At its worst, the oneness reinforced our hang-ups, mistrust of women, and lustful ways. Having identified our *baggage* and checked it allowed us to enjoy love—true love. Who would have thought it would feel so good?

FIFTY SIX:

B Check

Julian

A month later, Larry and Renee, Greg and Brianna, and Alexis and I decided to meet in Cancun for a mini-vacation. We swam, laid out on the beach, took shots of tequila (Larry and Renee had juice), partied and mostly just absorbed the beauty of friendship. We were like family.

When we left to head back to the States, we had to make a mad dash so we wouldn't miss our flights. Hey, trying to get three women to be on time is virtually impossible.

And the baggage we had was ridiculous. We had to be a sight running through the airport, struggling with all those bags. Every few steps one of us would drop one, and someone would try to pick it up. This led to more bags being dropped like some episode of "Three Stooges."

We were too macho to ask for any assistance, and we refused to let the ladies carry much more than their purses. I thought I might have pulled a muscle, but I wasn't about to act like I couldn't handle it. We had to catch that flight.

When we got to the counter, we were hot, sweaty, and tired, like after playing a good game of ball. We just dropped the baggage into a pile on the floor. It felt great to put all that baggage down. Release it. Get rid of it. Dispose of it.

We could see the women in the distance casually walking down the concourse before stopping in a Duty Free shop. And just then, for a brief moment, I thought about all the stuff that got in the way of our having good relationships. Most of it was caused by some of our very distorted views and compounded by negative experiences that we contributed to.

I looked at all the baggage on the floor that seemed to envelop the three of us, and it brought a smile to my face. I realized then that extra baggage can really slow you down—and not just when it comes to catching a plane, either. It can also stunt your growth as a person. And it can stop you from hooking up with a quality person who could enhance your life, make your life better. That's really what our existence should be about; being happy.

Greg and Larry seemed to have gotten the same vibe because I saw familiar expressions on their faces. We were so tight for so long that we just sensed what was on each other's minds. Did it so many times I can't even remember.

I said, "Yo G, you thinking what I'm thinking?"

"No doubt," Greg said, looking around at all the suitcases strewn all over the place.

"I know," Larry added. "It's a trip."

Even a superfine ticket agent could not break our telepathy. Her physical attributes were duly acknowledged—hey, we weren't blind—but they were dutifully, and I might add, happily ignored. In the past, we would have been compelled to try and get her number even if our women were around. But not then. No one even contemplated stepping to her. It wasn't about that for us anymore.

She said something about the obvious tans we got from a long weekend under the Mexican sun and then pursed her lips together and asked in breathy tones, "Baggage Check?"

She was talking about our luggage, but we were thinking about our past—and our present. All the hang-ups and immoral habits and general wildness were part of baggage that we carried from one woman to the next. It was exactly what held us back from social growth.

We had already checked our personal baggage, and believe me, it was more than that pile that rested on the floor before us.

"Baggage Check?" the woman asked again.

We looked down at the bags and then at each other.

"Yeah," we said in unison, "*Baggage Check.*"

THE END

The Craft

In the movie *Misery*, the author celebrated finishing a novel by enjoying a nice fat cigar. I remembered that when I began *Baggage Check*. Looking at the empty computer screen, writing the words "The End" seemed not only a long, long way from reality, but also pretty unreachable.

Still, I could not dismiss the notion of how I would punctuate completion of my first novel. About eight months later, I was done— but I still had not come up with just the right gesture to honor the moment.

I ended up doing something I do as well as most anyone: I fried some chicken wings. And so, forevermore, if I'm blessed to complete other books, that will be my celebration.

With one twist, however. On that occasion, I burned the wings and nearly set the kitchen on fire. Under ordinary circumstances, that would be cause for alarm. In this case, I simply put the fire out, discarded the wings and went out to a party. Such was the glory of a dream fulfilled; not even a near disaster could singe the satisfaction.

The feeling of euphoria was hard to maintain in this subjective business of book publishing, however. I look back on what it took to get to this point, and I'm filled with equal parts pride and frustration.

Between the hours of 1 a.m. and 6 a.m., I crafted 95 percent of "Baggage Check." It was after I had gotten my daughter to bed, made or received phone calls, and done some work for my main job as a sportswriter for The Atlanta Journal & Constitution.

Some writers need solitude. I needed the opposite. I always worked with the TV on, with *Law & Order*, *Homicide: Life on the Streets* and *Sports Center* functioning as my favorite distractions. All the while the characters burned a place in my creative conscience and became a part of me.

Months before I typed the first words of *Baggage Check*, I listened to the great playwright, August Wilson, tell an Alliance Theatre audience in Atlanta that the characters in his plays tell him what they would do or say. I took that as you probably would have: utter nonsense.

Oh, but it was not. When you're engulfed in the creative process of developing characters, they grow within you and reside there. They actually become a part of you, communicate with you at all hours of the day, no matter the time or circumstance. And they virtually write the book themselves. It is a process that flushed out my imagination, and took my creativity into the stratosphere.

That's how I executed a manuscript that touches the cornucopia of emotions: disappointment, frustration, joy, relief, happiness, confusion, dislike, love, respect.

Many of those emotions ruled me as I had to deal with and overcome a legion of rude, unprofessional, incompetent, and insensitive literary agents. (You know who you are.) Finally, I did a "*baggage check*" on them in that I realized the issues they carried around like luggage was theirs, not mine. And so, I pressed on.

For me, completing the novel was a minor miracle, an odyssey that began with an empty computer screen and ended with burned chicken wings. The smell of smoke was never so pleasing.

For you, I hope the finished product entertained, moved, and most of all, forced you to check your *baggage*.

Curtis Bunn

About the Author

CURTIS BUNN is a national award-winning sports columnist for the Atlanta Journal-Constitution. Having nearly two decades writing sports, Bunn, 39, has covered three Super Bowls, 10 NBA Finals, three Masters golf tournaments, two NCAA Finals, two heavyweight boxing championships, three World Series and two Olympic Games (1988 in Seoul, 2000 in Sydney).

The 1983 graduate of Norfolk State University also has worked at the St. Petersburg Times, The Washington Times, Newsday and the New York Daily News. Additionally, the southeast Washington, D.C. native worked for three years as a pre-game and post-game analysis at New York Knicks games for the MSG Network.

He is blessed with a son, Curtis Jr., daughter Gwendolyn (Bunny) and nephew, Gordon, who is like a son. Curtis Bunn lives outside Atlanta.